HISTORY
FROM THE
AIR

HISTORY FROM THE AIR

RICHARD MUIR

IN COLLABORATION WITH UNIVERSITY OF CAMBRIDGE
COLLECTION OF AIR PHOTOGRAPHS

MICHAEL JOSEPH · LONDON

First published in Great Britain by
Michael Joseph Limited
44 Bedford Square
London W.C.1
1983

ISBN 0 7181 2306 9

Filmset by BAS Printers Ltd, Over Wallop, Hampshire
Printed and bound by L Van Leer & Company Limited, Deventer, Holland

CONTENTS

LIST OF COLOUR ILLUSTRATIONS

Between pages 128 and 129
A ruggedly beautiful Scottish Highlands landscape near Loch Alsh
The landscape of the Southern Uplands near Melrose
Snowdon, the highest mountain in Wales
The famous technicolor cliffs at Hunstanton
A fine panorama of good old English countryside in the vicinity of Southwick in Wiltshire
The outlines of a deserted medieval village in the pasture at Lowesby in Leicestershire
Wandlebury, near Cambridge

Between pages 144 and 145
An area of peat bog near Powers Cross in Co Galway
Crop marks near Deeping St Nicholas in Lincolnshire
The Norman cathedral at Durham
Crop marks at Maxey in the north of Cambridgeshire
A panorama of Cambridge
Burghley House, near Stamford
Warwick Castle

Was a big high wall there that tried to stop me
A sign was painted said : Private Property,
But on the other side, it didn't say nothin'
That side was made for you and me

Woody Guthrie (1912–1967)

Air photography allows us all to see the heritage of landscape which lies beyond the signs and I would like to dedicate this book to all the harmless earthbound lovers of our countryside and monuments who have seen the 'No Trespassing' signs from the back.

A. *The great Iron Age hill fort of Emain Macha on Navan in Co Armagh is portrayed as a simple relief feature rather than as a crop mark and is photographed from an oblique perspective. The outer hedge ring traces the ditch and bank which defended an area of 7.5 hectares. The inner ring defines an artificial mound, built to cover a mysterious wooden structure which was ritually burned and then covered by a stone cairn around 300 BC. Shadow marks reveal the outlines of a second ditch-ringed structure, perhaps a house*

INTRODUCTION

The branches of photography are many, but air photography can surely claim to be the most versatile and effective of them all. These qualities are evident from the fact that, when judged purely by aesthetic standards, some air photographs are strikingly beautiful; many have become indispensable teaching aids in the presentation of subjects as diverse as geography, history, archaeology, botany, geology, town-planning, ecology and cartography, while others reveal information about the history and contents of the landscape which would be otherwise unobtainable.

In these ways, an air photograph can be a thing of intrinsic beauty, a means of counting individuals in a sea bird sanctuary, the revelation of an unsuspected Roman villa, the basis for constructing a map, a device for illustrating the stages in the growth of a town, or it may serve scores of other valuable purposes.

Air photographs come in different types appropriate to the varied uses to which they may be put. But the essence of the air photograph is the unfamiliar view. The landsman tends to see the landscape in profile. This perspective has its merits, for buildings great and small were all designed to be viewed from the ground, while the earthbound historian of the landscape is free – owners permitting – to peer and forage for evidence amongst the relics of different ages. But very soon the landscape enthusiast and photographer must crave the power of flight.

In a flat landscape like that of the Fens, the visible landsurface is seen as a narrow, ribbon-like strip and a mere hemline to the vast expanse of sky above. In fact this surface is richly and fascinatingly patterned by pale networks of former stream channels and punctuated with the subtle traces of Bronze Age, Roman and Romano-British life and settlements, all of which loom through the overlying patchwork of geometrical fields – but this view is reserved for the airman. Similarly, the town or village historian is confronted by a maze of physical and visual barriers: houses, hedgerows, walls and sheds. It is usually impossible to see from one street to the next and very difficult to recognise the plans and patterns which the scene contains, so that the settlement layout is poorly perceived and the tell-tale clues and alignments which it surely contains may be unrecognised. When air photography is brought to bear on an historically interesting settlement – be it a living one or a deserted village now blanketed by pasture – the result is more than a map but a compendium of evidence which may be contained in the shadowy outlines of former streets, in ditches or hedgerows which mark former boundaries, or in the instantly recognisable outlines of medieval house-and-land plots or 'tofts'.

The unfamiliar view comes in many forms. Most of the photographs that are included are low-level oblique views, mainly taken at altitudes of a few hundred feet and comparable to the sorts of views obtained from church towers or summits. They present a perspective view of their subjects along with fairly intimate details of the nearer features. Also included is a smaller number of higher level vertical views, revealing a more distant landscape in an almost map-like form in which the perspective distortions are – for our present purposes – insignificant. Such photographs are admirably suited to a book such as this,

B. *The huts and enclosures of an Iron Age village near Leuchars in the Scottish county of Fife revealed as crop marks. The huts appear as ring-doughnut-like features because the crop is growing more vigorously in the encircling ditches dug to catch the drips from the conical hut roofs*

but they only represent a portion of the 'remote sensing' techniques which are available. More specialised research may require the use of heat-sensitive media like infra-red line-scan which records the radiant heat at the ground surface. There is also a photographic technique using the near-infra red part of the spectrum which is able to differentiate between healthy and diseased crops before there are visible symptoms, allowing swift remedial action. The broad spectrum of remote sensing also embraces the sophisticated satellite, Skylab and space ship imagery, with a wide range of uses including weather forecasting, espionage, crop survey and the mapping of remote areas.

The emphasis of this book however is on man's occupation and transformation of the British landscape and the bias is, in the broadest sense, historical. Given access to the

c. *The 'double banana' outlines of semi-circular banks and ditches of a Neolithic henge temple at Hutton Moor near Ripon emerge as crop marks. The earthworks of a great prehistoric religious centre are virtually invisible from the ground*

vast resources of the Cambridge University archives, it would have been relatively easy to compile a book of visually striking landscapes and monuments. While seeking to do this, each photograph is complemented with an account of the fascinating information that each one contains, thus producing an unfamiliar view of the history of these islands. A number of illustrations from the Republic of Ireland have been irresistible and it is hoped that Irish readers will accept that the incorporation of the words 'Great Britain and Ireland' would become unwieldy.

Much of the archaeological information which is presented comes in the form of shadow, crop, soil and parch marks. Each of these phenomena can reveal vital and illuminating traces which are wholly or virtually invisible to the landsman. Shadow marks are formed of shadows cast by the sun, following the patterns of surface relief; where very subtle features are concerned, the effect is usually most apparent when the sun is low in the sky. Minute differences in terrain, notably the faint scarps and hollows of grass-grown ruins or earthworks, can then emerge as shadow marks, and if an archaeologically interesting area is under a dusting of snow as well as being sunlit, the faintest of ridges may become visible through being brilliantly sunlit on one side and darkly shadowed on the other.

Crop marks are produced by differences in the quality and rate of growth within a crop and these differences are a reflection of differences in the soil and subsoil immediately below. For example, grain growing on the rubble of old foundations will grow relatively feebly and appear stunted by comparison with the surrounding plants, while other crops growing in the deep rich silts filling up former ditches will tend to grow more vigorously and soon rise above their neighbours. Such variations in the heights of growing crops in turn cause shadow marks to be cast and are usually associated with variations of colour and density that are plainly visible from any well-placed vantage point as lines of darker or paler growth exactly following the course of an underlying buried feature. Vantage points at ground level are rare and seldom appropriately sited to allow the crop marks to be recognised, and it is usually impossible to recognise their plan, but from the air the clarity with which buried features like tiny pits and narrow ditches may be revealed is quite amazing.

Soil marks reflect differences in the composition of the soil at plough depth and such differences may be natural or the result of human activities like cultivation, digging, road-making or embanking. Because of disturbances caused by the action of the plough itself, soil marks tend to produce rather blurred images in air photographs and there may be difficulties of interpretation.

Parch marks are less commonly seen because they result from periods of drought. At such times, vegetation which is growing upon very dry, stony ground, such as buried foundations, will swiftly parch, while grass or crops growing in deep ditch silts will survive the parching of adjacent areas. The photograph of Old Oswestry hillfort (pl. 7.1) shows the effects of parching in the fort interior which reveals a network of twentieth-century wartime practice trenches.

Air photographs are so effective and informative that the medium will continue to support and enhance our appreciation of the environment long after the novelty value of the aerial portrait has been eclipsed. The earliest examples were taken over Paris by a balloonist in the 1850s, but it was not until the 1914–18 war that the practical applications of air photography were seriously explored, and in this war, the aerial reconnaissance of enemy dispositions and the prevention of such reconnaissance were the primary roles allocated to the opposed air arms. As a result of the improvements in technology and an enormous multiplication in the numbers of trained pilots resulting from the war, private enthusiasts began to explore the peacetime applications of aerial photography, several of them having discovered independently that unsuspected archaeological features were visible from the air. Most notable of the pioneer aerial archaeologists of Britain were Major G. W. G. Allen who compiled an important archive of photographs of the Oxford region and the outstandingly influential archaeologist O. G. S. Crawford who, with A. Keiller, published a remarkable collection of archaeological studies in *Wessex from the Air* in 1928.

During the 1939–45 war, air reconnaissance flights and the expert analysis of the results were again essential components of espionage and military planning, although cameras, emulsions and aircraft had greatly advanced since the previous World War. After the war, in 1948, J. K. S. St Joseph, one of the most respected of the wartime air reconnaissance analysts, was appointed to a Curatorship in Aerial Photography at Cambridge University. In the following year, the University constituted a Committee for Aerial Photography in recognition of the increasingly important roles that aerial photography was playing in teaching and research in history, archaeology and the environmental sciences. In 1962, an Auster aircraft was obtained and Mr A. G. Douglass was appointed as pilot. Three years later, a Cessna Skymaster which offered a superior range replaced the Auster.

Professor St Joseph has recently retired, but during his period of tenure, an incomparable collection of more than one-third of a million aerial photographs was compiled, including hundreds of archaeological sites discovered in the course of aerial survey. Mr D. R. Wilson has succeeded to the Curatorship, having served with the unit since 1965 and developed a remarkable expertise in the interpretation of air photograph evidence.

This book is entirely based on items from the Cambridge University Collection and although it only represents a miniscule fraction of the archive material, it provides a glimpse of the exceptional scope, quality and research value of the still-growing collection. I would like to thank David Wilson for his help in selecting subjects, commenting on my drafts and providing expert analyses of some of the most subtle and perplexing of the antiquities portrayed.

D. *The lost Roman town of Silchester. The polygonal hedgebank traces the line of the town's outer defences, while the street grid emerges as pale crop marks. Two closer views (pl. 9.1A & B) show that the outlines of the Roman buildings are also perfectly traced by crop marks*

1. THE FOUNDATIONS OF SCENERY

Human decisions have determined the course of British History, but Nature provided the stage upon which the successive dramas were enacted. The photographs in this book all testify to the handiwork of generations of settlers, farmers and urban workers who have helped to model and remodel the surface of these islands. All the pictures reveal the intimate relationship between man and the natural landscape, even if some seem, superficially, to portray a virgin countryside while, in others, the continuous townscapes appear unaffected by their physical setting. Nobody, having flicked through these pages, could be left in doubt of the remarkable diversity of the British scenes and, not surprisingly, Britain has been a fertile seedbed for leading geologists, geographers and naturalists.

Although Britain is less than one-ninetieth the extent of the world's largest state, the Soviet Union, her geological map is a finely detailed and brightly coloured tapestry of different rock types which cover virtually every age, structure and composition. It is no accident that all the oldest geological periods, the Devonian, Silurian, Ordovician, Cambrian and Pre-Cambrian, derive their names from British territories.

These photographs all testify to the potency of the air photograph as a means of probing and presenting the evolution of the natural landscape, but many of them stand in their own right as objects of beauty – works of art, almost. When appraised in this light, the textures of the land surface, the juxtapositions of high and low ground, hedgerows, walls and upland pasture, and light and shade endow each photograph with different aesthetic qualities. The first photograph, which is taken looking south-south-eastwards over Snowdon has a dreamy and strangely Japanese quality in the distant peaks which loom like mysterious islands above the swathes of mist.

While man is unpredictable, often apparently irrational and imbued with a will of his own, it is clear that in every locality Nature has guided the hand of human endeavour. In some places, the influences which stem from the natural landscape, its terrain, soils, climate and assets, may be subtle and difficult to discern. In others, particularly the exposed and thinly-soiled uplands where the limited opportunities restrict human choice, the voice of Nature has been more insistent.

In pl. 1.B of the Long Mynd in Shropshire, we see a striking juxtaposition of a rather barren upland and a fertile lowland. Surfacing along the right-hand side of our photograph like the back of a great whale are the incredibly ancient Pre-Cambrian sandstones and slates of the Long Mynd, reaching heights well above the 1500-ft contour. As a result of the altitude, exposure and steepness of the slopes, the Long Mynd is farmed as unenclosed rough pasture. An ancient track, the Port Way, can be seen following the crest of the ridge and in medieval times cattle driven from the Welsh uplands to market at Shrewsbury grazed beside this drove road. However, the Long Mynd is devoid of settlement. The only building which stands upon it, a white dot in the middle distance, exploits its own natural asset of exposure to westerly winds and cliff-face eddies for it is the local headquarters of the Midland Gliding Club.

1.A *Snowdon taken towards the south-south-east, with other peaks of the Snowdonia National Park just visible through the mist*

To the left of the Long Mynd, in the broad valley of the River East Onny, we see a completely different landscape of thickly-hedged pastures and ploughlands which are interspersed with patches of mature deciduous woodland. There are plenty of monuments to testify to the great antiquity of settlement in these relatively attractive farmlands. Some of the fields here may also be ancient as the rich, curving hedgerows in the foreground and middle distance suggest, while the more geometrical hedge patterns in the distance, beyond the scarp-foot hamlet of Asterton (right of centre), are typical of eighteenth- or early nineteenth-century Parliamentary Enclosure. This is one of the oldest photographs that is included, dating from 1947; most of this lovely hedgerow countryside still survives, but in view of the callous farming assaults on the counties to the south and east, one must fear for its future.

Although many of the landscapes which are portrayed may seem to be almost entirely natural, all are to a very considerable extent man-made. The deceptively 'natural' appearance of the countryside revealed in the photograph of Lake Thirlmere in Cumbria is quite

1.B *The Long Mynd in Shropshire: the Port Way, a medieval drove road, can be seen following the crest of the ridge*

transparent. Had man not interfered with the course of landscape evolution, we would see this countryside decked with lowland pockets of mixed deciduous forest including oak, elm and hazel, which once merged into the Scots pine and birch forest cloaking most of the uplands. The deforestation of the mountain slopes achieved by felling or burning was maintained by domesticated grazing animals and this clearance was probably largely accomplished before the close of the New Stone Age, around 4000 years ago. The small, walled fields which cluster in the lowlands may be of medieval and Dark Age vintage and are doubtless the successors of generations of prehistoric enclosures. The lake itself is not a natural feature but was created by the inundation of this glaciated valley to enlarge a tiny natural lake. This early exercise in what Miriam Shoard so tellingly describes as 'the theft of the countryside'* was enabled by an Act of 1879 in response to Manchester's needs for water. The trees surrounding the 'lake' are certainly not vestiges of Nature's wildwood, but alien conifers planted partly to stabilise the surrounding slopes.

The Theft of the Countryside: Miriam Shoard (1980)

1.c *Lake Thirlmere in Cumbria: a tiny lake was made into this huge reservoir in response to Manchester's need for water*

Like so many parts of the British countryside, the vicinity of Thirlmere is a 'no-go' area – and here again the airborne observer has a distinct advantage!

The countrysides which we struggle, usually vainly, to conserve are to greater or lesser extents the results of man's interaction with the physical landscape and in many of the photographs one can see that the most recent land-uses are superimposed upon the relics of earlier activities. The succession of changes can be compared to the pages in a book printed on grey tracing paper: the modern landscape is the open page but the creations of previous ages show dimly through. Beneath all the later pages is the one that represents the natural landscape, a forested wilderness which was still in the process of forming following the dramas of glaciation when, a little after 5000 BC, man the farmer set a new cycle of changes in motion. The vegetational relics of the natural landscape have virtually or entirely disappeared, but terrain, soil and climate continue to condition man's response to his setting and so a consideration of the physical environment is essential to this historically-orientated book.

1.1 WEST HIGHLAND LANDSCAPES

This scene, near Lochinver in the Highland region of the extreme north-west of mainland Scotland, is part of Britain's oldest landscape and also one which is almost unique in its scenic and geological fascination. The rocks portrayed were formed in the Pre-Cambrian era, before the dawn of recognisable life.

The barren, glaciated lowlands are composed of a tough, banded and silvery rock known as Lewisian Gneiss and before the end of the Pre-Cambrian period, around 600 million years ago, the Lewisian Gneiss land surface was virtually levelled by erosion to form a faintly undulating 'peneplain'. This plain in turn was blanketed by great thicknesses of pinkish Torridonian Sandstone which was deposited to form successive beds which were 2000 or more feet thick in places. All this was accomplished before the Pre-Cambrian period ended. In the geological eras which have followed, the overlying rocks have been eroded and the ancient Lewisian land surface is gradually being exposed. Thus, in the Highlands of the far north-west, one can tread upon a landscape which is apparently many millions of years older than life itself.

A great geological sandwich is revealed in the photograph. Dominating the scene is the precipitous mass of Suilven, its summit crowned by a slab of quartzite rock which protects the underlying Torridonian Sandstone that composes the bulk of the mountain, while the massive detached sandstone block stands amongst other Torridonian islands upon the basement of gneiss. The quartzite peak of Suilven reaches a height of 2399 ft, while Canisp in the distance is 380 ft taller.

The second photograph (pl. 1.1B) is taken from a position about fifty miles due south, above Loch Monar and looking north-westwards. The mountains that we see are almost entirely composed of Pre-Cambrian rocks and their ages increase with distance. The hard gneisses and schists in the foreground have been gouged and scalloped by glaciers, while in the middle distance are the more deeply dissected but loftier masses of Torridonian Sandstone. Lewisian Gneiss forms the less steeply rolling landscape of the island of Lewis on the distant horizon, while the northern tip of the Isle of Skye can be glimpsed just below the horizon in the upper left corner of the photograph.

A

1.2 TWO GLACIATED LANDSCAPES *Cumbria and North Yorkshire*

Each major glaciation of Britain resulted in the erosion of phenomenal amounts of rock debris from the exposed uplands of Britain, but glaciation was also a process which resulted in the deposition of this material in the lowlands as the glaciers and ice sheets waned. The photographs show two contrasting landscapes, one of which is characterised by glacial erosion, the other by deposition.

The first photograph (pl. 1.2.A), is taken from a position above the triangular lake known as Sprinkling Tarn, looking over the circular Angle Tarn towards the deep trough of the Mickleden valley and the summits of the Langdale Pikes in Cumbria. The scenery has been engraved in the tough old volcanic and altered or 'metamorphic' rocks which are termed the 'Borrowdale Volcanics' and the ef-

fects of glaciation are everywhere apparent. The mountain basin containing Angle Tarn was one of many upland collecting centres for ice. As the glaciations intensified, the glaciers advanced from these corries to gouge and steepen the existing valleys into which they slowly flowed and, at the same time, the corries themselves were steepened and deepened. As a result, several now contain lakes or tarns, while just above and to the right of Sprinkling Tarn there is a fine but tarnless corrie.

As the glaciers ground their ways forward, irregularities in the sides of the valleys were worn away and they developed their characteristically trough-like forms and 'U'-shaped cross-sections. Meanwhile, above the glaciers, frost-shattering prised slabs and flakes of rock from the

A

higher slopes and they retreated to meet at the rugged, crested 'arêtes' which superseded the more smoothly rounded watersheds. Such an arête runs from Angle Tarn towards the upper right corner of the photograph, via the bulky summit of Bow Fell at 2960 ft and Shelter Crags to Crinkle Crags.

The glaciers radiated outwards from the Lake District, their massive burdens of shattered rock debris being carried along in the body of the ice, while as the glacial conditions continued, glaciers and ice sheets from the Lake District, Southern Uplands and Pennines met and merged. In some places the rock fragments, which had become smoothed or reduced to innumerable flour-like particles, were plastered on the underlying landscape in a smear of boulder clay or 'till'. In others, they were moulded into recognisable landforms like the moraines which were dumped to mark the extents of the snouts or sides of the glaciers once the slow glacial retreat began. One of the most distinctive of the landscapes of glacial deposition and retreat is composed of masses of 'drumlins' and is fetchingly described as 'basket of eggs' topography. From the ground, one sees a smoothly pitching and rolling sea of hills but, viewed from the air, the aptness of the term is particularly apparent.

Above Horton in Ribblesdale in North Yorkshire, the view of the drumlin field also reminds one of a great shoal of stranded whales. This landscape was created at an early stage in the glacial retreat and the drumlins, which have aerodynamic forms like the blisters which cover aircraft wing and fuselage projections, were moulded from the masses of ice-bound sand, gravel and rock-flour debris by the receding glaciers.

B

1.3 BORROWDALE *Cumbria*

This photograph provides a more intimate view of the glaciated landscape of the Lake District than that of the broad panorama of Angle Tarn (pl. 1.2A). It was taken from a position about three miles south of Derwentwater; the small hamlet of Seatoller lies in the narrow lowland plain, lower right of centre, near the foot of the wooded spur. The photograph is looking up the valley of the Derwent river towards that of its tributary, Styhead Gill, which has its source in Styhead Tarn near the upper left corner of the photograph.

Between the 2949-ft peak of Great Gable and the spur overlooking Seatoller is the natural amphitheatre of a massive corrie which once contributed a river of ice to the glacier which advanced into the Derwent valley from Styhead Tarn corrie and other ice accumulation centres. Because the volume and erosive powers of the ice in the main valley exceeded those of the tributary glaciers, the Derwent valley is more deeply gouged than the tributary 'hanging' valleys. Glacial advance was a very slow process and the ice was welded to the rocks of the valley side. But the down-valley movement was remorseless and in the course of the gradual advance, fragments of rock were plucked from the slopes to produce the smoothed or rugged knolls which texture the landscape.

In the late- and post-glacial eras, sediments have been deposited in the valley floors, flattening the bases of the U-shaped valley cross-sections and supporting the sheltered enclosed pastures which present such striking contrasts to the barren, soil-stripped upland grazings. Despite the effects of at least 6000 years of grazing, pockets of woodland survive on the valley slopes. Some of them may be ancient and a few, in the neighbouring Keskadale and Rigg Beck valleys, may even be the relics of natural wildwood.

1.4 THE BLACK MOUNTAINS *near Llangorse, Powys*

This photograph is taken from a position about eight miles east-south-east of Brecon, looking south-eastwards into the Black Mountains which lie within the Brecon Beacons National Park. The scenery has been sculptured by ice and river action into a dissected upland of ancient, dark, reddish sandstone which is lapped by a sea of hedged fields. The sandstone beds are almost horizontal and minute differences in their resistance to erosion produces the faintly layered appearance.

The tallest summits in the Brecon Beacons, which lie to the south of the area, are around 2900 ft, but the highest ground in the photograph is the tabular peak of Pen Cerig-calch in the upper right quadrant, which reaches 2302 ft. The most striking division of the landscape is partly man-made, with the patchwork of old, hedged pastures extend-

ing upwards to the highest hedgerows which almost trace the 1200-ft contour, while above the hedgerows, the uplands are farmed as unenclosed rough grazings.

Although the region provides a convenient retreat from the battered industrial landscapes of South Wales, it remains one of the least celebrated of the British National Parks and its solitude is a valuable asset. The diagonally-trending valley in the foreground carries a tributary stream of the Rhian-goll river and the distant valley beyond Pen Cerig-calch is that of the Grwyne Fechan. This is essentially an area of dispersed settlement and the uplands provide pasture for the flocks owned by the occupants of the scattered white farmsteads which can just be glimpsed amongst the lower hedgerow country.

1.5 EGLWYSEG or CHURCH ROCKS *Clwyd*

Faulting along the line of this escarpment has juxtaposed two different rock types: the tough, silvery limestone which forms the uplands in the upper right half of the photograph and the softer shales which form the lower but quite steeply undulating country in the lower left section. The limestone scarp-face has a stepped appearance and this is due to slight differences in the resistance of the different horizontal limestone beds and also to the more rapid erosion of the thin sheets of shale which lie between some of the beds. During the Ice Ages, frost-shattering affected the exposed scarp-faces and vegetation maintains a precarious foothold on the unstable scree deposits near the foot of the cliff. When there is a heavy rainfall, the floods become channelled in fast-flowing streams which gradually engrave gullies in the scarp-face.

Contrasting landforms result from the erosion of the shale. The prominent hill of Dinas Bran in the lower left corner of the photograph is a natural feature, but its defensive potential has been enhanced by man-made fortifications. The masonry and earthworks of a medieval castle stand on the summit and can be seen on the left-hand margin of the photograph, while the hill is girdled by the ramparts of an Iron Age hillfort. The lushness of the woodland and pasture which grows upon the shale contrasts with the dry, springy pasture and scrub growing upon the limestone which is fissured by crevices that rapidly swallow most trickles of rainwater.

1.6 SALCOMBE *Devon*

During the Ice Ages, great volumes of water which would normally have formed a part of the oceans were locked upon the land in the form of gradually accumulating snow and ice. In the northern and western uplands of Britain which bore the brunt of the glaciations, the ice built up in some places to thicknesses of several hundreds of feet where the mountain peaks will have appeared as small islands adrift in a frozen sea. The weight of this land ice was sufficient to depress the northern portion of the British land-raft. When the glaciers and ice sheets waned, the resultant meltwater gushed back to raise the levels of the oceans, while the depressed land masses began gradually to rise once the heavy burden of ice was removed. Meanwhile, in a sea-saw like compensation, the southern territories which had carried little or no ice suffered a slight submergence.

In areas such as the west of Scotland, the gradual process of recovery is charted by the step-like raised beaches which mark stages in the re-emergence of the depressed land mass, while along the south and south-western shores of England, submergence is apparent in the drowned valleys or 'rias'. Here, rising sea levels have resulted in the inundation of low-lying vales to produce the sheltered, branching inlets so valued by medieval seamen and modern yachtsmen.

Salcombe, in the foreground of the photograph, is situated near the mouth of such a ria and the almost complete marine invasion of the courses of a number of small streams which previously converged in the vicinity of the town has created the complex of finger-like channels which, as the many white dots on the photograph show, are much exploited by members of the yachting fraternity.

The settlements which can be discerned in the upper left corner of the photograph are suburbs of Kingsbridge while the undulating landscape between Salcombe and Start Bay, which appears in the extreme upper right margin, is carpeted by the delightful patchwork patterns of well-hedged ancient pastures and cornfields.

25

1.7 KEYHAVEN SALT MARSHES *Hampshire*

When seen from the ground, this landscape will seem to most people but ecologists to be featureless, inaccessible and rather smelly. The shingle spit of Hurst Beach juts half-way across the south-western approaches to The Solent and, in its shelter, a salt marsh environment is developing. Most of the credit for the formation of this distinctive type of scenery can be attributed to the hybrid rice or cord grass *Spartina* which appeared here in 1870. By binding and stabilising the estuarine muds and silts, the plant is gradually causing the accretion of new shorelines.

Taken from different altitudes, the photographs provide views at contrasting scales and in the close-up view (pl. 1.7A), the line of the old coastline is seen marked by buildings and running along the upper margin of the picture. The loftier view (pl. 1.7B) provides an impression of the extent of the salt marshes. The stately rows of yachts are anchored in the tidal approaches to Keyhaven while the much larger port of Lymington is about four miles away and its south-eastern suburbs can just be glimpsed in the upper left corner of the photograph.

The salt marshes are traversed by the intricate dendritic patterns of tidal creeks; the gradients are minute and, consequently, as the tide falls the water pursues a lugubrious, meandering progress towards the sea. The yachts-man sees little evidence of these delicate patterns of rice grass, creeks and mudflats yet, from the air, the landscape resembles a masterwork of abstract batik.

1.8 LULWORTH COVE *Dorset*

Although beset by car parks (above), and a military training area (below), Lulworth Cove is one of our loveliest passages of coastal scenery. It is also a Mecca for students of geology. Closely paralleling the coast is an outcrop of relatively tough Jurassic limestone. It was intensely folded during the tumultuous earth movements which gave birth to the Alps, and the pleated patterns of folded beds can just be recognised in the cliffs above and to the left of the Cove. The back wall of the cove amphitheatre is formed of less resistant chalk which underlies the swelling Dorset downland.

Running between the limestone and the chalk is a narrow strip of soft clay, and at Lulworth the sea has breached the natural coastal defences provided by the limestone to carve out the great bay in the less resistant clay and chalk which lie behind.

1.9 FORENESS POINT *Kent*

Chalk cliffs, composed of the compacted, calcareous shells of minute sea creatures which were deposited in the geological age known as the Cretaceous, around 100 million years ago, provide a white frontage along the coastline of south-east England. This photograph is looking north-westwards to Foreness Point on the eastern extremity of the Isle of Thanet. The outlying Margate suburb of Kingsgate is neatly laid-out in the middle distance, while the castle, whose tower peeps above the cliffline on the nearer headland, dates from about 1680. A little below it can be glimpsed the broken walls of the stables of Holland House, built to resemble a decaying castle of Edward I. Follies such as this were scattered around Holland House,

but chalk cliffs being less resistant to the forces of erosion than many harder rocks, the greatest folly of all involved the construction of the mansion (above the main beach shown in the photograph) so close to the edge. Most of the house has toppled over the retreating cliff, leaving but a single range surviving.

The illustration shows how the action of the waves, which attack and undermine the bases of the cliffs in times of storm, have cut a smooth and gently sloping coastal platform as the cliff face has slowly receded. The dark blotches which carpet the sea shore consist of seaweeds anchored upon the shingles of the beach.

1.10 ORFORD NESS *Suffolk*

The low-lying coast of East Anglia is less stable than the rugged, cliff-girt shores of the north and west. This instability has led to the literal downfall of some coastal settlements, including the important medieval town of Dunwich which lay a few miles to the north of Orford Ness, while other old harbours were silted into redundancy as the waves rolled shingle spits across the outlets. Currents carry banks of sand and shingle southwards along the Suffolk coast and the creation of such a spit of shingle ridges is nowhere more dramatically demonstrated than at Orford Ness.

The photograph is looking north-eastwards along the sweeping spit of Orford Beach and it is clear that the gradual south-westward advance of the spit has diverted the outlet of the River Alde southwards. Known in its coastal section as the River Ore, the Alde parallels the shore for about ten miles before leaving the confines of Orford Beach and entering the sea.

The settlement of Orford, which lies above left of centre amongst a darker patch of woods and hedgerows, was developed as a medieval trading port which enjoyed the protection of a then much shorter spit. The tower of Orford Castle can just be glimpsed at the left of the village, and when it was built, between 1165 and 1171, the spit only reached southwards as far as the upper tip of the island which lies above the centre of the photograph. For a while, Orford Ness was stable in this position, before advancing southward and bringing decay to the old port.

In these three photographs are seen facets of a landscape which is relatively modern, both in physical terms and in its development by man. The Fens of East Anglia and Lincolnshire were created in the millennia following the last glaciation. The natural processes involved were complex, but around 6000 years ago, peat began to form in the slight hollows and valleys of the fenland clay plain, while 4500 to 4000 years ago, the area experienced a transgression by the sea, and layers of marine clays and silts were deposited. From this time onwards, peat continued to form until purposeful efforts at Fen drainage were accomplished in the seventeenth century. As a result of drainage, the fenland peats have contracted and have been greatly reduced by bacterial action and inappropriate modern farming methods. By the end of this century, the peat – and the profitable farming which it supported – will have virtually disappeared.

From the air, it is possible to survey ancient as well as modern Fen landscapes. Before the draining of the area was accomplished, the Fens were traversed by multitudes of slow-moving, meandering and branching rivers and streams. In the course of their wanderings, these watercourses became lined by accumulated tidal deposits of calcareous loams, silts and clays. Following the drainage and shrinkage of the surrounding peat, the sinuous watercourse deposits now stand above the peat surface as snaking ridges or 'roddons'. The roddons, whose main period of formation was the Iron Age, trace the tortuous courses of lost rivers and streams; they may stand up to 4 ft above their surroundings, but from the air they are recognised by the pale tones of their limey loams and clays. Thus, in the photograph of an area of Fen between Peterborough and Chatteris (pl. 1.11A), complete former river networks can be traced amongst the disciplined ranks of modern fenland fields.

At first glance, the photograph of an area of Fen near Littleport (pl. 1.11B) may seem quite uneventful, but on closer inspection one realises that it represents one of

A

B

the most striking illustrations of the close relationship between man and his environment. A monotonous tract of geometrical fenland fields is traversed by a straight modern road, while a roddon weaves to and fro across the scene. A typical series of dispersed fenland farmsteads punctuate the road – and soon the observer realises that a farm is sited at each point where the road and roddon intersect. Clearly, each farm has been deliberately sited to take advantage of the higher, drier and better-drained ground which the roddon ridge provides.

The most purposeful attempt to drain the Fens took place in the fourth and fifth decades of the seventeenth century, previous efforts at fenland drainage having had little success as a result of the piecemeal nature of the undertakings. The Duke of Bedford employed experienced Dutch engineers to carve a channel carrying the waters of the Bedfordshire Ouse across the Fens to the Nar valley at Denver near Downham Market, thus draining the entire South Level of the Fens. Two parallel channels were driven across the Fens, the Old Bedford River of 1631 and the New Bedford or Hundred Foot River of 1651. Sluices were

C

needed to regulate the outflow from the Fens and the inflow of tidal waters, while networks of ditches and channels conducted fenland water into the Bedford Rivers (pl. 1.11c). The scheme was pushed through in the face of powerful objections from common folk who flourished from the self-contained grazing, fowling, fishing and peat-cutting lifestyle. Also, despite its spectacular initial success, the Duke's scheme created a complex series of environmental consequences, beginning with the shrinkage of the Fen peat, and soon the new rivers had to be complemented by an elaborate pumping system, firstly involving windmills and then steam pumps.

2.A *The gigantic passage grave of Maes Howe on Orkney. The central dome-like mound which covers the stone-built entrance passage and burial chamber is 24 ft high and 115 ft in diameter and the entrance can be seen as a slit to the right of the mound. A roughly circular ditch encircles the Late Neolithic tomb*

2. ANCIENT TOMBS AND TEMPLES

Many of the most imposing monuments in the British landscape are the products of forgotten religions and, as such, they present serious challenges to archaeological interpretation. Excavation can tell us a great deal about the day-to-day lives of prehistoric people and about the nature of their environment, but beliefs exist in the mind and perish along with their adherents. While it is relatively easy to recognise the form and function of constructions like dwellings or livestock enclosures, monuments which have no obvious domestic or economic uses are bracketed together in the 'ritual' category – and we may never be able to recognise their precise places and uses in the religious and ceremonial lives of those who built them. Although we have been conditioned to think in terms of practical, rational 'economic man', the study of prehistory, particularly of the Late Neolithic and Beaker periods, leaves one in no doubt that the creative energies of most societies were devoted to the construction of monuments which produced not one iota of food, shelter or physical comfort.

Although the most central questions about the prehistoric ritual monuments concern the religious beliefs and practices which spawned them, these questions are still unanswerable. The relics do however provide other insights into prehistoric life. They shatter the myth of the inept aboriginal savage, for the greater monuments could only be the handiwork of people who were sufficiently numerous and adept in the techniques of farming as to be able to set the need for food-raising aside and despatch sizable labour forces for work on building tombs or temples.

They also tell us of communities with well-developed and purposeful political organisations. The great monuments are unlikely to be the products of peasant spontaneity or democracy but, rather, they commemorate the arrival of a class or caste system in which priest-kings or chieftains wielded powerful forces of command. The greatest of the ritual constructions, like Avebury, Silbury Hill or Stonehenge, could not have been built within a single lifespan and so they show that visions and powers could be passed on from one generation to the next. Also, we should not assume that preoccupations with status or territorial control are unique to the modern age. While monuments like long barrows, chambered tombs, causewayed enclosures and, perhaps, henges and stone circles are epitaphs to lost religions, they also proclaim the status of those who caused them to be built and demonstrate in a most telling manner the clan or tribal claims of ownership over the territories in which they stand. Only a tiny fraction of the people who lived in Neolithic Britain could aspire to burial in one of the great tombs, and the siting of these mausoleums in prominent, widely visible places hints strongly at their symbolic importance in the contest to control land.

It is very notable that some periods, like the Neolithic, Beaker, Earlier Bronze Age and Middle Ages, are associated with massive religious building enterprises, while others, like the Later Bronze, Iron, Jacobite and Georgian Ages produced relatively little. The monuments which are depicted in this chapter belong to the three first mentioned periods and recent developments in archaeology allow us to reconstruct the outlines of the social and economic context.

2.B *The magnificent Ring of Brodgar stone circle on Orkney. Of the sixty original stones, twenty-seven remain standing and their average height is 7 ft. The diameter of the area enclosed by the surrounding ditch is around 370 ft*

In Britain, we know of no important religious construction dating from the Old or Middle Stone Ages when man existed as a hunter and gatherer. The semi-nomadic hunting and gathering lifestyle will have precluded the amassing of possessions or establishment of imposing permanent temples. Early in the fifth millennium BC farming became established, but the farming era was around five centuries old before the great collective tombs and causewayed enclosures of the first generation of massive religious monuments were built. They appeared at a time when farming had advanced from its original favoured heartlands, becoming successful, productive and supporting unprecedentedly high levels of population. In the course of this triumphant revolution, stresses and competition intensified as groups struggled to win and hold land, and it was probably at this time that powerful leaders and a stratified class- or caste-based society developed. As well as being epitaphs to a compelling religion which required impressive ceremonial centres, the Neolithic ritual monuments must also be evidence of the arrival of powerful chieftains and the emergence of a society which was sufficiently efficient and capable as to allow the great investments of effort which the temples embody.

One of the strangest features of the ritual monuments is their diversity. Not only does one find great variations in size and design within a particular class, but there are also many different classes: tombs of varied designs, causewayed enclosures, henges, cursuses, stone circles, ritual pits and other monuments which overlap the categories. Monuments of all these types were built in the later part of the Neolithic period.

In the Beaker period, which arrived gradually in the centuries following 2700 BC, some monument forms fell gradually out of use; the rite of collective burial was slowly abandoned, but the interest in stone circles continued. It seems to have survived in the earlier part of the Bronze Age when solitary standing stones or monoliths were also erected and when round barrows became common features of the landscape.

In the course of the Bronze Age though, the practice of building impressive religious monuments apparently disappeared. However, it seems that the most important settlements of the Bronze Age were to be found in valleys and low-lying areas where, as a result of later ploughing and natural processes of deposition, the evidence is likely to have been destroyed or be masked. Although Classical writers have provided descriptions of Celtic religion with its many deities and Druidic cults, there is scarcely any evidence of imposing religious engineering in Britain during the Iron Age, when sacred sites seem to have been associated with natural features such as wells and groves. However, it is possible that the hillforts introduced in chapter 7 may have had some ritual significance.

Air photography has contributed enormously to our exploration of ancient religious foci. It has been particularly informative in revealing hosts of smaller or ploughed up monuments such as causewayed enclosures, henges and barrows which are quite unrecognisable from the ground. By lengthening the lists of such monuments, it has demonstrated the existence of scores of lesser 'neighbourhood' ritual centres and suggested vast numbers of potentially rewarding sites for excavation.

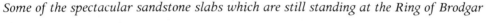

Some of the spectacular sandstone slabs which are still standing at the Ring of Brodgar

2.1 MAVESYN RIDWARE and CARDINGTON CAUSEWAYED ENCLOSURES
Staffordshire and Bedfordshire

In the closing centuries of the fifth millennium BC and around 500 years or more after the introduction of farming to Britain, an explosion of monumental engineering began which continued beyond the close of the revolutionary Neolithic period. The first of the massive creations were tombs and 'causewayed enclosures'. Although we know some of the functions of the tombs, the causewayed enclosures remain controversial.

The great enclosure at Windmill Hill, very close to Avebury, was excavated in 1925–9 and most of the early ideas about the 'causewayed camps' were inspired by this site. Subsequently, many new examples were recognised as a result of aerial photography, and new ones continue to be discovered. The monuments consist of a central area which is normally many acres in extent and which is surrounded by one or more rings of causewayed or interrupted ditches. Many of the sites, like these two, can only be detected

from the air, when their ditches emerge as crop- or soilmarks. The ditches served as quarries which were excavated in the construction of the ramparts or banks which lay on their inner sides. However, the banks tended to be poorly constructed and are prone to slump back into the ditches. As a result of these constructional foibles and the ravages of more than five or six millennia of erosion, the causewayed enclosures are hardly ever impressive when seen from the ground although they embodied tens of thousands of man-hours of labour and must have been very imposing in their day.

At the Mavesyn Ridware enclosure, the roughly concentric broken lines of the three ditches are apparent, although the function of the causeways is mysterious and they are certainly more numerous than the need for easy access to the interior would require.

The old term 'causewayed camps' which was applied

to such monuments is becoming unfashionable since it incorporates the original assumption that the enclosures were camps where pastoral peoples kept their livestock. It seems that the enclosures probably served a number of purposes. They had important ritual functions and corpses were exposed in their deep ditches, perhaps prior to the lodging of the bones in long barrows or megalithic tombs. They also had defensive uses and recent excavations, such as the one at Hambledon Hill in Dorset, have revealed evidence of burnings and attacks by archers. While the camps might have been used as livestock enclosures, their existence as great market places in association with the stone axe industry is more probable. They were certainly more important in the lives of the Neolithic communities than their poorly-preserved remains might suggest.

Some of the causewayed enclosures experienced a thousand years of use, during which time their silting ditches were periodically recut. The first photograph contains hints that the ritual significance of this example was still vaguely recognised in the Bronze Age for a pair of circular ditches representing the remains of round barrows can be discerned to the lower right of the enclosure.

The crop marks beside and overlapping the enclosure near Cardington are complex, but mainly of the Romano-British period. Although they tend to confuse the picture, the three sets of concentric broken lines of the causewayed ditches can clearly be seen in the lower left quadrant of the photograph.

Three distinct types of prehistoric monuments appear here, but the enclosure in the centre of the photographs, which is the most plainly portrayed in the picture, is invisible from the ground. To the visitor, by far the most obvious relic is the Pimperne long barrow, the sausage-like mound near the bottom of the photograph. This is an earthen tomb of the Neolithic period and is unusually well preserved. One can recognise the quarry ditches which run beside the long sides of the mound and provided the earth and chalk rubble from which it is built. In contrast to the majority of examples, these ditches are roughly parallel, while those of most long barrows converge slightly to define a trapezoidal mound. This long barrow will probably date from the fourth millennium BC and the simplicity of the external form could mask quite complicated internal structures, for several excavated long barrows are known to have been built on top of wooden 'mortuary houses' in which corpses decomposed before being interred in the earthen tombs.

Directly above the long barrow is an irregular, some-what heart-shaped enclosure which emerges as a crop mark and which is defined by the traces of double ditches; cross ditches link them and divide the intervening space, while the incurved entrance lies to the left. Without the aid of excavation, it would not be possible to deduce the date of this feature or discover whether it represents the defences of a settlement or a livestock enclosure. The diagonal lines across the enclosure are modern land drains whilst beyond, and just below the D-shaped spinney, the traces of 'Celtic' fields which probably date from the Iron Age can just be discerned.

These features lie just across the A354 from Blandford army camp. The barrow is some 330 ft in length and it remains a prominent feature of the skyline. Like other such barrows, it will have been thoughtfully situated to impress the traveller and, as well as a tomb, it was probably also a prominent symbol of territorial control, housing the remains of members of the social élite and thus demonstrating ancestral ownership of the surrounding lands.

2.3 BELAS KNAP CHAMBERED TOMB *Gloucestershire*

Around 4300 BC, the rite of collective burial under an earthen long barrow became established in Britain and, before very long, more sophisticated variants of the long barrow known as 'chambered tombs' were adopted in the stone-rich lands of the north and west. The tombs which were built in the region of the River Severn and Cotswolds repeated the elongated, trapezoidal shapes of the long barrows of the southern and eastern lowlands, but they had stone-lined passages and burial chambers and, unlike the long barrows, they could be re-opened from time to time to accept new burials. Before remains were interred, the corpses were allowed to decompose, perhaps in timber mortuary houses or in the ditches of causewayed enclosures.

The tombs seem to testify to a belief in the afterlife, a reverence and concern for the spirits of the departed and, perhaps, to a death cult. They were also important territorial symbols, sited in prominent positions and probably

announcing the claims of land ownership by the groups who built them. The Belas Knap tomb near Winchcombe is situated high in the Cotswold scarplands and commands fine views over the surrounding countryside. At first it seems to be a typical example of a chambered tomb of the Wessex hill country and, as with some other examples, it has an incurving entrance providing a small forecourt. However, this is a false entrance, perhaps constructed to frustrate tomb robbers. Excavation and restoration has enabled the actual burial chambers to be seen set into the long sides of the tomb mound. When the tomb was opened, at least thirty-eight skeletons were found and some of the skulls had been fractured by heavy blows. Whether these blows were struck just before or just after death is not known. An original low revetting drystone wall runs around the barrow clearly defining its shape but the enclosure wall is modern.

2.4 KING ARTHUR'S ROUND TABLE *Cumbria*

This seems to be a rather prosaic rural scene until one notices the circular earthworks in the centre of the photograph. Road widening has smashed through the upper rim of the monument which is otherwise a fine example of a Neolithic henge. An entrance causeway can be seen in the lower rim and a second entrance lay on the opposite side of the henge, now wrecked by the road. The car which is approaching the road junction provides an indication of the scale of the earthworks which have a diameter of about 300 ft.

The henge has been affected by nineteenth-century activities – including a period when it was used as a tea garden! – but an idea of its original form can be gleaned from a seventeenth-century plan and from excavations. The step-like 'berm' which separates the outer bank and inner ditch and the faint central mound are relatively modern features, while the obliterated entrance was flanked by a pair of standing stones. The enclosing bank still stands to a height of 5 ft, while the ditch was originally up to 5 ft deep. Presumably, the earthworks defined a

sacred enclosure within which rituals will have been performed – and it is worth noting that when the monument was intact, the congregation or celebrants will only have been visible to outsiders when glimpsed through the gunsight-like gaps provided by the entrance causeways. Near the centre of the monument, a trench was excavated which had been used in a human cremation ceremony and then covered by an indecipherable stone structure.

Although some henges were isolated, others often occurred in groups. The village at the top of the photograph is Eamont Bridge and just a quarter of a mile to the west (left) of the village is Mayburgh henge with a diameter that is 60 ft greater than that of King Arthur's Round Table and banks that are up to three times as high. In the medieval period, ancient earthworks such as these were woven into myth and legend; Mayburgh includes the Saxon 'burh' or 'fort' in its name, and of course there is no contemporary link between its henge neighbour and King Arthur.

41

2.5 THE PRIDDY CIRCLES *Somerset*

Seen from the B3134, running across the top of the photograph, the Priddy Circles are amost indetectable. Four great circles comprise the group, the fourth being partly destroyed and lying some distance away on the other side of the road. They are best interpreted as 'henge' monuments, and henges first appeared in Britain around 3400 BC. They are circular banked and ditched enclosures which must have been important in the religious and ceremonial lives of the Neolithic communities who built them. Even so, we know nothing about the detail of worship and ceremonies and perhaps the most puzzling feature concerns the way in which henges are often found in groups.

The Priddy henges are of the single-entrance type but they differ from the standard design. Firstly, their ditches lie outside their banks, in the Stonehenge manner. Secondly, the banks are not earthen and the excavation

of the most distant of the three henges in the photograph has shown that work began with the erection of a double circle of stakes. The spaces between the stakes in the rings was then filled with walling in drystone and, in places, in turf and then the central space of the bank was filled with stone and earth from the ditch. The roadside buildings give some impression of the colossal scale of these monuments and the point is underlined when one realises that the three henges are separated from each other by gaps of about 90 yds.

The unusual use of stone walling in the building of these henges may be explained by the fact that they are built on the thinly-soiled limestone of the Mendips. The surface here is pock-marked by circular depressions and these are not man-made, but solution hollows formed by natural processes which have dissolved the limestone.

2.6 ARBOR LOW *Derbyshire*

Arbor Low, a few miles south of Bakewell, is one of the most impressive of the British prehistoric monuments, but its remote location at a height of 1225 ft on a limestone plateau results in its being less visited than most others. It is a rather complex monument which has developed through a number of stages. The first is represented by a massive henge earthwork with opposed entrance causeways producing the typical 'double banana' form. These causeways can be recognised at the left and right sides of the great girdling banks which are still over 6 ft in height. As normal with henge monuments, the ditch was placed inside the banks and excavation has shown that it was originally up to 9 ft in depth.

At some time after the construction of the henge, an impressive stone circle was erected in its sacred interior, consisting of forty-six large and thirteen smaller stones and inside this circle a 'cove' – perhaps an inner sanctuary – of four large stones was built. The stones are now all lying flat; the circle could have been vandalised at some distant time in the past but it is also possible that the sockets which held the stones were insufficiently deep. The monument dates from the New Stone Age but, in the Early Bronze Age, members of a group of people who buried a ritual food vessel with their dead constructed a massive round barrow which intruded on the southern rim of the henge. It can be seen just below the left entrance causeway and its pocked summit results from the ravages of crude eighteenth- and nineteenth-century excavations. Running away from the upper rim of the henge is a much-decayed linear bank, perhaps a boundary marker of a later prehistoric era. Cattle graze in the surrounding fields.

Long after the original purposes of these imposing monuments had been forgotten, Saxon settlers often attributed them to the Devil or to giants. The 'Low' part of the name derives from the Saxon *hlaw*, a barrow or giant's grave and 'Arbor' may come from an earth fort or *eordburh*.

2.7 A CURSUS *near Scorton, North Yorkshire*

The apparently bland landscape around the wartime airfield at Scorton near Richmond was photographed in 1949. At first the area may seem to contain little of note, but then one becomes aware of the shadowy lines which trace the parallel courses of ditches defining a cursus monument.

The cursuses date from the late Neolithic and Earlier Bronze Age periods and they are almost totally mysterious. They seldom survive as impressive or even detectable monuments when seen from the ground and the discoveries which show that cursuses were quite numerous have mainly resulted from aerial photography. In their decayed and ploughed-out states, they make little impression on the senses, though when newly built they will have been dramatic and imposing features embodying many thousands of man-hours of toil. Their banks will often have

been over head high, and anyone standing between them will have had the sensation of being in a great trough which was heading far towards the distant horizon.

Various interpretations are on offer, some of them quite loony and none of them particularly convincing. The cursuses were named by the eighteenth-century antiquary William Stukeley, who thought that the example near Stonehenge was used for funerary games. More recently, it has been suggested that cursuses are processional avenues. They are often found to be associated with other ritual monuments such as henges and long barrows. In this case, the circular remains of a pair of Bronze Age round barrows can be seen right at the terminal of the cursus, and their siting here is unlikely to be coincidental.

2.8 CASTLERIGG STONE CIRCLE *Cumbria*

In revealing the geometry of the magnificent stone circle at Castlerigg near Keswick, this photograph is unable to include the magnificent setting, for the circle crowns Chestnut Hill and is surrounded by a beautiful amphitheatre of mountains and fells. Unlike many other great circles such as Avebury, the Ring of Brodgar or Stonehenge, the Castlerigg stones are freestanding for there is no embracing henge ditch and earthbank. The diameter is about 35 yds.

The circle lies in an area of fell pasture which is poor in arable land but which was associated, in the Neolithic and Earlier Bronze Age periods, with the vital stone axe industry, the axe quarries and factory sites of the Langdale Pikes being just a few miles away. While the stone circles

of the British Isles were probably temples, they could also have operated as market places associated with the axe industry.

The ring of slate boulders has a slightly flattened form that is probably related to the local terrain, which falls away to the upper right. The right-hand sector of the circle contains a rectangular arrangement of stones which form a group whose function is unknown. Although the circle probably dates from a late phase of the Neolithic period, as many as three Bronze Age stone cairns may have been added, and one of them is known to have been sited just above and to the left of the group. Medieval plough ridges can be seen approaching the circle in the upper portion of the photograph.

2.9 BARCLODIAD-Y-GAWRES PASSAGE GRAVE *Anglesey, Gwynedd*

In the centuries preceding 3000 BC, a new development in the evolution of the megalithic tomb appeared in the form of the 'passage grave'. The colossal and elaborate tombs of Newgrange, Knowth and Dowth in the Boyne valley of eastern Ireland may have been its culmination. The passage graves had long entrance passages which terminated in a central burial chamber with the stone-built interior structures being housed under a round mound of earth and rubble. Similar graves may be found beyond Ireland; Maes Howe on Orkney (page 32) is the most celebrated example and there are others in the Orkney islands and also in the west of Wales.

It has been suggested that the passage graves represent an invasion or migration of Irish passage grave-builders, but it may be that new ideas rather than actual settlers travelled across the Irish Sea. The tomb at Barclodiad-y-gawres on Anglesey is linked to the Boyne valley tombs not only by its form, but also by the carved examples of 'passage grave art' which appears in the form of spirals, lozenges and chevron designs carved on some of its stones.

The tomb is partly the product of modern restoration and a part of the round mound consists of a concrete dome erected to protect the internal tomb structures. It may be no coincidence that it lies just a few miles from the modern Irish Sea port of Holyhead, on a rocky promontory which juts westwards towards Ireland.

This ground level photograph shows how much more substantial the cliffs are than they appear in the air photograph

2.10 AVEBURY *Wiltshire*

Within the span of a single photograph is seen what are arguably the two most impressive creations of the New Stone Age. In the lower part of the photograph is the magnificent and elaborate Avebury henge, while in the upper right corner, the colossal mound of Silbury Hill (*see* page 50). Lying in this neighbourhood, there are also the causewayed camp of Windmill Hill and the imposing West Kennet chambered tomb. With such a concentration of great monuments, Avebury must be regarded as a great religious focus of Neolithic Wessex. Since a massive force of organised labour will have been needed to construct the Avebury and Silbury monuments, the area might also have been an important centre of political power.

The Avebury henge was constructed in the centuries around 2500 BC and consists of a roughly circular enclosure, around thirty acres in extent and embraced by an outer bank and an inner ditch which, in its original form, was a canyon-like gorge some 30 ft in depth. The enclosure was also ringed by a circle of massive sarsen stone slabs, some of which still stand and can be seen in the right hand portion of the henge. Inside, two more circles were constructed and the fragmentary remains of both can be seen above and below the dwellings of the modern village.

Running away from the circle towards the upper left corner of the photograph are the standing stones which trace the course of the West Kennet Avenue, presumably a processional way which continued for about a mile to The Sanctuary. This was probably a timber ceremonial building which incorporated stone circles within the structure and of which there are few visible traces remaining.

The modern roads still favour the henge entrances which were created some 4500 years ago. The medieval village developed inside the henge, overrunning the inner stone circles as it grew, while the villagers systematically vandalised the pagan stones. It may be significant, however, that the Christian church, which is visible near the right-hand margin of the photograph, was built in a position outside the prehistoric temple.

Silbury Hill stands 130 ft above the surrounding vale, contains nearly 9 million cubic feet of building materials and its circular base extends over 5½ acres of ground. It is man-made, but its function is one of the great mysteries of British prehistory.

The hill was commenced around 2750 BC and its construction may have continued for around a century. Calculations of the man-hours of labour involved suggest that a force of seventy would have been continuously employed if the hill took a century to build – in which case the labourers might then have been deployed on the monumental Avebury henge project. These statistics alone provide proof that our old and unflattering visions of late Stone Age society were false. Such daunting undertakings could only be contemplated by a capable and well-organised society which was highly motivated and disciplined and so able to see a great vision through to its fulfilment.

Silbury Hill is remarkably well preserved and more than four millennia of weathering have had little effect on its form. Excavations by Professor R. Atkinson in 1968–70 showed that the hill is constructed of tiers of quarried chalk blocks with the framework infilled by rubble, while an apparently random collection of chalk boulders lie at the heart of the monument. This, and several less competent earlier excavations have failed to reveal a burial inside the Hill. A burial in an off-centre position would easily escape discovery and the Hill could indeed be a tomb, but it could also be a massive and imposing territorial symbol, built to proclaim the wealth and might of the leader or society which caused it to be built.

Running diagonally across the photograph is the A4 which follows a Roman routeway, and it is notable that even the Romans were obliged to divert around the flanks of the great monument which they probably used as a sighting point when surveying the road and which is older than the pyramids and the greatest prehistoric mound in Europe.

Most readers will have viewed this scene from the ground, but from the air the geometry and less obvious structures at Stonehenge are more readily apparent. The monument has a long and complicated history. Work began around 2700 BC with the construction of a large henge earthwork which was unusual in that the quarry pits which composed the ditch were situated outside rather than inside the bank. This bank is only a couple of feet high today and will be unnoticed by most visitors, but its original height may have been over 6 ft. The henge almost fills the frame of the photograph. The entrance and the accompanying Heel Stone are in the upper left of the picture.

About two hundred years later, a double ring of bluestones was erected – the stones, almost incredibly, being brought by land and sea from the Preseli Hills in south-west Wales, although a recent geological examination of the stone has cast some doubts on this explanation. Then the bluestones were dismantled and the site was prepared to receive massive dressed boulders of sarsen which were brought from the Marlborough Downs. These were erected in an outer circle and inner horseshoe formation which was unique in that the vertical stones supported horizontal sarsen lintels or henges – the inappropriate generic term 'henge' for such sites deriving from the Stonehenge lintels.

In the second part of this phase, bluestones were reincorporated, but this oval arrangement was never completed and in the final building phase of the Earlier Bronze Age, the bluestones were re-used to provide an inner circle and a horseshoe setting which lay inside the sarsen horseshoe.

In the photograph, thirty of the fifty-six so-called Aubrey Holes can be recognised from white patches of chalk which mark their positions. They are named after their seventeenth-century discoverer and although their exact function is unknown, they seem to have been ritual pits and some of them held cremations.

Interest in this great Wessex religious and ceremonial centre waned in the second half of the Bronze Age. Although the circle's completion probably predated the Iron Age Druidic cult by at least a millennium, Stonehenge has become a focus for modern Celtic twilight eccentricities and the photograph shows Druidic goings-on in the centre of the circle. It was taken in 1948, long before it became necessary to fence off the circle to protect the turf from trampling and erosion by the feet of the tourist throngs. It is interesting to note that the pressure from visitors was far less in the early post-war period when the site was apparently quite unscathed.

2.13 LAMBOURN 'SEVEN BARROWS' *Berkshire*

The photograph opposite shows that the traditional title 'Seven Barrows' is misleading and, in fact, at least forty barrows were grouped in this important barrow cemetery. The bowl-shaped round barrow was the typical but not the only form of burial adopted in the Bronze Age. Although the smoothly-domed round barrow appears to be a simple monument, excavations show that such barrows often had complicated internal structures, including rings or lines of fencing which in some cases served to revet or support the accumulating mound. The form of burial found inside these barrows also varied, some corpses being buried in wooden coffins or scooped out logs, others interred as cremations in pots or bags.

In most parts of England, a rounded earth mound or cairn of stones was erected and the barrows had forms rather like inverted pudding bowls. The Earlier Bronze Age people of Wessex, however, were relatively advanced, active in Irish and continental trade and dominated by wealthy aristocrats, and in their territory a variety of different barrow forms were adopted. The significance of the various forms of burial mound is not known although it has been suggested that the 'disc barrows' covered female burials. Often the barrows were grouped in cemeteries.

A selection of different barrow forms are clearly portrayed in the photograph. A 'bell barrow', which is dotted with bushes, lies above the road and track junction at the extreme left. Nearest to the angle of the junction is a 'disc barrow' and right beside it, one of several 'bowl barrows'. A second disc barrow can be seen at the upper right of the cemetery and directly to its left is a 'double bowl barrow'. Masked by a line of trees in the upper right of the photograph is a damaged but extremely early Neolithic long barrow dating back to the latter part of the fifth millennium BC. Whether the association between the Stone Age and Bronze Age tombs is coincidental, we do not know.

A tree and some bushes partly obscure this bowl barrow at Lambourn

3. FIELDS: THE PATCHWORK LANDSCAPE

Although Britain is the most heavily urbanised country in the world, air travellers know that most panoramas of Britain are composed of patchwork field patterns. It is easy to assume that one field or network of fields is much like another, but on closer inspection it is plain that the landscape displays not only living fields of many types, but also fossilised fields of various different ages. Fields of one kind or another have existed in Britain for well over 5000 years, but each type tends to have its own particular features and so the airborne landscape historian can learn to recognise the fields of different periods. In some places he can see the relics of Bronze-Age or Iron-Age farming lying stranded in areas which are now only moorland or rough grazing. In others, he can clearly see that the latest generation of fields is really like the open page in a book of tracings and the evidence of older farming ages looms boldly or faintly through.

Farming arrived in Britain in the fifth millennium BC, but very little is known about the nature of the earliest fields or clearings. In the course of the New Stone Age, a landscape that was dominated by deciduous forest was gradually superseded by one in which fields, clearings and pastures at least equalled the extent of the woodland. Most of the information about the changes has come from ancient but well-preserved pollen grains. An extensive network of New Stone Age fields has been recognised in Co Mayo and traces of fields of this period are surely recorded on air photographs. However, to recognise them we would need to know more about the nature of the quarry as they are likely to be recorded only as faint and subtle details.

Much more is known about the fields of the Bronze Age. The image of prehistoric farmers who scrabbled away ineffectively in their efforts to farm tiny clearings in the primeval forest is quite false. Partly as a result of air photography, we know that Bronze Age fields carpeted vast extents of the countryside. They existed in a variety of shapes and sizes, but today they survive most obviously in upland areas, many of which have been abandoned by ploughmen for the last 3000 years. From the evidence of the Bronze Age field and boundary walls or 'reaves' recognised on Dartmoor, we know that networks of small fields here produced parallel patterns on the sides of the valleys, while the upper moorland plateaux served as common grazings. We know much less about the forms of Bronze Age farming practised in the richer lowlands and valley bottoms, where the evidence has usually been obliterated by later ploughing or masked by great thicknesses of river deposits.

Iron Age fields also existed in a variety of shapes and forms: sometimes the networks

---

3.A *Looking westwards across the foothills of the Cambrian Mountains from a position near Llandovery, we see a landscape which reminds one of a crumpled patchwork quilt. The fields, mainly pastures, are of various medieval and later ages and richly hedged. The rather strange 'quilted' effect is produced by the fact that here the hills are not sufficiently lofty to burst through the enclosure patterns as open upland moors and rough grazings* which air photography has revealed have regular, brickwork or ladder-like patterns, while others consist of irregular, cell-like forms. Often the fields were defined by banks and steps produced by ploughing and known as 'lynchets'. They are often termed 'Celtic' fields, but this is an unfortunate name since Celtic means no more than a family of languages. In the latest phase of the Iron Age of England and Wales – the Romano-British period – native farming communities with essentially prehistoric lifestyles created some remarkably well-preserved patterns of small, walled enclosures which can often be related to village or hamlet settlements and to the clusters of little paddocks which accompanied such settlements, while the old field tracks and droveways are also often recognisable. Such patterns can frequently be detected in the Yorkshire Pennines and western Pennine flanks.

Although the Romans created vast panoramas of rigidly geometrically planned fields in several continental areas, in Britain the existing native field patterns tended to endure and the evidence of a planned reorganisation of the countryside is seldom apparent. Though pagan Saxon settlers of the fifth and sixth centuries were previously credited with the transformation of the rural landscape, in fact they generally seem to have adopted the existing divisions, while considerable tracts of previously farmed land seem to have surrendered to forest and scrub around the time of the Saxon settlement.

While basically Iron Age farming practices endured in the uplands and west of Britain, the transformation of the countrysides of lowland England seems to have occurred around the eight or ninth centuries AD, with the establishment of open-field strip farming.

We must assume a rising population and perhaps a shortage of pasture were the spurs which encouraged a more productive and intensive organisation of arable land, which not only improved crop yields but also released some old croplands as pasture. Although the origins are still uncertain and controversial, the new method involved the division of a communal farming territory into areas, one of which was misleadingly designated as 'waste', with common grazings and woodland, while others were hay meadows, small hut-backing enclosures, and arable land. The cropland was divided into two, three or more vast fields, the fields into blocks or 'furlongs' and the furlongs into strips. Each tenant had his strips dispersed amongst the various furlongs, while each strip consisted of a small group of parallel plough-ridges. The ridges were created by the method of ploughing employed and the corrugated ridge-and-furrow which resulted assisted drainage. Corduroy-like ridge-and-furrow patterns are often obvious from the ground in areas where old ploughland has been preserved under pasture, but from the air one can see the organisation of the village lands into ridges, furlongs and unploughed areas.

In the north and west, where the croplands were more marginal and less productive, an alternative system of 'in-field out-field' farming was developed, with the in-field which surrounded a hamlet or small village often being fertilised and kept in production, while areas of out-field pasture were occasionally ploughed, cropped to exhaustion and then rested under a long period of fallow. On steeply sloping terrain, the medieval farmers often created 'strip lynchets' rather than plough-ridges and their contour-ploughing eventually produced staircase patterns of lynchets which ascend the hillsides to produce a series of more level terraces. Although strip lynchets are often described as prehistoric features, all the evidence points to late-Saxon and medieval origins.

In the course of the eighteenth and nineteenth centuries, individual Acts of Parliamentary Enclosure transformed almost all of the parishes where farming based on the open-field system still endured. As the Enclosure commissioners and surveyors moved from parish to parish, the old field patterns were replaced by the geometry of straight hedgerows and walls. Old commons were partitioned, meadows sub-divided and the ploughlands reallocated to provide a series of compact private holdings.

Much enclosure had already been accomplished, mainly by private agreements between farmers, landowners and tenants. 'Early enclosure' fields come in many forms. Some walls and hedgerows plainly preserve the outlines of older strips but others represent the forms of 'assarts' or clearings bitten out of the woodland apple. Particularly in the rolling countrysides of the south-west of England, much of the early enclosure is very old indeed and the wavy-hedged little pastures are indistinguishable from 'Celtic' field forms – in-

3.B *Largely as a consequence of air photography, we now realise that prehistoric field networks were continuous across large tracts of countryside. Showing through the unexciting pattern of modern fields in this section of Hampshire, we can see the evidence of a broad network of much smaller, probably Iron Age fields. Snaking through the photograph like a dark smudge is the course of a former stream, while the mark like a paper clip, lower left, is probably a motor cycle track. The ancient fields are displayed as crop marks and one can clearly detect the differences in their clarity from modern field to modern field. This is produced by variations in the nature and growth of the different living crops*

3.C *It has sometimes been said that the landscapes of medieval open-field strip farming must have been rather bare and monotonous. However, the verdant patterns of fallow land and the contrasting hues of strips bearing crops of oats, barley, wheat and legumes surely produced vividly varied scenery. This is suggested by the strip-like fields in the Great Field at Braunton in Devon, where some aspects of open-field farming endure. There are a few other local survivals, as around Epworth and Haxey in Humberside and also around Laxton in Nottinghamshire, where many of the complex institutions of communal farming also survive*

deed, this is what many of them may be – while others will date from the Saxon and medieval periods. Fields such as these are very hard to date, but the controversial species-counting technique of 'hedgerow dating' – which relates the age of a hedgerow to the number of species contained in a given length – will often suggest that the hedgerows are of a Dark Age vintage.

With scarcely a thought for the aesthetic consequences of their labours, generations of British farmers created a succession of entrancing landscapes, with vast sweeps of defor-ested upland pasture and tens of thousands of miles of winding walls and hedgerows to provide the delightfully intricate details which embellish the lowland countrysides. Now modern farming seems hellbent on destroying the beauty, interest and wildlife refuges which were centuries or millennia in their making. The prairie landscapes of suit-case farming have been transplanted from Nebraska and Oklahoma to disgrace the fine old settings of East Anglia, Wessex and the West Midlands. Countrysides whose beauty was a by-product of the labour of the peasant masses are now drab and featureless, raising Green Pounds for the few.

3.1 THE NEW STONE AGE *in the Langdales, Cumbria*

Agriculture appeared in Britain at an early stage in the fifth millennium BC. Very little is known about the first few centuries of farming in Britain – whether the first farmers were settlers from overseas or mainly converts from among the indigenous Mesolithic hunting and gathering peoples, and whether the earliest cultivation involved the use of only temporary woodland clearings. Farming seems to have become established in a number of favoured core areas on chalk, limestone and alluvial soils. From these agricultural heartlands it was diffused and quite rapidly was practised in many less hospitable environments. In all these endeavours, the stone axe, which could be hafted to serve as a chopper for clearing woodland or mounted on a curving branch to act as a ploughshare, was the essential tool of the Neolithic farmers.

From this vantage point above the Langdale Pikes in the Lake District can be seen some of the landmarks of the early farming landscape. The rugged mass of the Pikes contains a number of volcanic intrusions, and rocks formed of 'tuff' or volcanic ash had many of the desirable qualities of flint. A number of rock exposures were so systematically worked by Neolithic quarrymen and craftsmen that they are known as 'axe factories'. One of the most important of these factories lay just below the volcanic peak of Pike o' Stickle, which appears near the upper left corner of the photograph, where a bright streak of scree runs just below its distinctive bellpush-like summit.

The lake in the foreground is Blea Tarn, where research by W. Pennington has shown that a small clearance of the natural vegetation was made around 4500 BC and agriculture was established on a more permanent basis around 3800 BC. Unlike most of the favoured farming environments of Britain, the vegetation here was not deciduous woodland but birch and pine forest and the dates reveal the quite rapid expansion of agriculture into the remoter uplands of Britain. The landscape which is seen so magnificently displayed in the photograph is obviously unwooded, while modern arable farming is confined to a few fields sprinkled among the sheltered valley basins. The deforestation of the Lake District was largely the achievement of prehistoric farmers and graziers; the 'natural' appearance of the landscape is quite misleading and the area portrayed in the photograph has yielded evidence of the remarkable antiquity of man's refashioning of the environment.

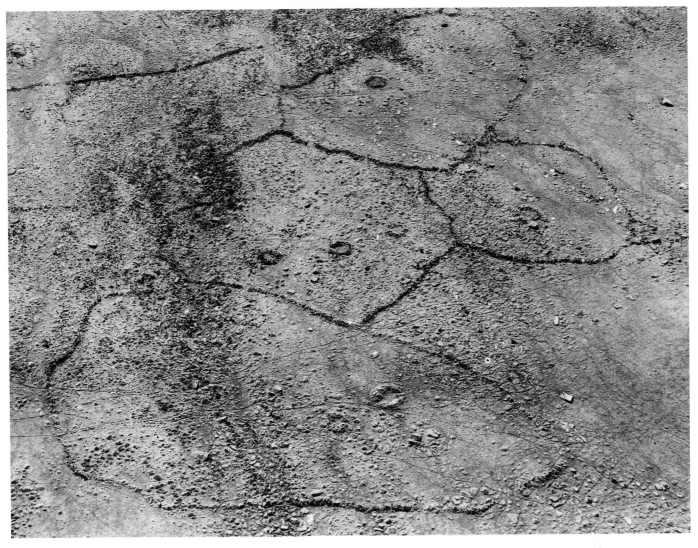

3.2 BRONZE AGE ENCLOSURES *near Walkhampton, Devon*

In the valley of the River Walkham, about $4\frac{1}{2}$ miles north-north-east of Walkhampton near Taverstock, is a common Dartmoor sight: a cluster of Bronze Age huts and enclosures. Rock outcrops and litters of moorstone create the stippled texture of the photograph, but the compact outlines of a number of stone-walled enclosures or compounds are clearly recognised. Within or occasionally in the walls of the enclosures can be seen the doughnut-like outlines of prehistoric peasant homesteads. In their original form, the huts were circular dwellings, ranging from 10 ft to 12 ft in diameter, with low stone walls and conical roofs of thatch. They were probably not all occupied at exactly the same time, but had they been, the settlement, which is too loose to be called a village or even a hamlet, would have been home to about ten families. Six of the huts are quite distinct, the other four less so, while a few other dwellings may have collapsed and merged with the moorstone litter.

Recent work on the surviving Bronze Age landscape in Dartmoor by Andrew Fleming has shown that settlements such as this one can be linked to extensive networks of fields which were defined by low walls or 'reaves' and ran up to the edges of the higher moorland commons. In the Bronze Age, most of Dartmoor was a well-peopled and productive landscape, although later in the Bronze Age, and in the Iron Age which followed, the moor was largely abandoned. It became a peat and rock-strewn wilderness largely as a result of climatic change in the direction of cooler, cloudier and damper conditions.

Some of the Bronze Age settlements on Dartmoor, such as Grimspound, are associated with more impressive compounds, although even these are probably best interpreted as stock pens rather than defenceworks. The enclosures shown in this photograph would have no defensive value and were surely stock pens, while the peasants from this little settlement will almost certainly have owned arable fields on an adjacent slope and probably valley meadows and rights of access to the moorland commons which were shared with the adjacent communities. If we imagine cones of thatch capping these hut circles and a more carefully managed and verdant setting, this ancient landscape is easily recreated.

3.3 DIFFERENT AGES OF FARMING
Little Siblyback, Cornwall

Sometimes the impact of change on the countryside was swift and drastic, but on other occasions the new emerged gradually from the old and facets of the previous landscape were preserved. At Little Siblyback on Bodmin Moor in Cornwall, we can recognise three ages of farming: the modern, the medieval and the prehistoric.

In the upper half of the photograph can be seen the relics of prehistoric farming, probably dating from the Bronze Age. There are several small, irregular, stone-walled enclosures, while at least six little rings of rubble can be detected and these are the remains of prehistoric hut dwellings. The area in which they lie is now rough and stone-strewn upland pasture, but on close inspection we can recognise the corrugations produced by medieval ploughing. Land such as this will not have offered great rewards to the peasant ploughman and it will probably only have been tilled occasionally, during phases of expansion into the poorer lands of the moorland edge.

In the lower half of the photograph, we see a zone of walled pastures and although the field walls here are still operational, this pattern of enclosures can easily be integrated with the prehistoric pattern above, suggesting that, with some small alterations, we are seeing a Bronze Age

field pattern which is still in use. A few of the prehistoric walls have probably been removed at some stage and it appears that the field in the lower right corner was previously divided by a number of them. In the bottom centre lies a ruined farmstead which may possibly be of a medieval vintage, representing a quite different phase in the exploitation of this rocky nook of the countryside.

3.4 'CELTIC' FIELDS ▶
near Grassington, North Yorkshire

Although this area has probably been farmed continuously since at least the Bronze Age, two different generations of fields are particularly obvious in the photograph. Firstly and most recently, there are the spidery black lines representing the field walls of post-medieval enclosure, charting the divisions of the upland commons, while a pair of eighteenth- or nineteenth-century hay barns can be seen in the lower-lying fields near the upper margins of the photograph.

Secondly, and more remarkably, we can see an uninterrupted network of 'Celtic' fields which has been shown by excavation to date to the Late Iron Age and Romano-British periods. Sections of the banks and lynchets which define the ancient fields can be recognised from the ground

but, from the air, the effect is quite stunning. It is produced by the low February sun which casts shadows behind the earthworks, while bright light is reflected from the crests of the banks.

Most of the 'Celtic' fields are roughly rectangular, but on close inspection one can also recognise the clusters of smaller paddocks associated with farmsteads and hut clusters (upper centre), the occasional remains of circular stone huts which appear as small, doughnut-like features and also the Iron Age field tracks and drove-ways which emerge as bank-flanked channels or holloways. The fields are not randomly arranged and one can recognise groups of fields which may represent properties or territories – note how a single (boundary?) bank links the top of the elongated fields at the bottom right of the photograph. As we follow this wall leftwards, it forms the top of a square enclosure which is separated from another square enclos-

ure (which has a small pen or hut built against its right-hand wall) by a well-worn drove-way.

The Iron Age inhabitants of this rugged limestone plateau were mixed farmers, but fell-walkers who have visited this area will know that hardly any soil now covers the fissured and treacherous limestone pavements; most of the soil has been flushed away down the labyrinths of clints and grykes. To what extent the degradation results from bad farming practices or from climatic changes, we cannot be sure, but it seems that this farming landscape, which extends up to and beyond the 1000 ft contour, has not been ploughed since the time of the Iron Age farmers who worked these fields. We should be grateful for this, for the absence of later ploughing activities has allowed one of Britain's finest networks of 'Celtic' upland fields to survive intact.

3.5 MANY AGES OF FARMING *on Fyfield Down, Wiltshire*

First impressions suggest that two ages of farming – the ancient and the modern – are apparent in this photograph. At the top, we can see the vast contemporary expanse of open downland pasture – which is thankfully free of the modern ploughing which has destroyed most of our lovely downland environments. Secondly, we can clearly see the outlines of banks or 'lynchets' which trace the boundaries of an extensive network of 'Celtic' fields, which probably date from the Iron Age and Romano-British periods although some prehistoric farming limits are marked by Bronze Age boundary ditches. The photograph is particularly evocative because it underlies the vastness of the original 'Celtic' field networks.

Although the old history books described prehistoric farming communities as scrabbling away in little clearings which were islands in the sea of primeval forest, by the Iron Age most English landscapes were scarcely any more wooded than today. Here, as in the Grassington photograph (pl. 3.4), we have visual proof of the great extent of prehistoric field networks. Field systems of some kind will have covered the greater part of England by the start of the period while many areas had already been farmed for two or three thousand years.

Closer inspection detects evidence of a third age of farming: the medieval. In the lower half of the photograph the remains of straight or slightly curving field divisions are faintly visible, cutting across the more prominent 'Celtic' field boundaries. The medieval long-house farmstead from which these fields were probably worked can be seen, just below the woodland nature reserve near the centre of the photograph. From the grid patterns which are just visible inside the dwelling, it appears that excavations were in progress at the time when the photograph was taken in 1960. This area has been intensively studied by the archaeologist Peter Fowler. He has distinguished between the Iron Age fields which are bounded by lynchets up to 12 ft high, formed as earth accumulated against their dry stone walls, which are in the middle and lower part of the photograph, and the more regular and orderly Romano-British field patterns in the upper part of the picture. The two networks are separated by a Romano-British field track which runs diagonally across the area skirting the upper margin of the patch of woodland centre left. The Old Bath Road which was closed in 1815 ran across the area from right to left and can be seen as a narrow, rutted track, cutting across the grain of the prehistoric fields.

And so, if we count the Bronze Age ditch, which is scarcely visible but which marked the prehistoric arable farming limit near the top of the photograph, we have evidence of five farming eras preserved in the landscape: the Bronze Age, Iron Age, Romano-British, medieval and the modern.

This ground level photograph shows the excavations of the medieval long-house

3.6 FIELD PATTERNS *on Malham Lings, North Yorkshire*

Most visitors to the charming Yorkshire Dales village of Malham are attracted by the geological dramas of Malham Cove and Gordale Scar. While the Cove lies outside the photograph, just above the shadowed area near the upper margin, and the Scar is beyond the top right corner, the aerial portrait is packed with interest in terms of the ancient field patterns displayed.

The fine networks of black (shaded) and white (sunlit) lines represent the enduring field walls created from the piecemeal enclosure of the medieval landscape. Looming through the wall networks and modern field patterns are the remains of older farming arrangements which date from several different ages.

Most obvious and widespread are the terrace-like patterns which endow some fields with a stepped appearance. These are strip lynchets, most commonly associated with the medieval ploughing of steeper ground. In the lower left part of the photograph can be seen a more common form of medieval ploughing in the corduroy traces of slightly curving ridged and furrowed plough strips. However, the relics of farming are not confined to the medieval

period, for in a few upland areas, most clearly in the top left-hand corner, we can see traces of farming patterns which seem to date from the Late or Roman Iron Age. These are represented by the outlines of small, irregular fields and close patterns of little paddocks of the kind that are associated with British settlements.

During the tiny fraction of a second when the shutter of the vertical camera was open, the main phases in the agricultural colonisation of this rugged limestone landscape were recorded. We can recognise the handiwork of small communities of essentially prehistoric mixed farmers, who produced some crops on lands which are now thinly-soiled rough grazings; also that of medieval Malham villagers who drove their ploughs into the steep limestone slopes and whose hunger and desperation produced the terrace patterns of strip lynchets, as well as the enduring pattern of irregular walled enclosures which are now almost entirely devoted to pasture. From the ground only a small proportion of the information can be recognised, with the strip lynchets as the most obvious features.

3.7 ROMAN PATTERNS *in the Fen, Lincolnshire*

The photograph provides clearcut information on two quite distinct eras of Fenland farming in the area just south-west of Spalding. Both have a regular and planned organisation of the land as their hallmark, but one pattern is modern, the other is Roman. The modern landscape is produced by post-medieval land colonisation associated with drainage and the establishment of large, perfectly rectangular arable fields and a sprinkling of dispersed and rather drab brick farmsteads. The Roman pattern emerges in the form of soil marks expressed by the deep silts lying in old ditches and channels. These come in two forms: the irregular, winding patterns which trace the outlines of former watercourses, and the organised, geometrical patterns which are a legacy of Roman planning.

Running from top to bottom of the photograph roughly parallel to the right-hand margin are the unmistakable outlines of an uncompromisingly straight Roman fenland road. It disappears beneath the garden and house of the farm which stands in the lower right-hand corner. Although the surface and raised bank or 'agger' of this road have disappeared, its course is traced by the dark silts which fill its flanking drainage ditches.

Above and to the left of the farm we see a Roman house plot as a rectangular feature which is linked to the through-road by a short and straight access road – one cannot resist the comparison with a modern 'desirable residence' set back discreetly at the end of a private drive! We can also see fragments of rectangular field patterns and at least three other side roads although other house plots are more difficult to detect. It is not known whether the owners of the ancient houses and estates were imperial settlers or members of the native élite but, in the lower right of the photograph, rather confused patterns of marks can be seen above right of the farmhouse. Some are produced by modern farming operations but others may be related to native peasant settlement.

These photographs may well baffle the layman, for they conjure memories of Mediterranean or oriental terraced farming landscapes or the stepped working faces of great American ore mines. In fact, the two photographs present different air views of the strip lynchets which are engraved in the sides of dry chalkland valleys near Mere in Wiltshire.

They were created gradually by contour ploughing, a form of arable farming which was better adapted to the cultivation of the steeper slopes than the more conventional ridge and furrow techniques. Although strip lynchets are commonly described as relics of prehistoric farming, they really date from the medieval period, while some were still being ploughed in modern times. Although the evidence does not emerge in these photographs, we know that these strip lynchets are younger than the era of 'Celtic' field cultivation because some of the lynchets cut across the outlines of older 'Celtic' fields. Strip lynchets similar to these occur in several other parts of England and there are particularly prominent examples near Worth Matravers in Dorset and Linton in North Yorkshire.

Strip lynchets are associated with difficult sloping ground suggesting that they were created during times of population pressure and land hunger, when peasants were compelled to plough even the least rewarding hillsides. In the years following 1348, the Great Pestilence provided a ghastly solution to medieval population problems and so strip lynchets are unlikely to have been ploughed into the hillsides after that time.

3.9 AN EARLY ENCLOSURE FIELDSCAPE *Luppitt, Devon*

'Early enclosure' is not a particularly glamorous phrase or one that can be guaranteed to quicken the heartbeat, but it describes some of the most delicious passages in the English landscape. Everyone may have their favourite type of scenery, but for myself and many other landscape history enthusiasts, nothing can surpass the delight of networks of small, irregular and venerable fields which nestle in the embrace of thick, mature hedgerows. Sadly, modern farming is waging war against this type of landscape while tax-payers are unwittingly subsidising the grubbing out of fine old hedgerows and the bulldozing of the details which brought such joy to the good old countryside. However, when this photograph was taken in 1955, an ancient, perhaps Saxon landscape flourished in this corner of Devon, four miles north of Honiton.

The air photograph alone does not allow us to date this pattern of fields and dispersed farmsteads, but research on various Devon farmsteads undertaken by Prof. W. G. Hoskins has shown that many of them stand on sites where Saxon farmers lived, while some of the hedgerows, boundaries and landmarks described in Saxon charters can still be identified. Certainly these field patterns are very old and one may guess that the dense and varied hedgerows date back at least to the early medieval period.

With its mild winters, early springs and moist climate, Devon favours the dairy farmer. Although faint traces of medieval ridge and furrow can be glimpsed in one field near the lower left-hand corner, the remaining fields may not have been ploughed throughout the historical era. The light-coloured fields are not bearing crops of grain; the month is June and they are newly-mown hay meadows.

3.10 MEDIEVAL FARMSTEADS *Duggleby, North Yorkshire*

Two types of farmstead were common in the medieval period: the long-house and the courtyard farm, and the differences between them partly reflect contrasting levels of status and prosperity.

The long-house form of peasant dwelling was remarkably widespread and examples are known from Cornwall and Devon to the Orkneys. Although late versions of the long-house occasionally survive in occupation in parts of upland Britain, this form of dwelling is known to have also been favoured in the eastern lowlands of England. In its simplest form, the long-house consisted of a mean, single-storey rectangular hut about the size of a small bus, which was partitioned to provide accommodation for livestock on one side of the entrance and a single room for the peasant family on the other.

The courtyard farm was associated with the more prosperous tenant families and with demesne farms; it is less

deeply rooted in antiquity than the long-house, but has a pedigree extending back at least to the thirteenth century. Here, the farmstead and the various out-buildings such as barns, byres and workshops are arranged around a rectangular courtyard which has at least one opening to admit livestock, wagons or carts.

At Duggleby, south-west of Malton and on the flanks of the Yorkshire Welds, we see the remarkably clear-cut remains of long-houses and courtyard farms at a deserted settlement which perished in the years following 1500. The reasons for the apparent segregation are obscure, but we can see that the two courtyard farms lie on the right-hand side of the winding stream, the much smaller long-houses on the other. Modern roads flank the stream and settlement, but it is possible that the stream itself served as a High Street for this straggling and ill-fated little medieval village.

3.11 LINGMELL *Cumbria*

In the field patterns of the Lake District, we see striking contrasts between the small, stone-walled fields of the valley bottoms and the vast expanses of upland grazing. In the sheltered pockets of lowland, the irregular little enclosures are medieval or perhaps sometimes older and provide superior pasture, hay meadow and periodic or occasional arable fields. Towering above the detailed field and farmstead landscapes of the low-lying areas are the bold panoramas of old upland common. The slopes which were once blanketed with natural woodland have been denuded by prehistoric grazing and clearance, and now the mountain masses are divided by far-striding walls which mark the divisions between medieval township or monastic lands or later enclosures.

The photograph is taken from a position just beyond the northern head of Wast Water lake, looking across the narrow, glaciated valley of the Mosedale and Lingmell becks towards the surging bulk of Lingmell Crag which culminates in a 2649-ft summit, while beyond lie the still loftier peaks of the Scafell Pikes which exceed 3000 ft.

Deep down in the foreground valley, the once larger glacial lake has retreated and the becks deposit a carpet of alluvial sands and gravels on the former lake floor. A hotel, a mountain rescue post and about four farmsteads share this little Eden.

The typical Lakeland farmstead snuggles in a valley bottom on a sheltered site which stands above the reach of flooding and the typical holding embraces three distinct and complementary packages of land. These are the 'inland' lying closest to the farm buildings where the cluster of small walled fields yield crops of hay and occasional crops of roots or oats; the 'intake' of walled pastures on the lower valley slopes, and the unimproved sheep grazings of the upland fell. When this photograph was taken, in the month of June, a couple of the little inland fields appear to have been cut for hay, a couple are under oats, while the remainder are serving as pasture. Dot-like hay barns and larger farmsteads can be seen amongst the valley bottom fields.

In the Aran Islands and in the Burren on the adjacent mainland in Co Clare one encounters perhaps the strangest and most compelling landscapes in the whole of the British Isles. It is formed of pale grey Carboniferous Limestone, resembling the limestone of the Pennines and Peak District. Tunnelled by underground water-worn caverns and with a surface which is fissured and finely partitioned by grykes, the limestone swiftly swallows the heavy rainfall which the area receives. And washed down with the rivulets of rainwater goes the soil as well. Nature is not entirely responsible for the barrenness of the Burren and Aran Islands countryside, for the removal of the natural woodland blanket and over-grazing in the latter part of the prehistoric period has exposed the landscape to the ravages of soil erosion.

Bare, silvery limestone pavement produces the lighter blotches which pattern the photograph, but the labyrinthine networks of field walls are far more striking for here, walling materials exist in an unwelcome abundance. No quarrying or shaping is needed, for angular and roughly rectangular slabs can be lifted everywhere from the surface of the limestone pavements. The multitude of walls partly reflect systems of inheritance which caused the progressive sub-division of land holdings, but the walls are also convenient repositories for the boulder litter on the surface. The absence of entrances to many of the fields may seem puzzling, but in this part of the world it is often more convenient to kick down and rebuild a wall than to install a costly field gate.

These fields are all but impossible to date. Some will date back to the pre-medieval or even prehistoric period while the almost continuous straight walls which cross the photograph diagonally from upper left to lower right reveal a later reorganisation of the farming landscape. The double walls trace the courses of winding field tracks and drove-ways which are probably amongst the oldest features in the man-made landscape.

3.13 TWO AGES OF FARMING *Padbury, Buckinghamshire*

Here, in the clearest possible fashion, can be seen two quite distinct farming landscapes: the older, medieval landscape of open-field strip farming, and the younger, straight-hedged landscape of Parliamentary Enclosure.

Let us give precedence to age and look more closely at the medieval pattern, disregarding the radial hedges shown in the photograph. Most of the landscape is corrugated by medieval plough ridges and furrows. In this particular case often singly, but elsewhere commonly in small groups of two, three, four or more adjacent ridges were packaged together to form strips. The strips in turn were combined in blocks or furlongs, and here the block which fills the lower central area of the photograph was called Downe Furlong; to its left lay Shelland Furlong (touching the photograph's left margin); above and to the right of Downe Furlong was Sprintes Lane Furlong, while above and to the left lay Padocke Furlong. We know all this from the information contained on a plan of 1591 in the possession of All Souls College, Oxford, which Professors M. W. Beresford and J. K. S. St Joseph have described.*

The ridge and furrow patterns terminate before the outskirts of Padbury village are reached and, in typical medieval fashion, small hedged enclosures or 'closes' lay behind the dwellings – some of them still survive. The furlongs were in turn grouped together within Padbury's three vast open fields. The 'balk' or headland field track which

Medieval England, An Aerial Survey: Beresford and St Joseph (1958, 1979).

marked part of the boundary between West Field (to the left) and East Field (to the right) can still be recognised, running from the upper right corner of the small, hedged field at the lower right-hand corner, diagonally towards the upper left. So detailed is the map of 1591 that even the names of some of the tenants are known – Pearson, Allen, Scott, Snowe, Walcotte and others.

One interesting feature which had not been built by 1591, and which no longer exists today, was the village windmill. However, we know that one did exist at some stage in the post-medieval period. The evidence can be seen inside the little square field already mentioned, where the circular feature is the remains of a 'windmill mound' upon which the mill will have been built. More puzzling is the levelled rectangle of ground amongst the ridge and furrow patterns in the field to the left of the windmill field. It certainly did not exist in 1591 and one can only guess that it may represent an old cricket square.

The essentially medieval pattern survived until 1795 when dramatic change arrived in the form of an Act of Parliamentary Enclosure. The enclosure commissioners produced the pattern of straight hedgerows which still endures, dividing the village lands by long hedges which radiate outwards from the main part of the village and completing the reallocation of the holdings by delineating cross-hedges between the radial lengths. As Professors Beresford and St Joseph remark, 'A landscape which had taken centuries to create was only a year in dying.'

3.14 FLECKNOE *Warwickshire*

This photograph is packed with interest. The Oxford Canal (upper left) cuts a group of older, straight-hedged Parliamentary Enclosure fields, which in turn are superimposed upon the fainter corduroy patterns of medieval ridge and furrow. The village meanwhile is a study in itself, with plenty of evidence of shrinkage represented by the roughly rectangular patterns of house-and-land plots or 'closes'.

We can see how the larger medieval village was surrounded by open-field ploughlands. The ridges were linked in small groups to form strips tenanted by individual peasants, while the strips combined in blocks or furlongs. If we try to ignore the later hedgerow patterns, the pattern of furlongs can be recognised. In the upper centre part of the photograph, immediately to the left of the white stripe of the narrow road, it seems that the direction of ploughing was changed, for one can just discern a pattern of narrow ridges running left to right and forming a block with a grain that is at right angles to the surrounding strips. Narrow ridges such as these are usually associated with post-medieval ploughing patterns. Most of the ridges in the photograph have distinctive 'C' or 'reversed S' shapes, created as the plough-team of two or more pairs of oxen were swung to begin their turn as the end of a strip was approached.

The Parliamentary Enclosure surveyors completely abandoned the old field and furlong patterns, dividing the lands into a network of geometrical fields defined by long hedgerows which radiate outwards from the village. Despite its planned and disciplined character, the new landscape which resulted is not unattractive, with the many miles of hedgerows providing refuges for wildlife with some hedgerow trees being allowed to grow tall as 'standards', providing shelter and timber resources.

The village itself offers a number of challenges. At its greatest extent, the medieval village will have filled the area which is defined by the limits of the ridge and furrow ploughland, and the pattern of closes, each of which will almost certainly have contained a peasant dwelling, reveals that this was a substantial settlement. The modern village is loose and apparently formless, with many gaps marking the abandoned plots. With shrinkage, the priorities in the village pattern of streets and lanes seems to have changed, and the present through-road follows the lower left margins of the medieval village whose original main street may be revealed by the largely empty lane which runs from left to right through the middle of the settlement, while holloways or shallow troughs mark the courses of some other village lanes.

The photograph of Flecknoe and its fields therefore underlines the fact that change in both slow and drastic forms is a vital factor in the history of the countryside.

3.15 WATER MEADOWS *Castle Acre, Norfolk*

The eye is immediately drawn to the remarkable earthworks of the Norman castle at Castle Acre: the circular motte and shell keep, the monstrous banks and ditches of the bailey and the strange rectangular package in which they sit – which makes one wonder whether the Normans had remodelled a Roman site. Certainly some Roman pottery has been found here. However, the photograph is included to show the well-preserved remains of a system of riverside water meadows, clearly visible in the lower half of the photograph.

Most systems of water meadows seem to date from the post-medieval centuries, particularly the seventeenth and eighteenth, and they were commonly associated with sheep farming. Until the cultivation of root crops for winter fodder became widespread as a product of the eighteenth-century Agricultural Revolution, the shortage of winter feed restricted the number of livestock which could be over-wintered. The sooner that meadowland could be

stimulated into spring growth, the less the burden of over-wintering and the more stock the farmer could keep. Water meadows, with their carefully engineered networks of major artificial channels or 'head mains' which fed parallel networks of lesser channels carried on the tops of artificial ridges, were associated with the controlled flooding of meadowland in the late winter. The flooding had the effect of encouraging an early flush of growth at a time when other pastures were still dormant and grass was in short supply. Sometimes the flooding was achieved by the simple practice of damming a stream, but at Castle Acre and many other riverside places (for example, all along the stream which accompanies the Bishop's Stortford to London railway line) a much more elaborate system of head mains, channels, ridges and sluices was created. Although costly in time and labour to create, maintain and operate, the effort must have been deemed to be well-spent in the days before efficient winter feed production.

3.16 LAND RECLAMATION *on Exmoor, Somerset*

At the start of the nineteenth century, Exmoor was a semi-wilderness, a vast upland common which provided summer grazing for multitudes of sheep which were driven in from the surrounding moorland edge parishes. The moor had enjoyed the status of a royal hunting forest since medieval times but in 1818 a large portion of the royal estate was sold to a prosperous Midlands iron founder, John Knight, following an Act for Parliamentary Enclosure which allowed the moor to be partitioned in private ownership.

In the course of the next three decades, the landscape was transformed with the Knight property being ringed by an enormous wall and divided into farm holdings. The farms were in turn divided into geometrical fields which were often defined by earthen banks, some of which were planted with beech to provide shelter from the fierce moorland winds. We can see how the short hedge lower right of centre has been shaved by winds blasting through a valley-side gully. John Knight's son, Frederic, designed many of the farm buildings which then appeared, favouring a functional courtyard layout of the kind adopted in the farm which is above right of centre, nestling behind a shelter belt of trees which protect it from northerly and westerly winds.

This photograph was taken at Exe Cleave fourteen years after the violent Exmoor floods of 1952 but one can still see the evidence of the destructive torrent in the bare scars and slumped ground on the valley sides all produced by landslips.

THE LORD AND THE LANDSCAPE

Most field and countryside patterns were the creations of local farming communities of many different ages or of the eighteenth- or nineteenth-century Parliamentary Enclosure commissioners. The landscape creations of the greater landlords are much more localised in their occurrence, but in the photographs of the agricultural landscape around Helperby near Ripon in North Yorkshire and the countryside surrounding Dundas Castle in the former county of West Lothian we see their handiwork. Although the results are quite different, both contain faint echoes of the medieval countryside.

Around Helperby, the slightly curving boundaries of some of the elongated fields suggest that they originate from the enclosure of medieval strips, although the earlier pattern is much altered. The most striking feature of this landscape concerns the orderly planting of trees which are grown freely as 'standards' at regular intervals within the hedgerows. The pattern extends far into the distance, showing a coherent estate policy. Although the patterns produced would have been much less regular, some hedgerow trees were also allowed to grow tall during the Middle Ages to provide valuable constructional timber, and post-medieval cartwrights and wheelwrights are known to have favoured the hard, resilient timber produced by hedgerow trees. Neat blocks of deciduous woodland punctuate the fields, while a small coniferous plantation lies to the right of the lawn of the small mansion, lower centre. At the foot of the photograph it seems that a formal garden has been converted into a plant nursery.

The country around Dundas Castle provides an excellent example of landscaped parkland of a type much favoured in the eighteenth century. In the area of park above the castle, the manufactured countryside is far from being natural, but the skilful juxtaposition of pasture and trees creates a superficially 'natural' appearance. The trees are sufficiently spaced to permit broad vistas while adding detail and distinction to the scene. To the right, the park is more thickly wooded, with rhododendron bushes providing a frontage to the woodland, this environment offering game cover and attractive woodland walks. There is a very loose resemblance to the type of medieval countryside known as woodland pasture, in which the grazings were closely interspersed with valuable timber-yielding trees, although in the medieval woodland pastures many of the trees were grown as pollards, producing timber poles from a crown which lay above the reach of grazing animals.

3.18 SPADE CULTIVATION
Lewis, Western Isles

The tangled patterns on the land surface, which remind one of maggots seething in an angler's bait box, were produced by spade cultivation. Both photographs are of Lewis in the Outer Hebrides: the closer view is of Garrabost on the Eye Peninsula in the east, while the more distant view is of Uig on the west coast.

One can hardly begin to imagine the desperation and poverty which compelled the inhabitants of these barren, peat- and rock-blanketed landscapes to create these corrugated epitaphs to sweat, spadework, over-population and land hunger. In such Highland and island locations, where many families could not afford to maintain draught oxen and the broken terrain made ploughing difficult, a form of spade or foot plough known as the *caschrom* took over the role of the ox plough. At first, one tends to assume that the ridge patterns shown in the photographs represent an ancient form of agriculture. On closer inspection though, the patterns seem quite fresh and little degraded by the passage of time. In the north-west of Scotland and western Ireland, the *caschrom* remained essential agricultural equipment during the nineteenth century.

Both these landscapes have since returned to peat moor and pasture. In the closer view, one can see tiny white dots which are sheep, while the movement of these animals

together with soil-creep have created little terraces running around the edges on the steeper ground. In the Uig photograph, no traces of peasant blackhouses can be discerned, although an apparently recently ruined farm, which probably post-dates the spade cultivation, lies amongst the frozen black ocean of peat ridges.

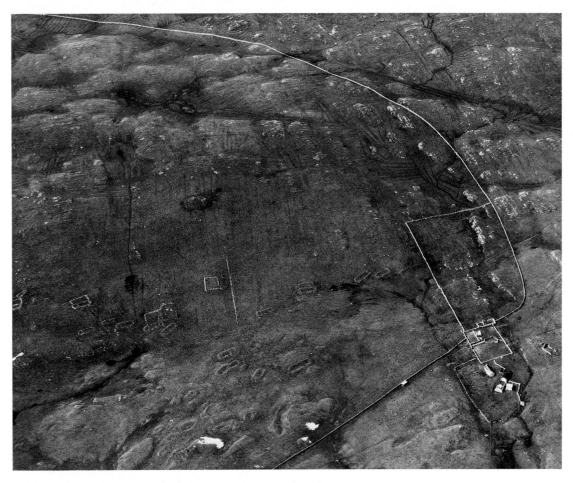

3.19 AN ABANDONED CLACHAN *Pabbay, Western Isles*

On the bare, glaciated and peat-carpeted island of Pabbay, which lies in the sound between North Uist and Harris, we see the remains of a Highlands hamlet or *clachan*. The abandoned dwellings are represented by the rectangular, slightly boat-shaped outlines of 'blackhouses'. The term only dates back to the middle of the last century when it was adopted to distinguish between the traditional thatched and stone-and-sod-walled dwellings and the newer, thin-walled and lime mortared 'white houses'. The blackhouse however has a pedigree that extends back though medieval long-houses to the rather boat-shaped long-houses of Norse settlers which can be recognised, for example, at Brough of Birsay on Orkney. The blackhouse had its roof of barley straw, heather or rush thatch weighed down by boulders slung on ropes, while its walls were built of double stone courses which were packed with earth or turf to provide insulation against the cold winds. In typical long-house fashion, it was partitioned to provide living quarters to one side of the side entrance and a byre, hog pen and poultry roosts on the other. Often a barn was built against one of the long walls, and such barns can be recognised paralleling three of these blackhouses.

The layout of this *clachan* is in complete contrast to that of the typical English village: there is no distinct lane and street pattern, few signs of close or toft-like plots and no green. Instead, the homesteads are similarly aligned, but scattered on the barren landscape in a haphazard fashion, like members of a stranded school of whales. We can just recognise that they are situated in a pocket of 'in-field' ploughland and some plough or spade ridge patterns can be seen.

Hundreds of *clachans* such as this perished in the scandalous Highland Clearances of the late eighteenth and nineteenth centuries. Here, however, the differing states of ruination amongst the blackhouses points to piecemeal desertion over a period of time. The group in the lower part of the photograph are in an advanced state of decay and beginning to merge with the knoll patterns of the glaciated land surface.

In the lower extreme right part of the photograph can be seen another deserted dwelling – apparently a 'white house' and a group of buildings, one unroofed. It seems that a single farmstead has taken control of this bleak landscape of bare rock and peat, which once provided bare subsistence for a small community of blackhouse-dwelling clansmen.

3.20 THE SOULLESS LANDSCAPES OF MODERN FARMING *Shropshire and Devon*

The old agricultural landscapes of both Devon and Shropshire, with their small, thickly-hedged old fields display the English countryside at its best. Here, however, the scenic ravages of modern farming can be seen. Many eastern counties, including vast extents of Cambridgeshire and Bedfordshire and a large part of the once lovely Suffolk, have surrendered to the drab anonymity of featureless 'prairie' farming. The photographs show that in the 1960s and 1970s the same visual and ecological vandalism erupted in the West Midlands and South-West.

In the photograph of an area in the east-north-east of Devon (*left*) a pattern of lines in the vast central grain field reveals how a network of winding, 'early enclosure' hedgerows has been grubbed out or bulldozed to create a bare extent of land more suitable for the operation of massive modern farming machines. The circular feature seen in outline just left of centre may represent an Iron Age farmstead enclosure.

In the above photograph, we see a vast prairie field with

an ant-like team of tractors at work. Two different sets of lines run across the field; those which trend slightly diagonally from upper right to lower left represent modern land drains and these are intersected by broader lines which are the boundaries of the former fields, hedgerows which were removed to create the featureless grain factory. This area lies amongst some still lovely countryside to the south-east of Bromfield near Ludlow.

The conservationist Marion Shoard has pointed out that between 1946 and 1974 farmers removed a quarter of England's hedgerows, destroying them at the rate of 4500 miles each year. Now the rate is accelerating and she recalls Richard Jefferies' view of 1884 that 'without hedges, England would not be England'. The country-loving public will deplore this facet of the theft of the countryside, and it is no consolation that a part of the massive public subsidies for farming is devoted to the 'improvement' of land through the removal of hedgerows.

4. VILLAGES PAST AND PRESENT

We could probably build several paper villages from the popular, romantic and scholarly literature which the subject of 'the village' has spawned. However, the mountainous literature belies the fact that we are only just beginning to understand the origins and evolution of the British village. The story which unfolds has some surprises – and many more interesting complexities than we might have imagined. Air photography has played an important part in this process of discovery, revealing unsuspected prehistoric settlements, portraying the fossilised outlines of the deserted settlements described in the next chapter and offering new and more telling perspectives on the layout of surviving villages.

Villages have existed at all stages in British history from the New Stone Age onwards. However, we must draw a line between the prehistoric and Dark Age villages and those of the medieval and modern periods. Villages in the former category tended to be short-lived and footloose, while the later villages were created to endure. Prehistoric villages were established infrequently, exceptions in landscapes in which dispersed hamlet-like hut groups and farmsteads were much more numerous.

Skara Brae in Orkney (below) is a remarkable and exceptional survival from the New Stone Age and has endured so well that we can still see the stone slab-built furniture of hearths, dressers and cots inside the sub-rectangular huts. A part of the village may have perished from the erosion of the nearby low sea cliff, but originally there were

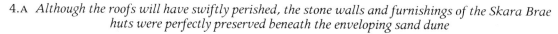

4.A *Although the roofs will have swiftly perished, the stone walls and furnishings of the Skara Brae huts were perfectly preserved beneath the enveloping sand dune*

4.B *Crop marks trace the outlines of huts and paddocks at an Iron Age and Romano-British settlement near Standlake in Oxfordshire*

probably about a dozen stone huts, connected by walled alleyways and insulated by the enveloping masses of household refuse – mainly shellfish debris. Until the middle of the last century, Skara Brae was preserved beneath a sand dune which had engulfed the ancient village, while its survival also owes much to the availability of the durable slabs of Caithness flagstone which were used by the hut-builders. Skara Brae is probably only typical of the New Stone Age in Orkney and it is rather too soon for us to be able to generalise about the contemporary villages of England, where timber will have been a more popular and perishable building material.

During the Ages of Bronze and Iron, village-sized settlements occasionally punctuated the hamlet and farmstead patterns. Dwellings were almost invariably circular, thatch-roofed huts; stone-walled in the boulder-strewn uplands or built of posts and wattle in the vales and scarplands. Each hut or hut cluster was almost always associated with a group of paddocks and stock-pens, while tracks led away to the nearby fields.

Fragments of ancient farming landscapes dating from the Iron Age and Romano-British periods are superimposed in the photograph of the crop marks near Standlake in Oxford-shire. The corduroy pattern of dark stripes running across the photograph from left to right represents the remains of medieval field strips. Looming through this pattern we can see older landscapes with small circular huts, larger less regular paddocks and enclosures, and the smudgy dots which mainly represent grain storage pits, while in a few places one can just detect the parallel ditches which flanked ancient trackways. Not all the prehistoric features that we see existed at exactly the same time, but the photograph helps us to reconstruct a vision of 'pre-Village England', in which the countryside was dominated by farmsteads and hamlets which might have persisted for a couple of centuries or less, until their sites were abandoned and new dwellings were built elsewhere.

While the Romans built some specialised commercial and industrial villages and provided the stable conditions which encouraged the growth of many native settlements, the Saxon settlers of the fifth and sixth centuries, contrary to popular belief, do not seem to have been greatly interested in the foundation of villages. A number of loose and unplanned Early Saxon villages are known, but on the whole the immigrants (who were probably much less numerous than the history books tell) tended to adopt the field patterns and settlement habits of the British. The revolution in English settlement patterns seems to have come later, around the eighth or ninth centuries.

In the course of what the less reverential archaeologists tend to call the 'Middle Saxon Shuffle', existing, impermanent settlements seem to have been abandoned, while new and lasting villages were created. The causes were probably complicated, if clear to everyone at the time. This seems to have been the period when co-operative open-field farming was established and so peasants may have gravitated from farms and hamlets to settle in the farmstead clusters and new villages which were situated at the cores of the emerging open-field systems. This was also the period when nobles began to establish parish churches, and the church will have reinforced the permanency of any village which gained one.

In the western uplands, Ireland, and the lowland heathlands and woodlands, where the emphasis on arable farming was much slighter, the dispersed patterns of farmsteads and hamlets persisted. Elsewhere, the process of village creation continued through the earlier medieval centuries, although by the thirteenth century the more inviting locations were largely exploited and population pressure led to the establishment of undernourished villages on the less fertile and more vulnerable soils where the prospects for village survival were often poor.

Throughout the whole of its history, the village has evolved apace with local conditions. For many villages, change implied abandonment or shrinkage, while others have physically shifted, gradually drifting across their fields to exploit new opportunities or moving to a roadside situation to tap the trade which might encourage a new village market. Although we cannot always discover the causes for the lively patterns of village growth, shrinkage, shifting and remodelling, the legacies of these little adventures are generally more strikingly and instantly apparent in the fossilised patterns of old streets, lanes, plots and house sites when they are seen from the air.

Many mysteries remain, but at least we know that most of the old village concepts can be discarded. Having looked at a good number of villages, one finds that the early inhabitants do not tend to have discovered and exploited the most favourable sites for settlement – most village situations are mediocre and, some, quite poor. Simple classroom village stereotypes also tend to be worthless, for on close inspection we do not find a few simple categories like 'green' villages (with greens) or 'linear' (elongated) villages. Instead, we find a staggering complexity of village forms; hordes of shrunken villages, plenty of shifted examples, lots which were planned, many which have changed their shapes to accord with changing local circumstances, and masses of 'polyfocal' villages which incorporate the nuclei of two, three or more previously separate dwelling clusters. In short, the village is much more exciting than the sleepy old stereotype that seemed to be so easily understood.

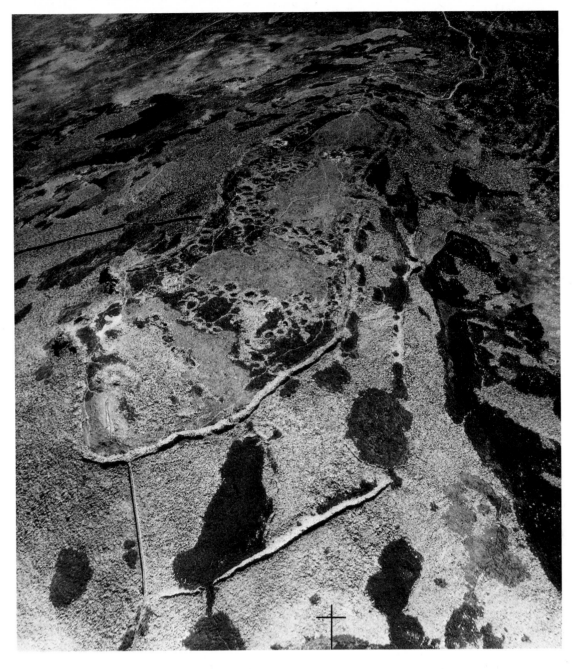

4.c *A large defensive village or proto-town lies within the double ramparts which guard the summit at Tre'r Ceiri on the Lleyn Peninsula in North Wales. The hillfort walls are clearly shown, as are the outlines of the circular and sub-rectangular stone dwellings which packed the interior. The settlement dates from the centuries before and after the Roman conquest*

4.1 THE ORTON WATERVILLE CROP MARKS *Cambridgeshire*

In an area of the former county of Huntingdonshire, doomed by gravel quarrying and designated for the expansion of Peterborough, this remarkable photograph was taken on a June evening in 1966. The crops growing in the deeper, richer soils of ancient ditches and pits have risen above their less favoured neighbours, while the sinking sun cast long shadows which portrayed the features of a long-forgotten landscape in an almost three-dimensional clarity.

The area concerned lies on a gravel terrace in a meander loop of the River Nene, an attractive site which stands above the reach of flooding and which was exploited by a sequence of communities in the later stages of the Iron Age. The settlement remains seem to represent successive hamlet or farmstead hut groups; we can see that these were successive from the way that some features cut across others.

A number of circles can be recognised and are probably best interpreted as the remains of circular, once wattle-walled and thatch-roofed huts, or of ditches which encircled the huts, catching the drips of rain which fell from the thatch. The huts were associated with trackways and small, paddocky enclosures. We can see how, at different times, one piece of ground near the foot of the photograph was occupied by part of a rectangular enclosure and by the larger of two irregular enclosures associated with the huts. The area is studded by small rectangular and circular blobs and these are produced by tall-standing plants growing in the deep soils of former pits, some of which will have been used for grain storage.

Running across the upper half of the picture is a hyphenated line which represents a 'pit alignment'. These rather puzzling features which sometimes take the place of a continuous ditch seem to mark prehistoric boundaries of various kinds; it is not obvious why particular land divisions should be defined in this way.

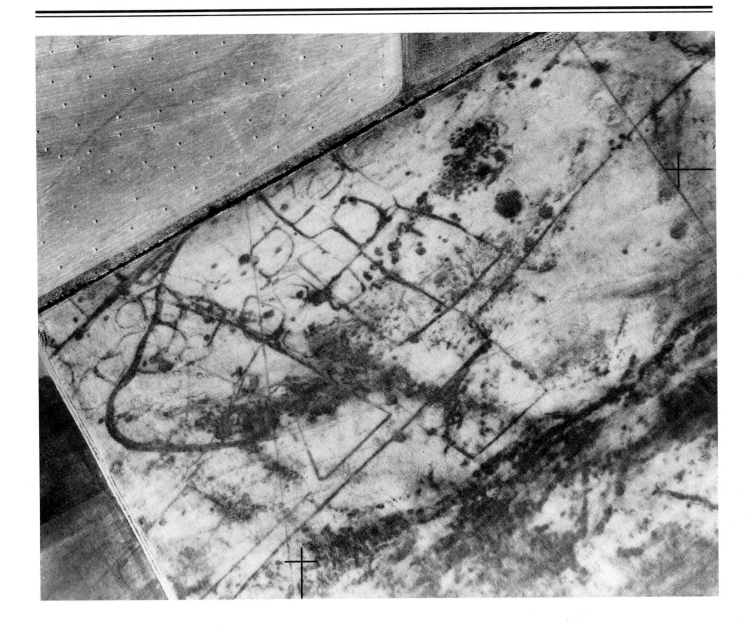

4.2 CROP MARKS *near Cople, Bedfordshire*

In reconstructing the Iron Age countryside, we must imagine a landscape that was well-peopled and productively worked, but in which villages were greatly outnumbered by farmsteads and small clusters of two or three huts. To the east of Cople, we can recognise a fragment from such a landscape. Although the remains are virtually invisible from the ground, from the air the crop-marks, which are produced by differences of growth between crop plants rooted in the silts of old ditches and elsewhere, clearly record an ancient rural scene.

At first, the pattern seems to be a mere jumble of dark lines, but on closer inspection we can recognise the circular outline of hut dwellings or, rather, of the ditch which

ran around the hut to catch the drips from its conical thatched roof (centre, far left). More obvious are the loosely oval or rectangular shapes, the remains of paddocks and small enclosures which will have been sited close to a farmstead, while larger, rather rectangular fields or enclosures can also be seen.

The pattern continues into the modern field in the upper left corner, where the orderly array of two-tone dots turns out to be made by bales of straw. This field, having been recently reaped and baled, scarcely reveals the secrets of its buried Iron Age remains, and the contrast with the display of evidence in the field that is still under standing crops is truly striking.

4.3 CHYSAUSTER *Cornwall*

Chysauster village dates from the late Iron Age and Romano-British period and is particularly worth visiting. To the extent that there is a village plan, it consists of eight dwellings set out on either side of a track, although some of the houses have their entrances in the 'side' rather than the track-side frontage. The dwellings are of a peculiar type known as 'courtyard houses', largely confined to Cornwall, although some have been found in Wales, and a few further north. The largest of the houses may be the oldest and the objects found in it have yielded dates ranging from the second century BC to the third century AD.

The form of the courtyard house is most clearly apparent from the air, whereas from the ground the compartmentalisation seems at first confusing. The nucleus of the house consisted of an open central courtyard and several chambers, workshops or other rooms opened on to this. These rooms would each have been roofed, either in thatch or by 'corbelling' of overlapping stone slabs. From above we can see how the boulder-rubble walls are thickened and scalloped to accommodate these rooms. The village has been excavated, and the state of preservation and restoration obviously varies, with the trio of huts in the upper

right portion of the settlement being particularly well-preserved.

Chysauster was essentially the home of peasant farmers who grazed livestock, grew corn which they ground at home in stone querns, and gardened. Courtyard houses are also found dispersed in Cornwall as free-standing farmsteads or in pairs. The village is also interesting because it can be related to its contemporary setting. There are well-preserved fragments of the old Iron Age system of fields round about and old field boundaries can just be discerned as overgrown ridges in the lower right of the photograph. More obvious are the garden plots which were attached to the huts, like those showing in the cleared ground to the right of the upper right dwelling, while 'clearance cairns', composed of boulders and rubble removed from the fields, lie further afield. Although it does not emerge in the photograph, Chysauster also had an underground passage or 'fogou'. Fogous are thought to have been used for storage or sheltering livestock, although a good example at the courtyard-house village of Carn Euny, further west in Penwith, seems to have been used in rituals.

4.4 EWE CLOSE *Cumbria*

While the Romano-British people of Cornwall were tending to favour courtyard houses like those at Chysauster (p. 88) the clusters of simple circular stone huts and oval or rectangular paddocks that we see at Ewe Close were more typical of the English uplands. On the Pennine flanks just to the east of the Lake District, a remarkable collection of well-preserved native settlements has been found – three villages around Crosby Garrett, others near Crosby Ravensworth and Ewe Close itself with Ewe Locks and Cow Green within easy walking distance. Along with others in the neighbourhood, these little village survivals tell us of a landscape which was well-peopled in Roman times, if never particularly fertile and inviting.

The outlines which emerge so plainly when seen from the air are not crop-marks, but the remains of stone walls. Ewe Close consists of various components: two roughly rectangular well-bounded areas to left and right, each containing small rectangular paddocks or stock pens and circular huts, while to the south (ie, above) is a third walled and embanked rectangular area, less tightly-packed with paddocks, but with some small huts and rectangular enclosures. A particularly large hut stands near the centre of the right-hand enclosure; its massive stone rubble walls are six feet thick.

Despite its walls and slight embankments, Ewe Close is not a heavily defended village like some of its Welsh contemporaries (Tre'r Ceiri) or English predecessors, and its 'paddocky' appearance and the rugged surroundings reflect the prominence of stock-raising in the village lifestyle. Although most of the remains excavated here are of Roman vintage, no real Romans lived at Ewe Close and the first British occupation of the site could predate the Roman conquest. Ten huts in varying states of preservation can be recognised and, if they were all occupied at the same time, we should expect a village population of about fifty. In that it envigorated the market for farm produce, the Roman occupation will have benefited villages such as this, although the people of Ewe Close were probably as prone as their neighbours to participation in the occasional flare-ups and conspiracies which made life difficult for the occupying forces. The Romans for their part will have been content to leave the villagers to get on with farming, though the Carlisle-to-Lancaster Roman road sweeps in to the right of the village, and would have allowed patrols to keep an official eye on affairs at Ewe Close.

4.5 ZENNOR *Cornwall*

To the extent that non-industrial villages exist in Cornwall, they tend to consist of small, loose farmstead clusters, some with churches and some without. Whatever influence the Anglo-Saxons may have had on lowland England, they scarcely penetrated Cornwall, while Cornish patterns of settlement tend to be ancient and finely adjusted to the pastoral lifestyle favoured by an environment of rugged upland grazings and damp hollows. With an old granite church as its only recognisable nucleus and a handful of farmsteads straggling beside the through-road, Zennor is quite typical, and dispersed farmsteads are numerous in the surroundings.

We are left to wonder just how old settlements like Zennor may be, but very recent fieldwork by members of the Cornwall Committee for Rescue Archaeology is showing that the farming divisions in the immediate vicinity of the village, near St Ives, are very old indeed. Most of the fields seen in the photograph seem to be derived from 'Celtic' fields. The farm territories tend to consist of a package of lower pasture which often has a frontage along the nearby sea cliff and then stretches inland to embrace an adjacent area of upland moorland. The remains of courtyard houses similar to those at Chysauster (see p. 88), dating from the Romano-British period, have been found by archaeologists amongst the 'Celtic' fields, while in places it can be seen that modern farm boundaries correspond to the limits of Romano-British fields. And so, while Cornwall is often Liberal in its politics, it tends to be very conservative in terms of its rural life!

4.6 BAMBURGH *Northumberland* ▶

The eye is immediately drawn to the magnificent medieval stronghold on Castle Rock, although here we are really concerned with the apparently unexciting village next to it. The historical importance of Bamburgh pre-dates both castle and village and, although our knowledge of Dark Age settlements is slight and our understanding of the defenceworks of the period less than we thought it was, we can be sure that little Bamburgh has a lineage surpassing that of almost all our great modern cities.

Anglo-Saxons became well-established in this part of England in the course of the sixth century. They seem to have been attracted by the craggy ridge of volcanic rock which is bounded on one side by the sea, while presenting a steep and stern face to the south and, as the Dark Age kingdom of Northumbria rose in importance, Bamburgh gained prestige as its capital. Until both kingdom and capital declined as a result of Danish raids, the 'town' and

defences probably occupied a part of the Castle Rock. Bede (c. 673–735), who lived as a monk at Jarrow, was well-versed in Northumbrian affairs and he mentions how the relics of King Oswald were kept in a silver casket at St Peter's church in 'Bebbanburh' or Bamburgh, 'the royal city, which is called after a former queen named Bebba'. He also describes how the warlike king Penda and his Mercian army attempted to storm, then besiege and then burn Bamburgh, piling wattle, rafters and thatch pillaged from neighbouring villages around the city wall, but how the attack perished when the prayers of Bishop Aidan produced a divine wind which turned the flames upon the attackers.

The walled royal city was probably little more than a wooden, village-sized settlement with a church that has since vanished and rubble ramparts. In 1095, William II is said to have attacked the Earl of Northumbria's fortress on Castle Rock, but was unable to storm it despite having built a wooden stronghold or 'Evil neighbour' outside its walls. The surviving medieval castle has the rectangular Norman keep as its old nucleus and it was extensively restored and adapted as apartments by Lord Armstrong in 1890.

In the shelter of the Norman castle, a medieval village developed in the area between it and the church. There were hopes that, having gained its market charter, the settlement might grow as a prosperous town and Henry II granted generous port rights to the burgesses. In the event, competition from Berwick upon Tweed proved too much, and the planned out-port of 'Bamburgh Newtown' which was sited about a mile to the north-west has perished utterly.

The humble village of Bamburgh was remodelled by Lord Crewe at the start of the last century and, the castle apart, the only obvious monument to medieval Bamburgh's status is the wooded triangle of land, lying in the fork of the village road by the church, which held the medieval market.

4.7 WHELDRAKE *North Yorkshire*

Wheldrake lies a few miles to the south-east of York, and although it has a thoroughly rural and village-like character, we must recognise that a village such as this could never be created by accident. The whole village landscape resounds to the tune of planning. From the air, we see clearly that the farmsteads and cottages tend to line up facing the through-road. Then we have the long narrow 'tofts' or plots which run back from the dwellings, their ends neatly trimmed by a pair of back-lanes which run parallel to the through-road to define the village package.

When and how did the planning take place? We can at least begin to tackle this question if we look at the medieval history of the region and the forms of other villages in east, central and northern Yorkshire. When we research the latter, it is found that Wheldrake is more typical than unique in being planned, and so we must look for an occasion when a sweeping and drastic remodelling of the northern countryside could have taken place. It is probably to be found in the vile Harrying of the North of 1069–70 when, provoked by lingering resistance to Norman Rule in Northumbria, the Conqueror launched his forces on a campaign of genocide and devastation which few Northumbrian communities escaped. Then it seems that the rehabilitation of the battered and depopulated countryside was undertaken by landlords who created processions of regularly-planned new settlements which were peopled by survivors and imported peasants.

However, because Wheldrake has been studied in great detail by June Sheppard, we have reason to think that the process might have been a little more complex. After the Harrying, in 1086, Wheldrake seems to have had only six tenant households, but there is the possibility that there was an earlier Saxon village at Wheldrake, perhaps with sixteen households. On the eve of the first outbreak of the Black Death or the 'Great Pestilence' which arrived in 1348, Wheldrake had probably grown to a size comparable to that of the nineteenth-century village, which had around seventy properties.

Old Wheldrake ends just beyond the church which can be seen near the top of the village. At first, the landscape history sleuth is tempted to suspect that the photograph shows a shrunken village, for it seems that the back-lanes can be continued in the hedgerow patterns to trace the outlines of a larger village which extended as far as the sharp dog-leg in the through-road near the upper right margin of the photograph. In fact, the hedgerow running to the right of the through-road, above and to the right of the church, is not tracing a 'lost' back-lane, but the course of the original through-road. The present road which runs beyond the church is known as 'New Road' and represents a straightening and diversion of the old routeway and the dwellings which lie beside it are relatively modern.

4.8 NEWNHAM AND BADBY *Northamptonshire*

There are few facets of the landscape more fascinating or challenging than the village and its layout. The more carefully that we look at the village, the more we become aware that it can be a dynamic and complicated subject. Many villages have contracted, expanded, reorientated themselves or drifted away from their original sites. A very frequent category is made up of villages which are described as 'polyfocal' in scholarly jargon; these are settlements which consist of two, three or more originally separate components.

The components may be represented by different churches, manorial clusters, planned and unplanned units or separate greens. Northamptonshire is one of the very few counties whose villages have been studied in considerable detail, thanks to a Royal Commission on Historical Monuments survey by the archaeologist C. C. Taylor. Here it is clear that most villages diverge from the supposed stereotypes and the majority display some form of individuality and oddness. Doubtless the villages of other counties are similarly complex.

Both Newnham and Badby, both lying near to Daventry, are good examples of the polyfocal village, while modern housing developments further complicate their layouts. At Newnham, the Church of St Michael with a parapet spire can be seen in the upper left portion of the village while a medieval manor house, less easily recognised, lies just to its left. A street running from the left of the photograph to the church and a tiny green beside it forms one of the old villages within this village. Beyond the church and separated from it by pockets of pasture lies a small cluster of houses. This was a separate and unconnected settlement and now consists of both dwellings and the overgrown remains of medieval houses. Just below the village's centre, we can see an old triangular green which lies at the junction between the village through-road and lanes arriving from north and south.

The church and manor cluster formed one district component of the village, the green and its flanking dwellings, another. However, modern housing, instantly recognisable by the bulky symmetry of the dwellings and their

possession of front gardens, now forms a bridge between the old, once distinct foci. Hidden by this recent development is yet another small triangular green which was the core of still another component settlement.

The situation at Badby is in some ways similar. The early eighteenth-century tower of the medieval church can be seen in the upper right section of the village where dwellings line the loop of road which encircles the church to form one component of the village. The plan of Badby – to the extent that there is one – resembles a pair of spectacles, and a line of roadside dwellings forms a 'bridge' linking the church cluster to a second house cluster which flanks a triangular green, just visible above the old rooftops and to the right of some very large trees near the left-hand margin. Below the green are two arcs of modern housing development. The road which runs along the bottom of the photograph is a post-medieval turnpike, wisely set out to by-pass the tangled lanes of Badby, while a broad ribbon of good, old, deciduous woodland preserves the medieval woodland pattern; beyond lie the lands of the deserted medieval village of Fawsley (see p. 130).

However, there are further complications to Badby for a now 'lost' village street ran diagonally from lower left to upper right just above the central section of the modern village. Its course can just be discerned and is marked by straggly rows of trees and bushes which line the top of a sloping field. Also, a tiny three-sided green lay to the right of the still-visible triangular green.

Both Newnham and Badby have grown from the merging of modest and tiny settlements which were once distinct. Some consisted of dwellings aligned along streets, others as small clusters of houses beside little greens. Many villages – and in some parts of England, probably most – are similarly complex. Modern housing may often seem to obliterate the evidence, but old maps, air photographs and the earthworks of abandoned streets and dwellings may help us to unravel the mysteries of village layouts.

4.9 LUDBOROUGH *Lincolnshire*

The saying 'Jack of all trades and master of none' cannot apply to this photograph, for it performs at least three tasks supremely well. Firstly, it provides an excellent portrait of an example of that very common resident of the English countryside, the shrunken village. The evidence of the internal collapse of what was apparently a quite substantial village is plainly evident in the fields to the upper left and lower right of the surviving village fragment. Traces of abandoned dwellings are scarcely apparent, but the obvious relics are the rectangular 'closes' which pattern the fields. Closes such as these will each have contained a dwelling and a patch of land which might have been used to pasture a cow, raise extra crops or vegetables or accommodate pigs and poultry, and the roughly rectangular form was typical of the English claylands.

Secondly, just below the village, the remains of the enclosing banks of a set of medieval fishponds are strikingly obvious, even though the ponds have long since been drained. Traces of the sluices which would be opened to pass water from one pond to the next can be recognised, while carp would have been transferred from one pond to another as they matured. Although the shadows cast by the artificial banks clearly outline the pond complex, such ponds were often very shallow, some holding less than a foot of water.

Thirdly, we can see how the modern road tends rather to disregard the emaciated village, for the village's original main street is the track which runs through the centre of the photograph from right to left before halting and becoming a holloway as it meets the old village earthworks. It is tempting to assume that, for reasons long-forgotten, old Ludborough fell on hard times and began to wither. Some other Lincolnshire clayland villages, such as Goltho, shrank or perished when climatic deterioration around the fourteenth century rendered the cold and ill-drained soils unsuitable for arable farming. In this case, however, the landscape historian Trevor Rowley warns that Ludborough might not be a shrunken village at all but a younger village which has taken over the site of a previously deserted medieval village.

4.10 ASHMORE *Dorset*

In the past, Ashmore might have been regarded as a 'typical' English village, but now we realise that each village has its own distinct personality. To the extent that the history of Ashmore can be traced, it seems to be rather unusual.

The village sits on the Dorset chalklands and its site is more than 700 ft above sea level – a very lofty position. The focal point of the village is a circular pond which must have provided a notable watering-place in the dry chalk countryside, while old and curving roads converge at this point, suggesting that prehistoric stockmen may have driven their beasts to the pond although the antiquity of the village itself is quite unknown.

Domesday Book tells us that a village of 'Aisemara' existed in 1086 and the name may mean 'ash-mere' – the pond near the ash trees. Place-names however are tricky and in this case one must remember that 'mere' could also indicate a boundary, and the Dorset-Wiltshire boundary follows the old hedgerow which runs diagonally across the photograph across the top of the fields which are above and to the left of Ashmore.

The village is something of a favourite in books about the rural landscape, but this vertical photograph shows another rather interesting feature: the ancient field pattern which emerges as crop-marks, notably just beyond the boundary hedge, above and to the left of Ashmore. Existing field and road patterns cut the ancient fields, while a feature resembling a Bronze Age round barrow can just be discerned, sitting in the corner of one of the little fields.

98

4.11 CHELMORTON *Derbyshire*

The medieval British village was bonded to the fields and commons which succoured it and enabled it to survive. Although the peripheral position of the church (upper left, within a tree-lined rectangular churchyard) is interesting, Chelmorton seems to have a simple plan which consists of farmsteads set at close intervals along a road which, today, goes nowhere in particular after reaching the church. The main fascination of Chelmorton concerns the surrounding fields. The village, like others in the Peak District, has a remarkably lofty position for the entire settlement lies well above the 1000-ft contour. Nevertheless, the situation of Chelmorton is to a certain extent sheltered and the original village was placed in an area selected as 'infield' ploughland, while the higher limestone plateaux around provided grazing.

The infield was divided into plough strips which ran back from the farmsteads at right-angles to the road and, at some later time but doubtless during the Middle Ages, the open infield was permanently partitioned and enclosed. Although the intricate farming arrangements associated with open-field farming no longer operated, the enclosure of the old infield strips preserved the earlier medieval strip patterns. The amalgamation of some of the strips and their division by cross-walls is obvious in the photograph, but it scarcely blurs the old, strip-based pattern. There are clear similarities with the fields around Middleton near Pickering in North Yorkshire (pl. 4.13), though at Chelmorton, we see field walls built from blocks of the ubiquitous Carboniferous Limestone instead of hedges. This rock is associated with thin limey soils, bright springy pastures but poorer ploughlands so the old infield arable fields were long since converted to grazings.

While the fossilised strip patterns of medieval enclosure dominate the photograph, in the upper right-hand corner can be seen the rectangular geometry of another form of enclosure: Parliamentary Enclosure under the Chelmorton Enclosure Act of 1809, which partitioned the surrounding upland commons and wastes. The photograph also offers a tidy little lesson in the archaeological principle of 'superimposition'. See how the straight road which runs from the church end of Chelmorton to the right-hand margin cuts right across the strip patterns, showing that the walled strips existed before the road was built. This is in fact an enclosure road, newly created as part of the arrangements of 1809.

4.12 DEEPING ST JAMES and NEIGHBOURS *Lincolnshire*

Much ink has been spilt in describing how geographical factors governed the siting of villages. More often than not, however, chosen village sites have nothing in particular to recommend them: there was no rule book and, had there been, it would probably have been thrown away! In the case of The Deepings, though, we do see the effects of geographical controls. The River Welland runs through the photograph which is looking westwards, over Deeping St James in the foreground which merges with Deeping Gate, which in turn links with distant Market Deeping.

At the time when Domesday Book was compiled in 1086, Deeping St James already existed as 'East Deeping', a substantial village of about fifty households. Early in the twelfth century, the village seems to have been enlarged, while the community of Peterborough Abbey created Market Deeping as a large and deliberately planned village. These changes were part of a more general colonisation of the western Fenland margins which took place in the twelfth and thirteenth centuries.

At this time, and for many years after, the land to the left of the Welland was Fen and so settlement and ploughland were confined to the slightly higher and better-drained ground to the right, while the through-road closely follows the river bank, linking and guiding the form of the riverside villages. From each roadside dwelling, a long toft of arable land ran towards the ploughlands and the surviving hedgerows trace this orderly and perhaps planned arrangement. Here, the local geography clearly favoured this 'linear' settlement pattern and the need for communal co-operation in reclamation and flood prevention projects underlined the importance of living in villages rather than dispersed farmsteads. Professors Beresford and St Joseph have described* how workers were responsible for maintaining the river bank, providing timber for bank defences and clearing the ditches and drains.

However, the forces of natural adversity also created advantages and the Fenland villages tended to be more prosperous than their Fen-less neighbours. The river carried the little craft which traded in Fenland produce like fish, eels and wildfowl, the willow wands or 'osiers' used in basket-making, while the spring floods stimulated early growth in the riverside meadows.

Medieval England, An Aerial Survey

4.13 MIDDLETON *North Yorkshire*

Middleton, lying about one mile to the north-west of Pickering on the southern flanks of the North York Moors, has interesting fields and a rather puzzling layout. Firstly the fields, for although they are now enclosed by hedgerows which contain some mature trees grown as standards, these are clearly survivals from the days of medieval open-field strip farming, and the pattern continues beyond Aislaby village on the left margin of the photograph.

Disregarding the small modern housing estate at the lower left end of Middleton and the triangular green-like area to the upper right (which contains the remains of a former pond), the village at first seems quite typical of a pattern which is common in the Vale of York. Each dwelling tends to be sited beside the through-road and has a slightly elongated plot or 'toft' attached, while back-lanes define the limits of the tofts. However, another row of tofts appears to run back from the lower left back-lane. One

is immediately tempted to assume that, at some point in its history, the village was enlarged with a new row of dwellings and tofts being established along the back-lane. This was a common form of village growth. However, a close inspection of the site by archaeologists of the Royal Commission on Historical Monuments has shown that there are no house relics along the back-lane, while the hedgerows at the end of the tofts beyond the back-lane are aligned with those of the tofts on its village side. And so we can only suppose that, at some stage, the villagers on this side of Middleton chose to enlarge and elongate their tofts, extending them across the old back-lane and taking in land from the village open fields.

In the north, such extensions were often known as 'Garthends' or 'Garrends' and they were frequently created during seventeenth-century enclosures of medieval open fields.

4.14 KIMBOLTON *Cambridgeshire*

In the popular imagination, the English village is an undisciplined or straggling place, the product of centuries of haphazard and piecemeal growth. In reality, however, we find that considerable numbers of villages are planned creations or show the planned reorganisation of an existing village. Very often, this planning is shown to date from the Middle Ages. It is commonly found in the cases of villages associated with Norman or later castles, or in places where the aristocratic landlord obtained a market charter and reorganised the village layout to accommodate a green, square or other trading area.

Kimbolton embodies both these planning factors. The vertical air photograph plainly reveals that Kimbolton is in two distinct parts: to the left, we see a planned and extremely regular component with the houses set out beside a spacious street with ample space for market trading, while beyond the medieval church, which lies in the angle of the dog-leg of this street, the properties preserve the outlines of a relaxed and unplanned village.

The reorganisation of Kimbolton took place in the medieval period and so none of the original village dwellings remains but the layout persists. The changes probably date to 1200 when Geoffrey Fitz Piers gained the right to establish a market here. His castle (which in a later form accommodated the rejected Catherine of Aragon as a reluctant guest) stood on the site of the large rectangular building seen to the left of the village. Now a school, this seventeenth- and eighteenth-century mansion incorporates the remains of an older castle. Not much imagination is needed for us to see the straight link-up between sectors of through-road to the left and right of the planned section of the village and it seems clear that the old road was diverted via two dog-legs to run through the centre of the planned village component.

Many market towns originated as deliberate medieval trading creations and, for a period after its elevation to the status of a market centre, Kimbolton seems to have grown, with new properties being erected along the back-lane which runs below main street. The River Kym can be recognised as a winding ribbon of trees and shrubs running from left to right below the village and above the fields, while below the river a track and field divisions trace the outlines of a rectangular package of land. Apparently there were hopes that the market town would be extended across the Kym in an organised expansion but, as was so often the case, the growth did not materialise and so modern Kimbolton is little more than a village.

The land around East Witton is a cornucopia of historical sites – Middleham Castle, Jervaulx Abbey and lovely Masham – which is probably why it always seems to be dusk when I arrive at East Witton. With its 'Gothic' church, stone cottages and long green, East Witton may seem to epitomise the traditional English village. The truth is much more complicated and therefore more interesting and, so far as it can be, it has been run to ground by Professors Beresford and St Joseph.

The church, built to commemorate the jubilee of George III, dates only from 1809 and it does not really form a part of the village plan. Neither did its predecessor, the Church of St Martin, which lay well below the lower left corner of our photograph, isolated and stranded in the village fields.

Alert visitors to East Witton will swiftly recognise that the elongated, two-row village which flanks the long and tree-studded green is a planned creation and the story might seem to end with the discovery that the attractive but stereotyped cottages were built, along with the church, by the Earl of Ailesbury in 1809. However, a village plan of 1627 shows that the village had the same layout then, even if its dwellings were rebuilt at the start of the last century.

The truth is partly to be found in the old road pattern. The modern visitor to East Witton negotiates a rather tricky dog-leg to enter the village from the A6108, which runs across the photograph from right to left, between the church and village. The original road from Ripon ran through East Witton village green and onwards into bleak Coverdale, up, over and down into Wharfedale. Traffic from Wensleydale also traversed the green. The narrow lane which can be seen curving away from the top of the green can be driven, providing that speed is not a major concern. A former lane, faintly marked by a broken row of trees and bushes just to the left of the village and parallel to the green formed a back-lane which is shown on the plan of 1627. At the top end of the village it turned sharply left and then right to run through the bank of trees and then along the hillslope and it may just be discerned as a faint holloway. At the other end of the village, it was joined by the main village street and led away eastwards, running just to the right of the straight hedgerow of the field which is to the left of the church. It was punctuated by a number of cottages which are no longer visible and continued to the original village church. Keen-eyed readers may just detect the abandoned holloway.

With a bustling road running right along its spine, East Witton will have been in a good position to exploit a medieval market. By the end of the thirteenth century, the monks of Jervaulx controlled almost all the parish, while a Monday market and Martinmas cattle fair were first held here in 1307. It is most likely that, rather than the market being slotted into an existing village, East Witton was shifted, planned and rebuilt in a position where it could best exploit the local trade. The monks of Jervaulx are the probable planners of the present East Witton which dates from around 1300. At the same time, since East Witton lies a couple of miles from the Abbey itself, it did not affront the Cistercian preoccupation with isolation from the laity.

The elongated, two-row village of East Witton which flanks the tree-studded green is a planned creation

Nun Monkton might have been designed on a Hollywood set to fulfil some director's vision of the typical English village. There is everything that the tourist might hope to find – a neat green with a circular duckpond; a pair of churches and a pub on the right-hand side of the green, albeit rather unobtrusive buildings; a former priory and, joy of joys, even a maypole on the green. Nun Monkton is a very pretty place indeed.

Whilst it is also a genuinely traditional village with a venerable layout, it is however even less 'typical' than most other villages. The average medieval village was home to a community of peasants who laboured on the surrounding lands, but Nun Monkton had its own special associations for it had a medieval priory and a small medieval weaving and tailoring industry. Also, until relatively modern times, it had a special role as a river transhipment port. It sits on a neck of land between the River Ouse and the smaller River Nidd, and the small port facilities lay on the riverside just beyond the present village, where goods moving up the Ouse, some coming via Humberside and the North Sea, were transferred to pack-horses for inland distribution.

Despite Nun Monkton's homely and relaxed appearance, when we see the village from the air we have reasons to think that this is a carefully planned settlement, perhaps set out in a single stroke of medieval reorganisation. Domesday Book often disguises the complexities of the numbers of smaller and larger settlements which can appear under a single entry, but it does list a 'Monchetone' existing hereabouts in 1086. We can see that the dwellings and plots are set out in three orderly rows which define the triangular green, while the slightly curving sides of some of the plots hint that they may have been carved out of older strip patterns.

After the Dissolution, the nunnery which lay beyond the apex in the village green was succeeded by a manor house, and the lords of the manor may have been responsible for preventing peasant encroachments on the green. There have been some small, more recent encroachments, mainly represented by the very un-medieval cottage front gardens, but the dwellings themselves trace out old property rows which reveal an even more geometrical and planned green. The circular pond is not a very common village feature although the motif is repeated in some villages lying further east in Yorkshire, like Newton on Rawcliffe and Wold Newton. The pond may be a later addition to the village, perhaps a watering place for stock but, now at least, a duck pond. Actually it is not a particularly effective duck pond, for a few years ago the villagers were compelled to erect an artificial roosting island on the pond in an attempt to entice the ducks away from their gardens. It was not a success!

As the result of maps and surveys described by Professors Beresford and St Joseph*, we know that this village layout already existed at the end of the Middle Ages. There were thirty-three rented tenements here in 1538 while the village which was described in a survey of 1567 closely resembled the settlement as mapped in 1607. The main differences in layout between then and now have been produced by the decay of some dwellings and the consequent amalgamation of some house plots. A few gaps are apparent on West Row, at the bottom of the green where there were seventeen dwellings. Tudor Nun Monkton will have consisted of more but smaller dwellings, mainly of timber and thatch, but the essential village layout has proved remarkably durable since it was first conceived, perhaps in the Norman period or High Middle Ages.

Medieval England, An Aerial Survey

4.17 STRICHEN and FOCHABERS *Grampian*

Residents of Strichen in the former county of Aberdeenshire and of Fochabers in the former county of Moray may jibe at the inclusion of these settlements under the 'village' rather than the 'town' heading. Both in fact are representatives of a form of settlement that is characteristic of north-east Scotland, but less common elsewhere. The plump and venerable villages which we associate with the English lowlands were scarcely found in this area. Instead, there were the large and small medieval market towns known as Royal Burghs and Burghs of Barony, and hosts of loose and straggly hamlets known as 'fermtouns', or – if they possessed a church or a mill – as 'kirktouns' and 'milltouns'.

In the aftermath of the English victory at Culloden Moor in 1746, the Highlands began to witness the ghastly Clearances as the farmstead clusters or '*clachans*' of the clansmen were erased by the landlords to create depopulated sheep ranges. In the more productive lowlands and plateaux of the north-east, there were also evictions, but the Clearances tended to take the more civilised form of 'Improvements'. The old fermtoun patterns were swept away in many extensive areas, but they tended to be replaced by a thinner scatter of much larger and completely planned villages.

These villages were the creations of the local landown-ing gentry and they provided superior accommodation for the peasant tenants who remained, while in many cases the landlords sought to establish new industries to improve the employment opportunities and prosperity of their estates. Most of this remodelling of the rural landscape took place in the second half of the eighteenth century and the new villages mirror the current preoccupation with orderly design and symmetry. The geometrical planning also provided layouts which could easily be expanded should the more optimistic visions of the future be fulfilled.

Strichen takes the name of its founder, Lord Strichen, who created the village in 1764 with the aim of 'promoting the Arts and Manufactures of this country and for the accommodation of tradesmen of all Denominations, Manufacturers and other industrious people to settle within the same'. The layout, which is based on a neat gridwork of straight streets, is typical although the curving course of the North Ugie Water river has governed the form on the left-hand side of the village. The towered church was provided in one of the grid squares at the upper left corner of the new village, while an old kirk can be seen in the foreground. When the railway arrived, about a century after the creation of Strichen, it could not be incorporated in the gridwork of the village and the depot lies near the

photograph's right-hand margin. We can see that later expansion beyond the geometrical confines of the original village was modest, although Strichen is much more substantial and successful than the hopefully named industrial village of New Leeds, built a few miles to the south-east by Lord Strichen's son.

The preoccupation with geometrical planning is even more emphatic in the case of Fochabers. The castle of the Duke of Richmond and Gordon lies on the outskirts of the village to the right, and Fochabers was partly created to improve the appearances of the Gordon estate. Fochabers provides a good example of how individual ingenuity and the accidents of history can influence the prospects of a town or village. In the early years of this century, shooting parties accommodated at the Gordon castle became very partial to the preserves made at Mrs Margaret Baxter's village shop. Business expanded as orders arrived from the south and just before the 1914–18 war, W. A. Baxter, Margaret's son, established a small factory on the far bank of the River Spey (which runs across the top of the photograph and the factory lies just beyond its upper right margin). This factory soon required much greater expansion as Baxter's tinned game and soups, jams and vintage marmalade gained a worldwide reputation.

4.18 FLAXTON *North Yorkshire*

This photograph of Flaxton in the Vale of York is included as a reminder that air photographs need not reveal all the evidence, while some of the little riddles in the British landscape may be very difficult to fathom. From the air, Flaxton seems a rather unremarkable village, essentially a row of dwellings set out beside a ribbon of village green flanking the through-road, while the long narrow tofts which run back from the dwellings suggest medieval village origins. In characteristic fashion, a back-lane defines the ends of the tofts, while the church and a small cluster of dwellings and farmsteads lie on the opposite side of the through-road. A measure of recent expansion is evident in the modern dwellings just below and to the right of the village.

What the photograph does not tell us is that the tree-lined strip of green to the left of the through-road is littered with the rectangular bumps and hollows which are the relics of former dwellings. This means that Flaxton was not the one-row village which we now see, but once had dwellings lining both sides of the road and green. I have not discovered what caused the destruction of almost half the village, but the changes must have come long ago, for the inset from a map drawn by Jeffreys about 1770 shows that the layout of Flaxton was, then, much as it is today.

The deserted medieval village of East Lilling (see pl. 5.c) lies just to the right of the through-road at the upper margin of the photograph.

4.19 BARTON PARK
Great Barton, Suffolk

The sentimental attractions of village life are deeply in-grained in the English consciousness, and here is seen a modern attempt to recapture the village ethos. The photo-graph shows a collection of individually designed upper-middle class dwellings almost guaranteed to test an estate agent's resources of superlatives. Each dwelling is sited within a substantial plot of land, while the variations in the maturity of the hedgerows and planting schemes at the edges of the plots suggest that the properties are of slightly different ages. An up-dated version of a village green which is 'landscaped' by pockets of surviving wood-land forms the village-suburb's focus – yet even if viewing the scene from a satellite, one could scarcely confuse Bar-ton Park with a genuinely traditional village. All other things apart, the spacious front gardens which separate the houses from the edge of the green and from the minor roads express a modern rather than a traditional concept of the proper relationship between house, plot and community.

5. DESERTION, MIGRANTS AND VICTIMS

The countryside of Britain is liberally sprinkled with the corpses of deserted villages and hamlets, but only in recent decades has it been realised that lost village remains are common visible features of the rural scene. We do not know how many abandoned settlements of the medieval and later centuries there are because the process of discovery is still continuing. It is only matched by the rate of destruction as farmers plough over these monuments to lost communities. Air photography has played the leading role in the search for former settlements; the first recorded aerial portrait of a deserted medieval village was taken by the great field archaeologist O. G. S. Crawford in 1925 following a request from a local vicar that he might like to photograph a presumed 'Roman Camp'. In later decades, the Cambridge University team working under the leadership of Prof. J. K. S. St Joseph accumulated a remarkable collection of lost village portraits, many of them showing sites which were actually discovered in the course of aerial photography.

These sites vary considerably in their appearance. A few recently abandoned places still contain recognisable houses and there are a small number of stone-built medieval villages where the house walls still stand knee high. At the sites were ploughing has utterly destroyed the remains, so that even from the air they are invisible, the only evidence of the former settlements exists as dense pottery scatters around the old house sites.

Most lost village sites lie between these extremes. They can be recognised by experts on the ground, but to the layman they appear only as faint bumps and hollows. Such places are much more clearly visible from the air, whether they exist as troughs and ridges which cast shadow marks or are outlined by crop marks. In the instant that the shutter of the aerial camera is open, not only is the existence of a former village or hamlet recorded, but also its form and layout. Often a good aerial photograph allows one to identify all the different village components such as roads and trackways, property divisions, the site of the church and other village earthworks such as fishponds or windmill mounds.

Aerial photographs, however, tell one little or nothing about the causes of village destruction or decay. In many cases, even contemporary documents are silent. The majority of deserted villages met their fates in the latter half of the medieval period. Different social attitudes prevailed and the men of substance and power who could employ clerks or scribes were interested in their possessions and the rents and services which were their due, but the death of a village or the eviction of a peasant community were seldom considered worthy of a written record. As a result, the landscape historian often finds the evidence in oblique references to villages. Their disappearance is often only marked by the evaporation of the settlement in question from contemporary tax lists, or the fate

5.A *Braybrooke near Besborough in Northamptonshire, where the earthworks on the outskirts of the shrunken village trace the outlines of former village streets, moats and ponds*

5.B *Jarlshof on Sumburgh Head, Shetland, where the jumbled relics of former settlements include stone huts of various Bronze Age and Iron Age dates, a Late Iron Age defensive tower or 'broch', a medieval farmstead and a sixteenth-century mansion*

of a community might be recorded in an ecclesiastical complaint to the landowner concerning lost tithes or glebe land.

We are still far from understanding the processes by which different villages have evolved to assume their present forms. Consequently, lost villages, especially those whose desertion can be dated, are of much more than antiquarian interest. The remains which emerge in air photographs reveal villages fossilised at their moments of death and therefore help us to chart the development of those villages which survived.

The deserted settlements are also archaeological storehouses where the relics of the lifestyles of our medieval forebears are entombed. Peasants being crushingly poverty-stricken as a rule, the lost village sites contain nothing that will interest the amateur skinheads of pseudo-archaeology with their vile metal detectors. But they do contain the prosaic fragments of pottery and stratified earth deposits and house-footings which allow us to peer into the world of the medieval peasant. The excavation of the deserted Yorkshire village of Wharram Percy has proceeded with painstaking precision since 1952 and although the task is far from being completed, it has transformed all our notions about English village history.

As with other fields of landscape discovery, the further that one enquires into the lost village riddles, the more complicated and elusive the truth becomes. In addition to the villages which surrendered completely, there are others which survive in a shrunken form, with typical 'lost village' earthworks on their outskirts. More puzzling are the migrant or shifted villages, which have forsaken one site for another. More often than not, the reason for the migration is a mystery, but the departure of the village to greener pastures will leave a legacy of remains that are quite indistinguishable from those of a village which has died rather than shifted.

Readers interested in lost villages should visit well-preserved sites on the ground. One does tend to envy the aerial archaeologist's immunity from the unprovoked wrath of certain farmers, and it is always best to seek the landowner's permission. The less damaged sites provide the amateur archaeologist with excellent opportunities to test his or her powers of observation and eye for terrain. Air photographs offer a wonderful introduction to the world of the deserted village, showing the sorts of features that one should look for, but in a much clearer form than they appear when viewed from the ground.

5.c *A dusting of snow intensifies the outlines of the deserted medieval village of East Lilling near York and its surrounding ridge and furrow ploughland*

A

B

c

5.1 SHRUNKEN AND DESERTED VILLAGES: A PASTICHE

The potency of the aerial photograph as a means of outlining deserted settlements and the varied forms of the settlement portraits produced by aerial photography are evident in this montage of examples.

5.1A The deserted medieval village of Godwick near Tittleshall in Norfolk, where a thin snow cover helps to outline the plan of the former settlement. The tower of the village church can be seen as a jagged stump, upper right, while the round pond just below it is a later marl pit which has been dug into the holloway which marks a former village street. Above the dark field, the earthworks can be seen to have a very regular, rectilinear character, and here one is seeing not village remains, but those of the post-medieval gardens of the nearby hall which were superimposed upon the lost village remains before being in turn abandoned. As is so often the case, a solitary farmstead now stands upon the lost village site.

5.1B The street plan of the deserted medieval village of Muscott near Long Buckby in Northamptonshire is clearly shown in this photograph; small rectangular features reveal the positions of some of the former dwellings, while a farmstead endures upon the old moated medieval manor site, upper right.

5.1C The village of Overstone near Northampton was removed shortly before 1775 and relocated on a site beside the Northampton road in the course of 'improvements' at and around the manor house. The church stood midway between the house and the lake, and the present mansion was built in 1861 to replace a seventeenth-century building. The ornamental lake was constructed early in the nineteenth century, and the holloway of the old village's main street disappears into its lower arm.

D

E

5.1D & 5.1E Two deserted villages, Wolfhampcote at the top and Braunston Bury in the centre of pl. 5.1D, appear in this picture of a section of the Northamptonshire/Warwickshire border, north-west of Daventry. The curving earthwork in the lower left-hand corner marks the course of the old Oxford Canal, while its successor cuts across the upper right-hand corner. The village of Braunston Bury, left of centre, seems to have been short-lived, but the pattern of earthworks suggest a rectangular planned form, distorted in the course of village growth. The level expanse between the village and the corrugated patterns of its ridge and furrow ploughland was a vast fishpond. The closer view of Wolfhampcote (pl. 5.1E) reveals the outlines of an unplanned village. The most obvious feature is the unusual hexagonal manor moat; an elongated fishpond lay just below and to its right, while the church, below and to the left of the moat, has been isolated by the desertion of the village.

F

5.1F The desertion of failed medieval villages is frequently incomplete, with a solitary farmstead or mansion often enduring among the overgrown village relics, as here, at Testerton which is south of Fakenham in Norfolk.

5.1G Thousands of medieval villages have perished completely, but there are also many which have shrunk or have shifted. Work by the archaeologist Peter Wade-Martins suggests that Mileham in Norfolk has shifted its position. The dominating feature of the photograph consists of the earthworks of the imposing Norman motte and bailey castle, and the photograph shows that the greatest concentration of dwellings lies below and to the left of the castle. However, the archaeological evidence of pottery fragments shows that in the Middle Saxon period, Mileham village lay around the church site, where the tower of the medieval church can be seen near the top of the photograph, to the right of the farmsteads and trees which border the road. During the Late Saxon period, the village began to develop along the through-road and, in the course of the medieval period, it grew to reach the vicinity of the castle. The original core of the village around the church is almost deserted.

G

H

I

5.1H & 5.1I Milton in Dorset was one of many victims of emparking (*see* page 134), unusual only in that the fated settlement was a town rather than a village. Lord Milton had his home at Milton Abbey (pl. 5.1H) and during the year 1771–85 he systematically destroyed the adjacent town as the leases of his tenants expired. The destruction of Milton allowed his Lordship to enjoy the solitude of the resultant park while the dispossessed families were rehoused in very congested conditions in the purpose-built village of Milton Abbas, nearby (pl. 5.1I). Milton Abbey is now a school, as can be guessed by the number of goalposts.

5.1J Destroyed in the early years of this century by a Ramsbury butcher, Henry Wilson, who purchased the surrounding lands for use as a sheep-run. Snap near Aldbourne in Wiltshire was a remarkable throw-back to the days of the medieval sheep clearance. Around seventy years after the evictions, Snap has the appearance of a deserted medieval village and the relics of house sites and small enclosures can be discerned in the hedged area, left of centre.

5.1K Imber in Wiltshire is one of a small number of modern village victims, destroyed in the creation of military training areas in the Salisbury Plain. Now tank tracks trace weaving patterns, enmeshing the doomed settlement.

5.2 OLD SARUM *Wiltshire* ▶

Here we see a stronghold and former settlement which has known many different masters. The photograph is looking towards the south-west and the most obvious feature is also the oldest: a 'univallate' Iron Age hillfort – that is, one with just a single earthen ditch and rampart ring. As is always the case, the ditch lies outside the ramparts, but the photograph shows how some of the ditch material has been diverted from the main rampart to form a counter-scarp bank on the outer side for added strength. The origi-

nal eastern entrance to the hillfort seen on the left is used by the modern access road and the oval ramparts enclose some thirty acres.

The Romans recognised the advantages of this position in the construction of their famous road network and it lay at the junction of routes to Badbury near Swindon, to their towns at Dorchester, Silchester and Winchester and to the lead mines of the Mendips. The settlement of Sorviodunum developed near the crossroads, though its traces are not evident in the photograph. Its fate during the Dark Ages is uncertain, although King Alfred defended the site, Aethelred II had a mint here and Saxon artefacts of the ninth century have also been found upon the spot.

The Norman Conquest was succeeded by an outburst of ecclesiastical and defensive projects throughout most of England, during which Old Sarum resumed a central position upon the Wiltshire stage and about a decade after the Conquest, it succeeded Sherborne as the diocesan centre. Shortly afterwards, St Osmund caused the cathedral to be built within the Iron Age ramparts (upper right), and an imposing moated castle motte was constructed in the centre of the ancient defences, which now served it as a bailey. During the first third of the twelfth century, Bishop Roger enlarged the original cathedral and had a stone keep constructed upon the motte. The improvements to the cathedral are plainly evident in our photograph which shows the successive stages outlined upon the turf. The cathedral which was consecrated in 1092 was quite small, just 173 ft in length. The east end terminated in an apsed chancel and apsed aisles which flanked it. Their rounded ends can be seen within the cathedral plan, level with the cross limbs of the transepts, which supported towers. The three apses and the towers which flanked them must have presented an unusual and impressive appearance, but they soon disappeared in the course of Bishop Roger's eastward extension of the church which, with his addition of a new western façade, brought the length of the cathedral to 316 ft.

The days of medieval growth and grandeur at Old Sarum were short-lived. Bishop Roger opposed King Stephen and was deprived of his castle as a result. The Iron Age ramparts then embraced a royal garrison and an ecclesiastical community which were forever squabbling. Further disenchanted by the poverty of the terrain and the shortage of water, the clerics chose to abandon Old Sarum for greener, more tranquil pastures. At the very end of the twelfth century, Bishop Poore decided to move to a new cathedral site in the valley; papal approval was given in 1219 – though the foundations of Salisbury cathedral had been laid in 1200 – and the new cathedral was consecrated in 1258.

The royal garrison remained. The castle was improved in the 1170s, a gatehouse was added towards the end of the twelfth century, and the castle improved again in the 1240s. During the fourteenth century, however, it became derelict, and by the sixteenth it was ruinous. Only a chapel then remained at the cathedral site and the small settlement which had surrounded the ecclesiastical focus crumbled and decayed. Faint traces of the chapel's flint-packed walls can be glimpsed through the blanketing turf. Old Sarum came to be the most famous of the notorious 'Rotten Boroughs', represented by the elder Pitt in the 1730s and 40s.

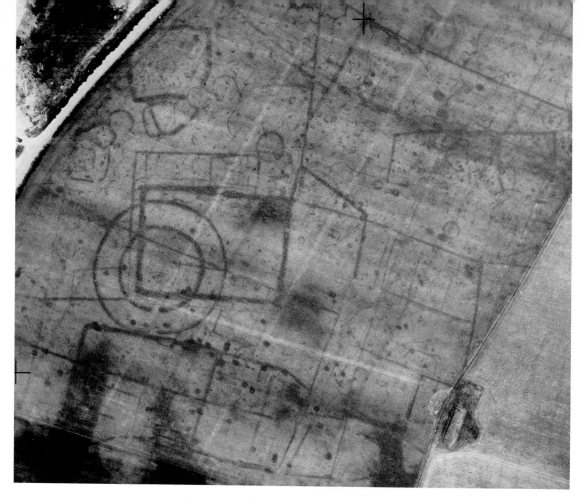

5.3 THE MUCKING CROPMARKS *Essex*

When prehistoric and pagan Dark Age people created settle-ments, it was not their intention to found permanent vil-lages or hamlets. Invariably, homes were deserted after a site had been occupied for a few years or decades or, occa-sionally, a few centuries. We have still to learn the reasons for this 'desertion habit', but we do know that villages which were to prove durable did not appear until quite late in the Saxon period. At Mucking, on the northern side of the Thames estuary near Grays, in an area encroached upon by gravel quarries, the nature of the soil is such that unusually prominent crop marks develop. The photograph shows a complex of marks which represent many different stages in man's occupation of the land and reveal the ways in which the relics of one period overlie or underlie those of others.

Among the most prominent of the outlines are those in the form of two concentric circles, lying just left of centre. An archaeological team has been working at Mucking for several years, and excavation has helped to establish this feature as a 'mini-hillfort' of the Later Bronze Age. It is one of a pair which guarded the Mucking creek and a ridge routeway in the ninth century BC. The rectangular out-lines of fields which were worked from a nearby villa in the Romano-British period are superimposed upon those of another field system which dates further back, to the Bronze Age. Scattered around the site in an apparently haphazard manner are the small circles which outline huts occupied at different stages of the Iron Age.

The most interesting features of the photograph are among the least obvious: the small smudgy dots. These are the remains of small Saxon huts. More particularly, they represent silts which have accumulated in the scooped out or sunken floors which were a feature of early Saxon dwellings. At least 112 of these hut traces have been recognised, suggesting a substantial if sprawling settle-ment. The village dates from the period of Saxon settle-ment which followed the collapse of Roman power in Bri-tain, but the character of Saxon Mucking is controversial. Some experts see it as a 'transit camp' which received Saxon settlers arriving from the continent; to others it was a seasonally-occupied settlement used by wandering Saxon graziers, while still others regard it as a simple peasant settlement.

It would be wrong to think of any of the abandoned settlements revealed in this photograph as 'failures', for they all belong to periods when villages, hamlets and farm-steads were, by their nature, impermanent. Following the inundation of the land bridge which linked Britain to the continent in the Mesolithic period, many different bands of settlers will have found the Thames estuary to be a use-ful thoroughfare leading towards the English interior and many will have made their landings near Mucking. The crop marks tell us more than these immigrants will have known about the previous tenants of the bleak estuarine lands, where gravel-digging now advances across one of our most revealing archaeological sites.

5.4 HOUNDTOR *Devon*

At most deserted medieval village sites, the remains of actual peasant dwellings tend either to be unrecognisable or marked by roughly rectangular platforms or depressions. Dwellings of timber, mud and thatch quickly decayed, but in some stone-strewn areas where more durable materials were available, the rubble of walls may still stand knee high. At Houndtor deserted village, which lies on Dartmoor south-west of Moretonhampstead, almost in the shadow of the great natural rock pile of Hound Tor, the dwellings have been excavated, the foundations restored and the humble houses are easily recognised.

In the Bronze Age, Dartmoor was well-peopled and quite productive, but a marked deterioration of the climate caused the uplands to be deserted in the Iron Age when the moors became waterlogged and blanketed in peat. Apparently the climate improved in the Dark Ages and after about 800 AD colonists began to return. In the thirteenth and fourteenth centuries, however, the climate took a turn for the worse and again refugees abandoned the uplands. Houndtor village was one of the casualties listed in a tally of deserted farmsteads, hamlets and small villages which now numbers more than a hundred.

Excavations by the late Mrs E. M. Winter showed that the Dark Age recolonisation of the area began with the establishment of three sunken-floored huts which may have been the summer shelters used by herdsmen. A permanent village of turf-walled huts was established later, but in the middle of the thirteenth century the dwellings were superseded by stone-built long-houses – single storey dwellings partitioned to provide a living-room and a byre beneath the same roof.

The villagers were mixed farmers working vulnerable, marginal lands which extended above 1000 ft, and the faint corrugations in the moor around Houndtor show how they struggled to plough its steep, rock-littered slopes. As the climate decayed, the pastures will have become muddy and churned by the hooves of the livestock; winter fodder will have been in short supply and the villagers built corn dryers out of deserted barns and dwellings in an attempt to preserve their late-ripening crops. But it was a losing struggle and in the course of the fourteenth century the failed farming families drifted away and the site became deserted.

The long-houses are about the size of motor coaches and although several are aligned to the north-east, like many small West Country settlements, Houndtor had no distinct plan. Small garden plots and paddocks were close by the dwellings, while the small circular feature lying near the lower left margin of the photograph seems to recall earlier, Bronze Age tenants of the moor: a prehistoric enclosure perhaps converted into a stock pen by the medieval villagers.

127

A comparison between this photograph and the one of Houndtor (pl. 5.4) shows that the desertion of a village will leave different patterns when it occurs in the claylands of Lincolnshire rather than the peat and rock-covered slopes of Dartmoor. Even so, the villages of Goltho and Houndtor met similar fates. The climatic deterioration which afflicted the West Country was also experienced in the east. Particularly vulnerable were the claylands which tended to be poorly drained and slow to warm in the spring and therefore most sensitive to changes in the direction of cooler, damper and cloudier conditions.

Before its decline, Goltho will have been a settlement of mixed farmers, able to raise good arable crops when conditions were favourable. With the decay of the climate, some villagers will have drifted away, seeking tenancies on the lighter lands. Others stayed and excavations show that they turned to livestock farming, constructing open 'crew yards' where the cattle could over-winter, the yards being carpeted with straw brought from ploughlands on the lighter soils. Most of these families endured at Goltho until the fifteenth century, but eventually the site was abandoned early in post-medieval times.

On first impressions, the photograph may seem to show a meaningless jumble of bumps and hollows but, in fact, there is sufficient evidence to allow a reconstruction of the medieval village. The moated blister lying to the left of centre was the manor site and immediately to its lower right and sheltered by trees is the village chapel site which accommodates a basically sixteenth-century brick chapel. Shallow trench-like depressions are recognisable as hol-loways, tracing the course of the old village streets. One leaves the modern road in the upper left of the photograph and almost parallels this road; other streets can be seen to intersect it roughly at right angles and more streets or lanes ran from left to right to link them. Scarcely any dwelling remains can be discerned, although the outlines of some of the roughly rectangular plots or 'crofts' in which they stood can be recognised.

Although this is an important archaeological site, it fell victim to modern farming practices in the early 1970s and the medieval earthworks were all bulldozed – this photograph having been taken in 1965. Before the destruction, a rescue excavation was directed by Guy Beresford. It showed that three circular farmsteads were occupied successively in the first and second centuries AD, but that the site was then deserted and, like many other villages, Goltho came back to life in the eighth century. The moated Norman manor site proved particularly interesting, showing that the Norman manor house was preceded by an unusually large Saxon hall and that the Norman defences stood inside the remains of substantial late Saxon earthworks. This was most unusual, because the Saxons tended to fortify towns rather than the dwellings of the nobility.

Goltho was not the only Lincolnshire victim of the worsening climate and some twenty clayland villages lying within a nine-mile radius of this village were also deserted. The future of a medieval village was no more secure then than that of valuable archaeological sites appears to be in this modern period.

A panorama of the ruggedly beautiful Scottish Highlands landscape near the sea loch of Loch Alsh

A panorama of the landscape of the Southern Uplands near the old Scottish abbey and market centre of Melrose

Towering to a height of more than 3500 feet, Snowdon is the highest mountain in Wales. Note how the erosion of the backwalls of glacial cwms has scalloped the highlands

The famous technicolor cliffs at Hunstanton are composed of horizontal beds of chocolate-olive greensand, red chalk and white chalk. In the background is a section of the planned suburbs of this Norfolk holiday resort

(Opposite) A fine panorama of good old English countryside with networks of hedgerows in the vicinity of Southwick in Wiltshire. In the background is the distinctive chalk figure of the Westbury white horse and above it, the Iron Age hillfort of Bratton Castle

The outlines of a deserted medieval village can be clearly discerned in the pasture at Lowesby in Leicestershire and one can detect how the former roads which served the village were abandoned after its desertion

Wandlebury near Cambridge. At the centre of the photograph, a circular Iron Age hillfort was transformed by the construction of a mansion in its interior in the eighteenth century, and, in the early nineteenth century, ornamental beechwoods were planted all around. The area above is now a golf course, while below can be seen 'patterned ground' produced by periglacial conditions

5.6 CUBLINGTON *Buckinghamshire*

Although Britain contains several thousand deserted medieval villages, most people think that lost villages are rare features of the landscape. Country folk are sometimes aware of a nearby lost village; almost invariably they blame its demise on the Black Death but in the vast majority of cases this is a folk myth disguising the true facts.

This is not to deny the fearful voracity of the Pestilence and there are sound reasons for believing that during the Great Pestilence of 1348–51, between a half and a third of the English population was destroyed. Cublington exemplifies what may have been a common course of events at stricken villages. At first appearance, the photograph seems to show a shifted or migrant village which has wandered from the centre to the top of the area, leaving typical lost village earthworks behind it; but the truth is rather different.

Many of the villages which perished in the Middle Ages from various different causes were small and ailing before misfortunes sealed their fates. They might be deprived of a crucial component in village semi-sufficiency, like pasture or ploughland; be sited on poor, marginal land, or be otherwise vulnerable. Cublington was declining before the Pestilence intervened; the reasons are not clear but the worsening of the climate in the fourteenth century may have played a part. Some of the land in the immediate vicinity of the village can be seen to be rough and overgrown today, while winter visitors to the village earthworks are likely to sink shin-deep in mud. Professor Beresford points out that the site was abandoned soon after 1341 and the Black Death, arriving in this area in 1349, could have delivered the *coup de grâce*.

At the start of the fifteenth century, however, Cublington was resettled and similar recolonisations of deserted village lands and sites must partly explain why there are so few villages which can be positively identified as Pestilence victims. The new settlers had the good sense to rebuild the village on the higher, better-drained land where Cublington survives to this day, peopled by folk of substance who were able to dispose of threats like that of the planned Third London Airport, which they ran out of town in 1970.

The most obvious feature of the village earthworks is the small motte and bailey castle, unusually squared-off, perhaps to fit into a village plan of rectangular components. Just below and to its right is the scrub-grown fishpond which still holds water in winter. Rectangular platforms and depressions can be seen in the lower left side of the bailey earthworks; superficially, they resemble

house sites but seen from the ground they appear too prominent for this explanation and they could be stew tanks for fish fry destined for the large pond. The village was divided into roughly rectangular property units and the one above and to the right of the motte has been shown by excavation to have housed the church and churchyard. The village's main street appears as a deep holloway which passes between this plot and the castle.

The photograph does not reveal the actual relief, but the area with the lost village remains is low and level and the lane leading up from the holloway to living Cublington is quite steep. The medieval church tower of Cublington can be seen near the village centre, while the fields around still display the corduroy patterns of medieval ploughing.

5.7 FAWSLEY *Northamptonshire*

After the Great Pestilence of 1348–51, peasant labour, which had hitherto been cheap, cowed and over-abundant, became scarce and fractious. The political establishment attempted to peg wage-rates but the efforts to coerce the depleted and discontented peasant ranks met with little success. Many landlords sought new sources of income. They did not have to look far, for wool was already the mainstay of English wealth and trade. Between the arrival the Black Death and the end of the Tudor period, countless hundreds of peasant villages were destroyed as the flocks supplanted the ploughmen. Thousands of families became homeless beggars overnight; the roads were littered with shuffling victims; the stability of the realm was threatened, while scores of hard-faced landlords counted their profits.

Lying in a heartland of village destruction, Fawsley was one of dozens of Northamptonshire casualties, but the place has a special notoriety both as a victim and base of the Knightley family, one of the most avaricious and destructive of the sheep-rearing dynasties. The poll tax records tell that in 1377 some ninety villagers over the age of fourteen lived here. In 1415, the manor was bought by Richard Knightley and shortly afterwards the peasants were complaining of an intolerable burden of rents and services. It seems that Knightley was using rack-renting as the means to winkle out his tenants. Fawsley Hall, which lies south of Daventry, then became the base from which Knightley and his descendants expanded their empire and a later Sir Richard Knightley became the most wickedly successful of all the evictors, running up to 5000 sheep in the county in 1530. The records show that in his time there were only seven taxpayers living in this parish and most of them were Knightleys or shepherds.

About in the centre of the photograph opposite is Fawsley Hall, built by Sir Edmund Knightley who died in 1542; the house is in disrepair and a factory lies behind it. Below the Hall, on a peninsula flanked by artificial lakes is the old village church of Fawsley, a thirteenth-century building modified and adapted as a Knightley chapel. The landscaping of the Hall grounds has removed most traces of the medieval village while the direction and angle of lighting in the photograph is not helpful in revealing what little remains. A village lay around the church and a holloway representing one of its streets runs from the church to the causeway between the lakes to the left. Other lost village earthworks lie in the pasture to the left of the Hall, while from the ground one can detect faint traces of ridged and furrowed ploughland in the ground between the church and Hall. Taken together, these remains suggest that the Fawsley whose name features briefly in medieval documents was in fact composed of two neighbouring villages which were separated by a small area of ploughland.

The 13th-century church of Fawsley was modified and adapted as a Knightley chapel

5.8 CASTLE CAMPS *Cambridgeshire*

The important thing about the village of Castle Camps near Haverhill is that it has gone. It has not disappeared; it is alive and well today, but lies several hundred yards from the scene of this photograph. Castle Camps is one of the migrants, a shifted village which has drifted or leap-frogged far from its original site around the village church shown in the centre of the photograph. As is often the case, the reasons for the shift are quite unknown but it seems to have been accomplished in medieval times.

A massive Norman motte and bailey castle seems to have provided the original focus for settlement. It was built soon after the Conquest by Aubrey de Vere on one of the higher ridges in this slightly undulating countryside. The outlines of the stronghold can be traced by prominent banks and ditches but, from the air, the trees and bushes which delineate the fortifications are the most prominent features. The motte, which now accommodates a large farmstead near the left margin of the photograph, is defined by a ring of trees overhanging the still partly water-filled moat. The

bailey was a two-stage construction. The first bailey looped out from the motte, and the church stands on the line of its outer edge, while bushes trace its form. It was superseded by a much larger defended enclosure, trapezoidal in form, but D-shaped in the photograph because of perspective distortions and, again, its limits are plainly traced by the trees.

The church cannot have been built until after the expansion of the bailey. Even from the air, it can be recognised as a fifteenth-century building, but it contains some masonry from a twelfth-century predecessor. The original village of Castle Camps occupied the area between the church and the right-hand margin of the photograph; old property boundaries can just be discerned in the unploughed area, and the ploughland is rich in medieval pot fragments. They tell us that the village once nestled beside its church, but the reason for its departure remain mysterious.

5.9 ARGAM *Yorkshire*

Argam produces a photograph as clear as the fate of the village is uncertain. It had a simple plan being set out along a through-road which runs across the photograph from lower left to upper right. Running diagonally to intersect the old village's main street is a feature which at first resembles the holloway of another abandoned road, but it is something quite different: it is the ditch of a prehistoric 'linear earthwork', the Argam Dike, which was probably constructed to define an ancient boundary. It runs from just below the middle of the right-hand margin of the photograph. The rectangular outlines of former peasant dwellings can clearly be seen, while the much larger and more distinct rectangle perhaps outlines the yard of the medieval church although it reminds one of a walled garden.

Although little is known about the cause of Argam's demise, Prof. M. W. Beresford has described documents showing that priests were inducted long after the church and village had passed out of existence. The village layout is clearly preserved but there are some puzzling features. The sudden broadening of the through-road just below its intersection with the Argam Dike suggests a village green. One dwelling, apparently a long-house, lies just to the right of this 'green', but other green-side dwellings are not revealed, while the land above the 'green' has been ploughed over with short ridged strips. Perhaps the village drifted away from this 'green' before it perished. Though there are doubts concerning the causes of destruction, a sheep clearance is strongly suspected. The Yorkshire Wolds were severely affected by the Tudor clearances and in the area just south of Humanby there are many other deserted villages including Bertindale, Caythorpe, Swaythorpe and Octon.

5.10 HINDERSKELFE *North Yorkshire*

The village of Hinderskelfe lay near the centre of the photograph. It has been completely obliterated, but in this case we know how the village perished and details of its layout. The mansion of Charles Howard, 3rd Earl of Carlisle, burned down in 1693 and the Earl approached John Vanbrugh to provide designs for a replacement. The choice was a surprising one, since although Vanbrugh had gained a reputation as a comedy playwright, he had little architectural experience. Wisely he sought the assistance of Nicholas Hawksmoor, Clerk of Works to Christopher Wren.

A superb site was available and the presence of the living village of Hinderskelfe was a minor impediment, for many villages perished beneath the grandeur of a stately mansion and landscaped park. The birth of Castle Howard was heralded by the death of Hinderskelfe. However, Prof. M. W. Beresford discovered a plan of the village as it existed in 1694 in the Castle Howard archives and so it is possible to recreate the position and layout of the doomed village.

Its main street entered the photograph from the right, along the line of the Terrace Walk which joins a little 'roundabout' at the lower right of the Castle Howard frontage. From the roundabout, the main street turned, running through the ground now occupied by the circular pond and fountain and continued on this course. The sides of the street were flanked by dwellings set in slightly elongated crofts, while the village church lay just to the left of the mansion.

In some instances of 'emparking', particularly the later cases, a replacement village was provided to accommodate the dispossessed tenants and estate workers. The villagers of Hinderskelfe were not compensated, however, although plans for a bizarre circular settlement focussing on a church in the form of a Classical temple were produced by George London. A different estate village, Coneysthorpe, can be seen near the upper margin of the photograph beyond the waters of the ornamental lake.

A

5.11 HAREWOOD *West Yorkshire*

In the case of Hinderskelfe (pl. 5.10), emparking deprived the villagers of their homes and there was no replacement village, but in those of Harewood and Milton (pl. 5.11), new settlements were created to house the displaced folk. Harewood is unusual but not unique, sharing with Wimpole in Cambridgeshire the distinction of having been emparked on more than one occasion. Both villages survived the traumas and emerged in new forms.

The original Harewood was a small agricultural and market centre which tapped the trade on a routeway passing through Wharfedale. It prospered until the start of the fifteenth century when a form of emparking robbed the dwellings of their valuable surrounding lands. This was achieved by a process of 'engrossment', whereby Gascoigne, a prosperous freeholder, bought out the remaining freeholders to extend his demesne. The village withered but did not die and had become revitalised by the eighteenth century when local turnpike trusts improved the

communications in the locality. Two of these roads met at Harewood, promising good potential for economic expansion but the village, which lay in a now tree-grown area near the right-hand margin of pl. 5.11A was fated.

A *nouveau riche* sugar trader, Edwin Lascelles, gained elevation to the peerage as 1st Earl of Harewood and sought a home and setting fit to proclaim his new status. John Carr of York was appointed to design the mansion and work began in 1759. Robert Adam helped to fancify the design and the house was occupied by 1772. Unfortunately, the old village intruded upon the surrounding expanse of landscaped parkland and it was destroyed and replaced. Carr of York provided plans for the replacement which partly overlapped the site of a pre-existing settlement and was aligned along the Skipton to York turnpike.

In contrast to the contemporary situation at Milton Abbas, there was nothing mean about the new village of Harewood, which remains an attractive if rather bizarre

B

creation. Both Classical and terrace concepts were embodied in the stone-built village, where the severity of a straight terrace roofline was avoided by creating dwellings of two, two-and-a-half and three storeys. It was also intended that the settlement should be provided with an inn to tap the passing coach trade and a school as well as new employment opportunities and the potential for industrial growth – although the ribbon mill that was incorporated in the village plan failed to prosper. The church remained in its original position, stranded in the park not far from the mansion.

Harewood House (pl. 5.11B) sits in parkland landscaped by Capability Brown although the formal terrace gardens were added later. Although the north front of the mansion preserves Carr's design, the south front which is shown in the photograph was altered by Charles Barry in 1843. The old village church is largely hidden by trees and lies at the very top of the photograph, but the landscaping of the park has obliterated the traces of the village which once accompanied it.

5.12 BURNHOPE *Co Durham*

Compared with the settlement carnage of the Middle Ages, relatively few villages have perished in the twentieth century. Recent victims include the handful of settlements which fell foul of plans to create reservoirs and military training areas and a rather larger number of villages whose livelihoods were narrowly based upon a vulnerable local industry. This latter group includes a number of failed coal mining centres.

In the 1950s, villages in Co Durham were designated according to their economic prospects and those consigned to 'category D' effectively had their life-support systems switched off as the authorities withdrew finance for development and replacement. In 1969, the designation was changed to 'group 4'. The doomed mining villages were weak in prospects but strong in community spirit and efforts were made to rehouse their populations together in neighbourhoods within new and expanded towns. Any villagers remaining in the depleted settlements faced dangers from vandalism and fire. Fittings were pillaged from the abandoned dwellings, many of which were built without fire walls – walls which continued up into the roofs of houses to stop fire spreading from loft to loft – while the emptied terraces could have become refuges for disturbed or dangerous elements. Consequently, the deserted villages were completely bulldozed out of existence and within a decade it has been found that vegetation has advanced and completely colonised the acres of brick rubble.

Burnhope was an unexpected casualty, for in the early 1950s it seemed safe in 'category B', its mine was working and there were hopes that other industries might be established around the pit head. In the following decade, however, its economic prospects collapsed and when the photograph was taken in 1969 its site had been levelled. Amongst the rubble, one can trace the outlines of the old terraced rows of miners' dwellings. The church has been preserved, but the only other building still standing is associated with a scrap yard – a very common landmark at the sites of vanished 'category D' villages.

5.13 WEST WHELPINGTON ▶ *Northumberland*

At least four abandoned prehistoric settlements lie within a couple of miles of the deserted village of West Whelpington, which has been a lost village only since the early eighteenth century. The remains lie fairly close to Kirkwhelpington on a table-like spur of higher ground with the valley trough of the River Wansbeck defining its southern flank and running across the top of the photograph. West Whelpington had a simple, seemingly planned form with a long rectangular green as its centrepiece. Dwellings lined the green and some of their outlines can still be seen, although the walls defining their crofts are more prominent. Excavations suggest that the planned village was preceded by an irregular scatter of dwellings.

Field access lanes can be recognised running from the central green, between crofts to the village lands beyond, while the ridge and furrow patterns are very well preserved. A furlong block of plough ridges terminates at the bottom of the photograph and one can plainly see how the ends of the plough ridges curve, the effect being produced by the turning of the plough team as the end of a furrow was approached.

The village is portrayed during its destruction by stone quarrying, which can be seen to have obliterated the upper left section of the settlement. A rescue excavation directed by M. G. Jarrett explored a cluster of house sites in this section in advance of the quarrying, but stone is scarcely a rare and precious commodity and it does seem a sad commentary on official attitudes to the heritage that one of our best-preserved monuments to peasant life should be vandalised in this way. The medieval village was the ancestral home to most people living in Britain. We still know remarkably little about the life and evolution of our villages, and deserted village sites are treasure houses of archaeological information. Many of the best sites have been recently destroyed by ploughing and the protection of even officially-designated sites often proves little more than nominal.

6.A *The Scamridge Dikes run diagonally across the scarp face of the North York Moors to link Trouts Dale and Kirk Dale and almost certainly represent a prehistoric territorial frontier. The triple-ditched form of the earthwork is unusual, producing a very imposing boundary marker though having few apparent military advantages*

6. BOUNDARIES AND BARRIERS

Struggles to gain or hold territory may be as old as mankind. Archaeology is certainly able to demonstrate that in Britain they are as old as the later part of the Neolithic period, when some hills were fortified and defenders fell in attacks by archers. In recent years, prehistorians have emphasised the importance of territory and there have been various attempts to understand the patterns of the ancient earthworks which mark old territorial frontiers. Such work is extremely important, because if we can use these relict frontier works to define and so resurrect the former communal territories, then we will learn much more about the sizes of clan or tribal units, their relationships with one another and the political problems which they faced.

Although many of the old frontiers survive in the form of quite well-preserved dykes or 'linear earthworks', interpretation is seldom easy because similar ditch-fronted embankments were built in all periods between the Bronze Age and the Dark Ages, while some Irish examples are of a Norman vintage. Some are many miles in length and it would have been quite impractical to attempt to man their entire length with defenders. Although many have defensive proportions, the majority are best interpreted as forbidding but symbolic frontier markers of which only short sections might occasionally have been defended. Thus they fill the role of a 'Keep Out' noticeboard rather than that of a stronghold.

The construction of such frontier works seems to have begun in response to population pressure and land shortage in the Bronze Age and in a few places, such as the North York Moors, it can be demonstrated that purely symbolic boundaries marked by alignments of ridge-top round barrows were later demarcated by alignments of pits which were then superseded by dykes as social tensions increased. Other linear earthworks delimit Iron Age territories or represent the outer defences of Late Iron Age 'towns' or *oppida*. The Antonine Wall (pl. 6.2), is a refined Roman version of the linear earthwork; some of the supposedly 'Saxon' dykes, although appearing less professional, may also be Roman creations, while other dykes still are the frontier works of early Saxon kingdoms or were created in attempts to resist the Saxon penetration of British territory.

We are only beginning to appreciate the functional durability as well as the historical importance of the comprehensive array of British territorial frontier works. Although the origins of many dykes have long been forgotten, a large proportion of them still mark the extents of political units such as parishes or counties and many still serve as estate boundaries. Also, it is quite probable that many of the boundaries were already venerable when the frontier works were first erected to emphasise their positions in the landscape. Thousands of documents and charters survive to remind us that land was the essence and preoccupation of medieval life and there is no reason to doubt that the importance of land ownership was any less in the preceding periods.

Begun in 122 and virtually completed six years later, Hadrian's Wall was much more than a solid, defensive stone wall. It was initiated during Emperor Hadrian's visit to Britain and although Aurelius Victor, Hadrian's biographer, stated that it was created 'to separate the Romans from the barbarians', it was part of a broader political and military strategy, while the stone wall itself was just one element in a formidable defensive complex of frontier works. Although its defences were overrun in 197, 296 and 367, the wall, when properly manned, was a fearsome obstacle to barbarian invasions from the north. But it also served as a base for raids or advances into Scotland and as an effective means of policing the frontier and exerting customs controls.

It ran across the north of England from coast to coast for a distance of seventy-three miles and the stonework generally stood to a height of 15 ft and was possibly crowned by a 6-ft timber palisade. Sixteen forts guarded sections of the wall and there were eighty turreted milecastles recessed into the stonework. Standing in front of the wall was a ditch which was generally 28 ft wide by 10 ft deep, while a second ditch, the so-called Vallum, lay some distance behind the wall. The area between the wall and the Vallum was designated as a military zone and travellers were obliged to enter and exit via controlled crossing points. Military roads lay beyond the Vallum and the complex of wall defences was backed by an earlier system of forts and supply depots (the Stanegate system).

The photograph shows a section of the wall lying to the west of Housesteads fort. The wall itself is seen as a narrow thread meandering along the crest of the Whin Sill, a natural outcrop of igneous rock which climaxes in the famous Hotbank Crags at the upper margins of the photograph. The small rectangular outline of a mile-castle can be seen just above the quarry which has destroyed a section of wall near the foot of the photograph. The deep gouge of the Vallum is particularly well-displayed and near the top of the photograph it carries the B6318. The Stanegate road ran some distance beyond the right-hand margin of the photograph, while Roman temporary camps lay in the angle between the Vallum and the modern B6318. Parts of three of them are visible as small rectangular features.

Housesteads fort, lying just beyond the Hotbank Crags, is shown in close-up in pl. 6.1B and is the best-preserved and most rewarding to visit of the Roman forts in Britain. The typical 'playing card' shape and the defended gateways are plainly apparent. The remains of fourth-century barracks can be seen in the lower right corner and directly above are the ruins of the granary. To the left of the granary in a central position lay the headquarters building and, to its left, the commanding officer's dwelling, while above

the headquarters are the remains of the hospital.

The stepped landscape which exists outside the walls of Housesteads reveals cultivation terraces, as well as the remains of a sizable civil settlement which developed in the third and fourth centuries housing tradesmen and the families of servicemen as well as boasting a number of temples and taverns. The settlement was destroyed during the great barbarian raid of 367 when the wall was overrun and it was not rebuilt when the wall was repaired in 396. The town had previously been ravaged in a raid of 296 and rebuilt on the alignment leading to the lower of the two gateways on the left (southern) side of the fort. The outlines of former streets and buildings are evident in the terrain around the fort.

6.2 THE ANTONINE WALL *Strathclyde*

Roman policy towards Scotland was marked by a degree of uncertainty that one does not normally associate with the Empire. In the aftermath of conquest and consolidation in England during the decades following the successful Roman landing in AD 43, successive generals appraised the northern lands. In the early 80s, Agricola led his troops against the Caledonii and their confederate tribes. Roman roads studded by forts were established as far north as Strathmore but, although a great victory was won at Mons Graupius (perhaps near the prominent hill of Bennachie in the former county of Aberdeenshire), in the winter of that year Agricola was recalled to Rome. Then, before the end of the decade, Roman reverses on the Danubian frontier necessitated the recall of one legion from Britain and the redeployment of the three remaining legions. A series of military reverses in Scotland may have followed and the Romans appear to have lost the Southern Uplands early in the second century.

Hadrian's Wall was built to consolidate the British frontier of the Empire following the emperor's visit in 122. However, around 143 the limits of the Empire were again pushed northwards with the establishment of a new defensive line, the Antonine Wall, which ran for a distance of thirty-seven miles to link the Firth of Forth and the Firth of Clyde. Perhaps the advance accomplished under governor Quintus Lollius Urbicus during the reign of Antonius Pius was influenced more by the desire to gain plaudits in Rome than by the necessities of the local British situation and, after about fifteen years of garrisoning the Antonine Wall, the legions returned to Hadrian's Wall. There was a shortlived reoccupation of the Antonine line before the wall was finally abandoned around 180.

The Antonine Wall was nowhere as imposing as its southern counterpart and although sections of its ditch were cut in rock, the ramparts and all but two of the sixteen associated forts so far known were built of turf. The earthen ramparts were about 12 ft tall by 4 ft wide and were fronted by a level 'berm' about 20 ft wide and then a very broad ditch which was around 12 ft in depth. The supporting forts were placed at two-mile intervals.

Largely as a result of its earthen construction, the Antonine Wall seldom survives as a truly imposing landscape feature. The section portrayed in the photograph lies near to the Croy Hill fort on the middle section of the wall, near Cumbernauld. Here can be seen the ditch which was excavated from solid rock surviving as a well-marked feature although the earthen ramparts have virtually disappeared, leaving no appreciable traces to be glimpsed to the right of the ditch. Moreover, it can clearly be seen that while the ditch is well-preserved in the rocky uplands of Croy Hill, on the lower, ploughed-over land in the top quarter of the photograph, the destruction of the frontier work is almost complete.

In this area of peat bog near Powers Cross in Co Galway one can recognise the geometrical indentations of recent peat cuttings and the gradual recolonisation of the older cuttings by bog vegetation

Many monochrome illustrations of crop marks appear in the book and this photograph of an area near Deeping St Nicholas in Lincolnshire reveals Romano-British crop marks as they appear in full colour

The Norman cathedral at Durham, built on a wonderfully prominent and protected site which is almost surrounded by a meander of the River Wear

Crop marks at Maxey in the north of Cambridgeshire, lying in an area of the Fenland margins which has revealed a wealth of archaeological information for periods from the Neolithic to the Saxon

(Opposite) A panorama of the Roman, Saxon and Norman town and medieval university centre of Cambridge, looking across the city in an east-north-easterly direction

Burghley House near Stamford, said to be the largest Elizabethan house in England, was begun by William Cecil in 1552. He died in the house in 1598 as Lord Burghley following service for forty years as Secretary of State

Warwick Castle is mainly a formidable stronghold of the Beauchamp family dating from the thirteenth century, although it had Norman and Saxon predecessors

6.3 OFFA'S DYKE *Shropshire*

While several prehistoric or Dark Age dykes were attributed in later centuries to the handiwork of mythical deities or the Devil, there is little reason to doubt that Offa's Dyke was built on the instructions of the Mercian king whose name it still bears. The attribution of the dyke to Offa of Mercia (757–96) is a very old one and derives from Asser, the biographer of King Alfred. Asser tells that Offa built his dyke to run from sea to sea, but it now seems probable that a part of Wat's Dyke, which was built by Offa's predecessor, was incorporated as a northern extension of the great frontier work.

As with other great linear earthworks, it is hard to imagine that there was ever an intention that the ramparts should be manned along their entire length. Rather, Offa's Dyke should be regarded as a showy and unambiguous frontier marker which proclaimed that the land to its east belonged to Mercia and that unauthorised Welsh penetration beyond the dyke would not be tolerated. Having surveyed the frontier work in detail, Sir Cyril Fox suggested that the line of the dyke might have been negotiated between Offa and the Welsh provincial rulers. There is

also an intriguing possibility that in building his dyke, Offa may have been re-enacting the deeds of another Offa, who was famed in legend for his military prowess and for the construction of a great earthwork in Schleswig.

The dyke runs from Treuddyn, north-west of Wrexham, southwards to a point near Chepstow on the Severn. It is not completely continuous and the breaks may represent areas of former dense forest and difficult terrain. The span is some 120 miles and the dyke is therefore forty-seven miles longer than Hadrian's Wall.

The photograph shows a section of the dyke running in a north-western direction near Llanfair Waterdine, where the earthwork is well-preserved and passes through lovely hedged pastures and upland grazings. The complete lack of integration between the later field systems which have developed on either side of the barrier demonstrates that, although the political boundary between England and Wales loops back and forth across the old Mercian frontier, Offa's Dyke has remained a crucial estate and property boundary.

This photograph of Wansdyke shows the bank on the left, the ditch in the middle and the 'counterscarp' bank just beyond the ditch

6.4 WANSDYKE *Wiltshire*

Wansdyke is the most massive of the various Wessex dykes and, although it is almost certainly an imposing frontier work of the Dark Ages, its precise origin and function are still debated. It was previously thought that Wansdyke was a single great earthwork running from Maes Knoll in the Mendips through Wiltshire to the Savernake Forest on the Berkshire borders. Field surveys accomplished by Sir Cyril Fox in 1958 demonstrated that Wansdyke really consists of two dykes, West Wansdyke which terminates just to the south of Bath, and East Wansdyke which traverses the rolling chalk country of the Vale of Pewsey, with a stretch of undefended Roman road running between the two earthworks. The section in the photograph opposite lies about six miles east-north-east of Devizes, where the dyke runs along the ridge of Tan Hill.

Even a modern army would have difficulties in manning the dyke continuously along its length although sections of Wansdyke are of formidable, defensive proportions, measuring 90 ft across the breadth of the rampart and ditch and with a smaller 'counterscarp' bank lying just beyond the ditch. The great ditch is on the northern side of the main bank and this demonstrates that the dyke was constructed in anticipation of a threat from the north. As yet, we do not know the identity of the builders or that of their northern adversaries. East Wansdyke almost certainly dates from the fifth or sixth centuries and a section of West Wansdyke takes account of a stretch of Roman road, demonstrating a Roman or post-Roman date. It is probably either a British creation of the Arthurian period, constructed to bar Saxon penetration from the Upper Thames valley into southern Wiltshire, or a very early frontier work of the West Saxons.

7.A *The massive hillfort and Iron Age tribal capital of Maiden Castle near Dorchester in Dorset*

7. CASTLES AND STRONG PLACES

Preserved in the landscapes of Britain are the relics of many conflicts, threats and conquests. Some of the overgrown or decaying strongholds are the last enduring epitaphs to rivalries and insecurities which are long forgotten and now mysterious. Others can be linked to familiar episodes in the history of the nations of Britain. All are monuments to human fears and anxieties, and all are considered responses to the means of waging war which were current when they were built. Each citadel or defencework represents an attempt to face a challenge or secure a territory, yet each one was likely to be devalued by improvements in the methods of attack or by the emergence of an even greater and unanticipated challenge.

While these features are held in common, the castles and strongholds of Britain comprise a remarkably varied collection. In terms of age, they range from the oldest hillforts which appeared well before 1000 BC, through the rapidly evolving forms of medieval castle to the fall-out shelters of the modern age. In scale, there is similar diversity: at one extreme are the massive and overbearing hillforts with ramparts enclosing twenty or more acres and the gigantic Edwardian castles in Wales, the construction of which strained the resources of the English realm; at the other extreme are the small tower houses, pele towers and moated homesteads of the lesser nobles, as well as the myriad small pill-boxes of the last war.

Although the practical defensive qualities of many of these relics seem to be quite clear-cut, we must remember the close psychological links between social status and the means to protect oneself and others against outside threats. With this in mind, we may doubt the true defensive values of the circular embankments of the Irish 'raths' or farmsteads of the prehistoric and medieval periods, the flimsy drystone walls of the smaller Irish ring forts or the shallow moats surrounding many medieval English manor houses. Turrets and battlements were features of many of the noble mansions of the sixteenth and seventeenth centuries which were built after the private fortress had been shown to be redundant.

From familiar viewpoints on the ground, we may be in a good position to appreciate the awesome dimensions of medieval castle walls or the problems which faced attackers hoping to storm a hillfort across a precipitous series of rampart banks and ditches. Almost invariably, however, we are ill-placed to appreciate the totality of a stronghold or the way in which it has been constructed to exploit the advantages of the local terrain. The photographs which follow demonstrate the unique attributes of the aerial view. Ramparts or walls which, from the ground, may seem to be constructed with scant consideration for the subtleties of the landscape can be seen at a glance to be closely adapted to the individual character of the site, or planned and combined as parts of a coherent defensive complex. Often too, it is possible to recognise the successive stages in the development and adaptation of a stronghold. Therefore, the aerial view may be total, comprehensive and charged with potential for new and revealing insights. That the aerial views are also often visually stunning is a point that need not be laboured.

The capability of the airborne camera is nowhere better illustrated than in its portrayal of hillforts. Not only can we see all sides of a defended hilltop, but we can also appreciate the ways in which ramparts may loop out to secure a strategic spur or how complex entrance defences are designed to reinforce a major weak spot. Although much-studied, the important problems which the hillforts pose may only surrender eventually to excavation. Thus far, however, they have tended to become more puzzling as the relevant information increased. We can no longer accept that the 'bivallate' and 'multivallate' hillforts, with two or more roughly concentric ditch and rampart rings, are relatively late sophistications in response to the introduction of sling warfare towards the end of the Iron Age. Nor can we still envisage the hillfort as a bolt-hole to be occupied only when invasion loomed. Some of the larger examples are known to have accommodated sizable settlements which were actually more permanent than a typical Iron Age village. Perhaps the most puzzling facet of their history is the uncanny frequency with which hillforts are found to occupy the sites of Neolithic causewayed camps, as described in Chapter 2. Recent excavations suggest that defenceworks may have guarded some of these camps also.

The hillfort was certainly a stronghold, the construction of which will have imposed enormous demands upon the time and energy of the population of its surrounding territory. The first examples seem to have been constructed in the Later Bronze Age, before 1000 BC. Their appearance coincided with the onset of a prolonged period of climatic deterioration and so the hillfort can be seen as a response to the turmoils and pressures to be expected in an overpopulated countryside at a time when agriculture was retreating. However, the hillfort could be much more than a simple stronghold. It would probably act as a political focus and could sometimes even become the capital of a tribal territory. In some cases, it was also a settlement which like the walled town of the Middle Ages could serve as a centre for trading and the distribution of goods. It is even possible to imagine that some hillforts might be monumental public works erected partly to proclaim the powers of compulsion of a particular chieftain. Certainly such vast constructions testify to the purposeful organisation of Celtic tribal society and we suspect that their organisation was imposed by chieftains. We are left to wonder nevertheless why the forts are relatively rare in eastern England, which was well-peopled and not devoid of defensible hilltops?

Each age has given rise to its own distinctive fortifications and, therefore, we associate hillforts with the Celtic tribes, mottes with Norman conquerors and pele towers with medieval raiding on the Anglo-Scottish border. Often, however, we may fail to appreciate how defensible terrain may continue to retain its currency, how old citadels may therefore be adapted to meet new challenges, or how senile strongholds were sometimes hastily pressed back into service to face an unexpected threat. A number of hillforts which were abandoned before or during the Roman conquest and the occupation of Britain were hurriedly renovated during the traumas of Dark Age conflict and resettlement. Several of the photographs which follow portray the medieval adaptation of Roman strongholds, some of which were themselves sited within Iron Age defences.

The Roman defenceworks come in a number of distinctive forms and they were the creations of a heterogeneous but highly-organised people, experienced in many aspects of military engineering if perhaps somewhat inflexible in matters of design. Their strongholds can be related to changing political circumstances: the initial conquest of lowland Britain; experiments in the establishment of a secure northern imperial frontier while the productive lowlands were being assimilated into the system of empire; and the attempts to safeguard the British province in the face of seaborne raids and invasions from many quarters, climaxing in the (supposed) withdrawal of the legions around AD 410. The advances of the legions through England to Wales and then into Scotland as far as the Moray Firth are commemorated in the surviving earthworks of rectangular temporary marching camps, while the consolidation of power through the control routeways and domination of intervening ground is evidenced by the remains of more permanent

7.B *The rectangular outlines of a Roman camp on the moors near Malham in North Yorkshire*

7.C *The well-preserved Roman fort which guarded Hard Knott Pass in the Lake District*

fortresses with specialised buildings. The Antonine Wall and Hadrian's Wall and their related fortresses in part reflect the imperial preoccupation with stable, defensible borders, while the Saxon shore forts are clearly related to the mounting threats of barbarian raiding.

These Roman defenceworks come in many sizes and forms but they have one feature in common: they are all manifestations of the Roman vision of the British mainland as a single unit. Even if the conquest of Scotland was judged to be impossible or unworthy of the effort needed, at least the Romans had a far wider conception of Britain than its earlier inhabitants.

After the decline of the power of Rome, Britain hurtled into the period which is justifiably, if unfashionably, known as the Dark Ages. The rise of Saxon dynasties and the often ephemeral and precarious attempts to create a unified Saxon kingdom in England in the face of Norse and Danish assaults will be familiar to most readers. We know less about the defenceworks of the Saxons than we do of those of the Romans. Hastily refortified hillforts played a role in some of the campaigns which successively deployed Saxon war bands or armies against the British, other Saxons and the Danes. Four types of military settlement using a protective ring of earthbanks played an important part in the attempts of Alfred and his successors to secure and expand the English realm, and a number of such settlements have endured as towns. At a much more local level, some protection would also probably have been afforded by church towers built of stone.

In the course of the Middle Ages, the castle passed quite swiftly through a long sequence of evolutionary changes. The most ruthless of Darwinian principles governed its destiny, and as the stark techniques of siege warfare were improved and refined, so castle design advanced quickly, or the castle itself faced a gruesome fate.

In the early stages of the Norman occupation, the local magnates were generally content to construct small earthen mounds or 'mottes', which were crowned with a palisade of stakes, adequate for the modest task of cowing the local peasants. Soon rivalries between local dynasties and struggles for the throne encouraged the construction of more imposing mounds and the addition of bailey enclosures. The motte no longer carried a mere palisade but a square stone tower or keep, while the bailey earthworks were sometimes strengthened by the building of a stone curtain wall. In turn, the vulnerability to sapping of the corners of a square tower spawned a new generation of round towers, generally either embraced by or set in curtain walls. In the course of four medieval centuries, the sophistications produced in castle design by its enforced and essential evolution were many and various, but the main stages in the process can be followed in the photographs presented here.

A number of factors – the development and improvements of cannon, the ravaging of the ranks of the aristocracy in the course of the Wars of the Roses, the concentration of power under the Tudor monarchy, and the royal recruitment of large mercenary armies – contributed to the redundancy of the baronial fortress. In the course of the Tudor period, the emphasis in fortification shifted in the direction of the royal coastal fortress, designed as a bastion against foreign invasion and embodying a wealth of accumulated experience in military engineering. The periodic recurrence of such external threats has left a diverse legacy of fortifications which range from the Martello towers of the Napoleonic era through massive nineteenth-century shore batteries to the coastal installations constructed in our own times.

Nowhere more than in the relics of fear and conflict written in our landscape do we see the theme of challenge and response so vividly illustrated. The remains of outmoded strongholds of many ages serve as reminders to an insecure and turbulent past. Progress left these citadels and defenceworks stranded in obsolescence – and the same progress has now left the great mass of people bereft of any bolt-hole, less secure than the bygone occupants of the smallest hillfort, as we face the next developments in offensive warfare.

The two photographs opposite of the lowland hillfort which lies just outside Oswestry not only portray one of the most accessible and visitworthy of the British hillforts, but they also reveal how differences in weather conditions can influence the revelation of buried or overgrown features in aerial photographs.

The natural hill is only about 550 ft in height but it commanded a number of routeways running into the hills of the Welsh Marches to the west. The sculptured hillfort earthworks to be seen today were preceded by an Iron Age timber hilltop palisade but, around 250 BC, a more formidable 'bivallate' stronghold was constructed, the outer rampart and ditch rings and gate defences being added later.

The Roman peace made the stronghold redundant, but after the collapse of Roman power a number of settlers made their homes in the shelter of the ramparts. The strategic importance of the site endured in the Dark Ages, and the Christian king of Northumberland fell in a battle with the Mercian forces of King Penda which was fought nearby. When the Normans constructed a new town almost beside the old hillfort they named it Oswestry: 'the tree of St Oswald', the canonised Northumbrian king.

The photographs show that Old Oswestry did not entirely withdraw from the military stage. In the upper photograph, hardly any features are recognisable in the level hillfort interior. The lower photograph was taken during a drought and the patterns which emerge are produced by 'parch marks'. Much of the pasture has parched out for lack of moisture, but deep silts which have accumulated in former ditches provide richer, damper soil to sustain the overlying turf which remains green. The 'ditches' are, however, twentieth-century practice trenches of different types, excavated by soldiers training for trench warfare.

This ground level photograph is taken looking up towards the ramparts of the hillfort

155

7.2 TWO LOWLAND ZONE HILLFORTS
South Cadbury (Somerset) and Cissbury (West Sussex)

Seen from the ground, South Cadbury hillfort is impressive, a wooded platform which looms above the tower of the local village church. The airman, however, is in a far better position to appreciate the concentric rampart banks and ditches which so enhance the natural defences of the broad hilltop. Partly because of its conjectured associations with King Arthur, the excavation of this Somerset hillfort in 1966–70 did much to stimulate public interest in archaeology and it revealed a remarkable sequence of occupations.

Work on its construction began in the fifth century BC, but the hilltop was shown to have been occupied for much longer than this. In the New Stone Age, there was some form of settlement on the hill, while the discovery of pits containing human remains suggests that the hill also had religious and ritualistic associations. Some Later Bronze Age folk discarded their pottery and lost their bronzes and a gold bracelet here; and Iron Age peasants, perhaps emigrating from France under a warrior leader, established an

undefended settlement at South Cadbury around 700 BC.

A less formidable version of the existing inner rampart ring represented the first stage of hillfort-making, in which twenty acres of the hilltop were enclosed by a rubble bank with a near-vertical revetment made of horizontal logs supported by vertical posts. Subsequent improvements replaced these ramparts with more impressive banks composed of rubble, reveted by heavy upright posts, faced with drystone walling and topped with a paved walkway; the three outer rampart rings were eventually added. There were two entrances, the north-eastern one (right-hand corner), leading down to the present South Cadbury village, the one in the opposing corner looking out over Sutton Montis.

About two decades after the Roman invasion of England, the hillfort must have harboured insurgents for the gates were burned and sections of ramparts cast-down. Excavations at the south-western gate also revealed evidence of an earlier Roman assault, which left the bodies

of men, women and children to be torn apart by scavenging beasts. In the war-torn Dark Age period traditionally associated with Arthur, the defences were periodically renovated, while during the tenth and early eleventh centuries, a Saxon township with a small mint existed within the same ramparted area which, some 1400 years earlier, had harboured the huts, storage pits and out-buildings of an Iron Age community. Some form of occupation continued until about AD 1200.

There are Roman sources which describe the Celtic hillforts as being wooded. This seems odd, since the woodland would seem to have facilitated a surprise attack. If these records are correct, however, then the wood- and rampart-girdled summit, rising above a long-cleared agricultural countryside might have appeared to the Roman legions much as we see it today.

Though the single rampart ring is simpler at Cissbury hillfort near Findon in West Sussex, the central area enclosed is three times that at South Cadbury. This stronghold dates from about 350 BC and had a broad, flat-bottomed ditch that was sunk some 10 ft down into the native chalk. The associated ramparts were allowed to crumble during the Roman peace (when ploughing produced the faintly discernible field patterns inside the ring), but were restored at the close of the Roman rule, presumably to face the threat of Saxon raiding.

The sizable hut-dwelling communities which several hillforts contained might almost be likened to fortified towns. In some cases, air photographs reveal the hollowed pock-marks within the defended area which denote the positions of Iron Age huts – Hod Hill in Dorset is a good example. At Cissbury, too, pock-marks are clearly visible in the lower section of the hillfort and outside it, but on a far larger scale than those of hut remains – and even more interesting. They are, in fact, the remains of shafts which were sunk to depths of as much as 40 ft by flint miners of the New Stone Age. Dated to quite an early stage in this formative period, the shafts, and the horizontal galleries which radiated from them, were engineered in search of good quality flints for tool and axe-making.

◄ 7.3 FOEL TRIGARN HILLFORT
Dyfed

7.4 TRE'R CEIRI ▲
A Highland Zone Hillfort, Gwynedd

In this Iron Age hillfort on the Preseli Hills, a craggy summit outcrop of rock has been incorporated into the inner ring of ramparts which covers about 3 acres. Further defended enclosures were created by constructing an outer rampart of gathered stones, although the bare rocky ground prevented the digging of conventional rampart-fronting ditches. On close inspection, it can be seen that the summit surface inside the ramparts has a dimpled texture. The dozens of little depressions represent the scooped bases of Iron Age circular stone huts. Had they all been occupied at the same time, then a settlement of almost town-like proportions would have existed on this windswept Preseli hilltop.

Three mounds or 'cairns' of stone rubble are aligned on the summit. They predate the hillfort and must belong to the Bronze Age. Cairns such as these sometimes contain burials, but both the tombs and the tombless cairns are probably best interpreted as prominent symbols of tribal territorial control or as boundary markers at the junction of tribal lands. As such, they represent a stage in the political life of Britain when land had become a scarce and valuable commodity: the hillforts of the Iron Age result from an intensification of the competition to win and hold territory.

In the Highland zone of Britain, communities were probably always smaller and more thinly-spread than in the Lowlands, while the thin soils often rest on a hard bedrock. Not unexpectedly, the hillforts of the highlands contrast with those of the more favoured lower zones. They tend to be smaller, while the earthen ramparts and deep ditches of the English downlands have their highland counterparts in drystone walls built of rubble gathered from the hillside screes, sometimes fronted by shallow, rock-cut ditches.

Tre'r Ceiri, sitting upon Yr Eifl, one of a trio of summits which tower above the sea from the coast of the Lleyn peninsula, is a gem among the ancient monuments of Wales. A settlement of circular, drystone-walled huts, enclosed by a drystone rampart more than 12 ft tall, was constructed before the Roman conquest. It persisted during the Roman occupation, when the number of dwellings increased to around 150. The inhabitants may have been impressed by the rectangular Roman buildings seen elsewhere, for the later stone huts adopted this shape, while an additional wall was added (left-hand side), to form a new enclosure.

This aerial view clearly portrays the accumulations of decaying huts clustered like ring-doughnuts within the ramparts. Their occupants must have been hardy, for Yr Eifl rises to 1849 ft and the ascent is quite steep. Presumably the defensive advantages were deemed to be worth the effort.

7.5 BURNSWARK ROMAN CAMP AND HILLFORT *Dumfries & Galloway*

With the ramparts of an Iron Age hillfort showing on the hill and a Roman camp lying on the slopes, this photograph taken near Lockerbie symbolises the temporary change of mastery in southern Scotland which the Roman invasions achieved. However, the photograph contains much more than symbolic interest. The camp is of the standardised playing card shape, but showing clearly are three mounded protrusions or salients along its upper slope and a rectangular enclosure in its upper right corner. The latter is a small Antonine fortlet, built at some time during the years 143 to *c*.158 when legions advancing from the Hadrian's Wall frontier occupied southern Scotland. The three mounds are artillery platforms which housed ball- and bolt-firing *ballistae*. Their date and that of the rectangular camp of which they are a part are uncertain, but the archaeological evidence suggests use in the late second or third centuries.

A second camp, which is less well-preserved, lies on the other side of the hillfort and the entrances of the hillfort were found to be peppered by arrowheads, ballista balls and lead sling-shot. However, the evidence does not tell of a bloody Roman siege and assault of the native strong-

hold; the camps were practice installations used for training troops in siege techniques and were probably used by legionaries stationed at Birdoswald, Chesterholm and Corbridge. The hillfort entrances must have been used as targets and Roman tactics in the storming of hillforts would have involved a preliminary artillery barrage of the vulnerable entrances.

7.6 PORTCHESTER CASTLE ▶
Hampshire

At Old Sarum (pl. 5.2) we have seen the medieval re-use of an Iron Age hillfort; at Portchester, and at Pevensey in East Sussex which follows, we see the medieval conscription of Roman defences. Portchester Castle stands at the northern extremity of Portsmouth harbour, which it helped to secure. The rectangular complex sits inside a nineteen-acre snout of land partly severed to landward by the ditch and ramparts of an Iron Age fort of the promontory type. While this fort was almost certainly built to provide its defenders with security from attacks by their land-

ward neighbours, the tactical advantage of location within Iron Age ramparts attracted the Romans, whose Saxon shore-fort was built to oppose barbarian attacks from the sea. At one stage, however, the usurping Emperor Carausius is thought to have used Portchester as the base for his navy and it seems that some other shore-forts also served as naval bases.

This Roman fort is arguably the most completely surviving Roman monument in Britain; the rectangular walls enclose nine acres and were punctuated by twenty round bastions, of which fourteen remain; the walls rise to 25 ft and are in places 10 ft thick. Whether the legions of the doomed Empire ever did embark from the shores of Britain around the supposed date of about AD 410 is now a matter of dispute but, in any event, Professor Cunliffe's excavations show that the fort was occupied at about this time by Germanic people, perhaps mercenaries.

Within the pink-mortared walls of flint, limestone and red tile-like bricks, Henry I began the construction centuries later of a massive square keep, bounded on two sides by the original Roman walls and on the others by a great new wall fronted by an 'L'-shaped moat which was filled by water entering from the original Roman moat. King John, in turn, doubled the height of the keep, which now stands complete as a dominating example of Norman architecture, 100 ft tall and faced by typically broad but shallow buttresses. Richard II destroyed most of the subsidiary buildings which had clustered around the base of the keep, replacing them with his own works, including a banqueting hall. The fine Norman priory church and its yard occupy the opposing quadrant of the Roman fort; the church was constructed a little after the foundation of its priory in 1133, and the white dots which surround it on the photograph are tombstones.

7.7 PEVENSEY CASTLE *East Sussex*

At Pevensey, as at Portchester, we see a remarkable combination of Roman and medieval military architecture. The Roman presence is represented by the enclosing curtain wall of Anderida, a late third-century Saxon shore-fort built to shield the south-east, and Chichester in particular, from seaborne barbarian raids. The Anglo-Saxon Chronicle tells that Pevensey fell in AD 491 and thereafter the picture mists over until the Norman Conquest.

The Roman defences consist of walls standing some 20 ft in height and studded at intervals by ten great bastions, embracing an oval, somewhat kidney-shaped area. Whereas the flat terrain of Portchester permitted the Romans

to employ their standard rectangular plan, the rolling landscape of Pevensey determined a sweeping, slope-girdling shape.

The Conqueror granted Pevensey to his half-brother, Robert of Mortmain. At the start of the twelfth century, a great stone fortress was constructed in the north-eastern corner of the fort and, as at Portchester, the existing Roman walls provided a ready-made outer bailey.

Of the keep that was built at the beginning of the twelfth century, nothing remains standing above first floor level, and what is left supports a concrete emplacement of 1940, when the south-east was again threatened by invasion.

One weakness of the keep as a defensive form was its vulnerability to the sapping or undermining of its corners, where great weights of masonry were concentrated. Sufficient remains of the Pevensey keep to show the adoption of a novel counter-measure. The original keep lies in the north-eastern (upper right) portion of the medieval castle and one can see the great spurs or buttresses which projected from its angles to thwart the sapper.

Early in the thirteenth century, Pevensey became one of the Cinque Ports and, about this time, an imposing gatehouse was built to control the bridge between the inner and outer baileys. The exceptionally fine curtain wall and towers of the inner bailey perimeter date from about 1250 and display another twist in the spiral of defensive advance. Square wall-towers (such as seen at Framlingham Castle in Suffolk) suffered from the same weaknesses as did square keeps. Circular towers lacked vulnerable corners, but provided awkwardly shaped internal accommodation. At Pevensey, we see an early exploration of the superior 'D'-shaped form, which presents a rounded space to the hostile world outside, while providing more conveniently shaped room spaces within. The illustration shows the footings of a simple chapel of about 1300 lying within the inner bailey and curtain wall.

All this fine and costly military masonry soon proved to be a needless extravagance, for about the time that the castle was completed, the adjacent port silted up and Pevensey shrank with it. The castle lapsed into obscurity and decay although this was interrupted when the senile stronghold was briefly manned in 1587, in anticipation of the Spanish Armada.

The final stage in the military life of Pevensey is represented by what appears to be a pile of tumbled masonry to the right of the lower gateway, where the trees begin. Visiting the site, I realised that a Second World War pillbox lies buried and camouflaged in this apparently innocuous pile of stones.

7.8 DÚN CHONCHÚIR (DOON CONOR) STONE FORT *Inishmaan, Co Galway*

Massive stone forts, like this example from the Aran Islands, date from the Late Iron Age and early medieval periods. They seem to be the big brothers of the relatively flimsy 'ring forts', which are so numerous in stone-littered areas like the Burren that one seems to stand in every other field. The ring forts were defended farmsteads rather than fortresses and the stone forts, which are also known as 'cashels' and 'cahers', also contained dwellings. Chambers were built in the walls of Dún Chonchúir and inside the fort one can see the remains of stone-walled huts. The walls are terraced, with the greater thicknesses of stone at their base.

Although the size and sturdiness of the fort suggest that it was a major undertaking in military engineering, the necessary stone was available in abundance. The island consists of a hard limestone which supports only the thinnest covering of soil; bare limestone pavements can be seen as light patches at the top, left and bottom of the photograph and the close networks of field walls also tell of the excess of limestone slabs which litter the fields. Most of the surrounding land is poor pasture, but where the soil covering is thicker and the land has been improved, the fields which grow crops of potatoes emerge as darker, closely-ridged patches. Despite the poverty of the land, the stone forts and ring forts tell of struggles to win and hold territory.

7.9 THE BASS OF INVERURIE *Grampian*

The weird geometry displayed in the central expanse of the photograph is almost guaranteed to baffle the reader. In fact, it represents the handiwork of two quite different periods. The flat-topped, bowl-like mound in the centre is a Scotto-Norman motte. Following the conquest of England, a number of Norman adventurers penetrated far into Scotland, where they were often welcomed by Scottish kings who were keen to impose a feudal order upon the unstable Celtic provinces of their realm. Originally, the motte will have been crowned by a circular timber palisade inside which the Norman overlord and his supporters could have taken refuge during local insurgencies, while in more settled times they will have dwelled outside the motte, in its poorly discernible bailey. The little stronghold is sensibly situated, with the River Urie protecting it immediately to the north. In fact the site was better endowed with natural defences than our low-level photograph can show, for the motte is in the neck of a narrow peninsula bordered by the Don and Urie rivers.

The remainder of the geometry in the photograph is produced by a skilfully landscaped modern cemetery in which the circular theme of the motte is repeated in two groups of concentric pathways.

7.10 CASTLE RISING *Norfolk*

Although the remains of Norman defenceworks are prominent at Castle Rising, there are some puzzling and unusual features. They include the way in which the stone keep is sheltered by tall earthbanks which encircle its mound. Thus we see a strange and sophisticated example of a larger motte and bailey earthwork. The stronghold was built in the middle of the twelfth century by William de Albini, who married the widow of Henry I and became Earl of Sussex.

The formidable stone keep is also not typical, being more ornately embellished than most other, normally quite austere examples. Longer and broader than its height of 50 ft, it is an unusual variant known as a 'hall keep' and one of the most impressive of its kind. The keep is a little younger than its motte, which was probably originally fortified with a wooden palisade. The bailey to the right of the keep supported a great hall, offices and a tower, all of which have perished. The dot-like cars which can be seen in the photograph parked in the bailey provide a sense of the scale and majesty of the well-preserved Norman castle, the top of which stands some 175 ft above the bottom of the moat.

The villages which sit in the shadow of great Norman keeps are often seen to be planned creations, set out at the behest of those who built or occupied the castles – Castleton in Derbyshire is a good example. At Castle Rising, too, the village is clearly not the product of piecemeal, organic growth. Although the modern broadening of the main road and the rounding off of its sharp bends have blurred the pattern, it is clear that the village consists of neat rectangular plots. The gabled tower of the church of St Lawrence can be seen in the bottom right-hand corner of the photograph, and this too is a Late Norman building.

In the dark patch below the castle, just inside the rim of the motte, a debatably Saxon or Norman church has been exposed by excavation.

7.11 PEMBROKE CASTLE *Dyfed*

Claims of English suzerainty over Wales go back at least to the time of the late tenth-century Saxon king Edgar. After the Conquest, Wales provided a safety valve for the rapacious and warlike instincts of the Norman barons who, rather like the Cossacks of post-medieval Russia, enjoyed almost complete autonomy in return for securing and advancing the marches of their new realm. From the Earldoms of Chester and Shrewsbury and from Herefordshire, freebooting Marcher Lords advanced into Wales seeking new lands to conquer and control – although a greater number were interested in conquests and adventures upon the continent.

Although its site is uncertain, a slender fortress of stakes and turf was established at Pembroke by Arnulf de Montgomery in about 1090. An Earldom centred on Pembroke was created by Gilbert de Clare (Gilbert Strongbow), a powerful and wolfish Marcher Lord, in 1109. In 1138, the Pembroke lands became a County Palatine within which the Earl exercised sovereign rights. The County Palatine existed until English central power was sufficiently strong, and the threats of Welsh insurgency became so remote that the sovereign was permitted to abolish the autonomous status; this took place under Henry VIII in 1536.

The oldest part of the surviving castle at Pembroke was built in the years following 1207 by William Marshal, Earl of Pembroke and Striguil, and the entire castle was complete by the end of the century. The circular plan of the keep, some 75 ft high and virtually intact apart from the decay of its internal timber floors, represents a development intended to remove the vulnerable corner angles of the more conventional rectangular form. As with the older keeps, the entrance remained at first floor level. Its walls are 19 ft thick at the base.

The keep is ringed by a turreted curtain wall; a town was developed in its protective shadow and fragments of the wall which guarded the town survive, while the division of the settlement into regular plots is still apparent in the illustration. The main street, half a mile in length, runs along a narrow tongue of outcropping limestone, which is flanked by inlets from Milford Haven to form a superb defensive position. A deep ditch insulated the castle from the town. Located near the south-western extremity of Wales, Pembroke was an important stepping-stone for the Norman invasion of Ireland.

In the course of the Civil War, the mayor of Pembroke, John Poyer, switched from the Parliamentary to the Royalist side; the defences remained sufficiently effective to resist a bombardment by Cromwell's troops for seven weeks. The siege of 1648 succeeded only after the capture of the water supply; the defences were then partly dismantled and Poyer was shot. The castle was restored after 1928.

The keep of Pembroke Castle is ringed by a turreted curtain wall

Dover provides perhaps the most striking illustration of the re-use of old strongholds. An Iron Age fortress site, it was developed as a shore-fort and naval base by the Romans and maintained a garrison until 1958! From the unfamiliar vantage point opposite, we look south-eastwards over the medieval castle in the direction of the cliffs and sea. The Iron Age ramparts extend beyond the bounds of the photograph and, although the castle is the focus of our attention, it is interesting to note the base of the Roman *pharos* or lighthouse (upper margin, just right of centre) and the walls of a Saxon church, immediately to its left.

The nature of the post-Roman defences at Dover is uncertain; a fort of some type existed here two years before the Conquest – probably an earthen mound with a timber palisade – for the doomed King Harold is said to have promised to grant it to Duke William of Normandy in 1064. (One doubts that this capable king would have been so foolish as to fulfil the promise.) Directly after his victory over the Saxons at Hastings, William proceeded to this castle.

The keep which stands today was initiated by Henry II; the work began in 1168 and it was garrisoned within fifteen years. By this time, the tower keep had ceased to be an innovation; the 'shell keep', consisting of turreted curtain walls, was emerging as an alternative, but it seems that Henry had his reservations concerning both designs – and consequently chose to combine them. The formidable castle which resulted was unusual – a large tower keep with corner turrets surrounded by curtain walls which were studded with eleven rectangular towers, the whole standing upon a massive earthen mound. Perhaps the Norman concepts of castle-making were influenced by the walled towns and turreted curtain walls which had deeply impressed the first Crusaders in the Holy Land? Whatever its inspiration, Dover Castle was a dominating and costly construction; the 95-ft keep had ragstone walls some 20 ft in thickness, strengthened by dressings of expensive white stone imported from Caen.

The quest for impregnability for this immensely strategic Channel port proceeded with the construction of the second curtain wall to surround the outer bailey, begun in Henry's reign and continued in that of his wayward son, John. Close upon its completion, a severe deficiency in its design almost proved fatal when, in 1216, King Louis's French raiders almost breached a gateway which lay in the outer curtain at the lower left of the picture. The photograph clearly shows how this fault was remedied: the gate was sealed and replaced with beaked stone spurs which plug the gap between the two rounded mural towers. The access to the castle was then shifted (lower right), and the Constable's Gate and Tower which we now see was built to guard it as a formidable citadel in its own right (*see* photograph below).

The military significance of Dover Castle continued to be maintained over many passing centuries. The photograph shows barrack blocks belonging to the eighteenth century clinging to the walls of the inner curtain (left-hand side), while the tops of the outer curtain walls were shaved-off at the time of the Napoleonic invasion scares around 1800, when gun positions were created with little respect for the antiquity of the ramparts.

The gateway to Dover Castle is a formidable citadel in its own right

7.13 BEAUMARIS CASTLE *Anglesey, Gwynedd*

Beaumaris has often been described as the most perfect of our medieval strongholds and from the air more than from the ground the concentric plan is plainly apparent. It was one of the ten magnificent strongholds built at the behest of Edward I in the course of his conquest of Wales. The castles were concentrated in the northern heartlands of Welsh resistance and Beaumaris, Conwy and Caernarfon formed a formidable triangle of citadels guarding the Menai Straits.

Master James of St George was the principal designer of these Edwardian fortresses, but he was not wedded to a single plan. Flint Castle was built to an individualistic design, Conwy and Caernarfon had features in common and were integrated in the defences of planned new towns while the remaining castles explored concentric themes and were influenced by Byzantine concepts.

Building began at Beaumaris in 1295 and work continued until around 1330, when it was suspended for lack of funds and motivation. The towers were never built to their intended height and, as the castle was never assaulted, it remains well-preserved but incomplete.

The flatness of the chosen terrain allowed the use of an unadulterated concentric plan. Themes repeated at several other of the Edwardian castles include an inner ward with tall curtain walls which are studded by lofty round towers and have heavily defended entrances. The outer ward, which is also punctuated by round towers, is much lower and lies just a few yards beyond the more formidable masonry of the inner ward. Proximity to the sea allowed the construction of a sea-fed moat which originally encircled the castle completely. The plan for Beaumaris included several spacious and well-appointed suites of domestic and administrative chambers and, despite its destiny of redundancy, Beaumaris was as expensive to build as the castle of Conwy *and* its accompanying town.

This photograph shows the difference in height between the inner and outer walls

7.14 LEEDS CASTLE *Kent*

Leeds Castle competes with its Wealden neighbour at Bodiam for the title of England's leading fairyland castle. The name may derive from that of Ledian, chief minister to a mid-ninth-century Kentish king who had his estate hereabouts. A stone castle was built on this site in Norman times, but the surviving architecture dates mainly from the thirteenth century; there are many later medieval alterations and an extensive restoration was accomplished in the twentieth century.

For most of its life Leeds Castle has existed as a genteel and romantic mansion rather than as a formidable bastion. It passed into royal ownership in 1278 when it was bought by Edward I as a gift to his wife, Eleanor of Castile. For the remainder of the Middle Ages, it was a favoured abode of the Queens of England and the contrast between Leeds and the heavily fortified castles which Edward built in Wales is quite striking. The addition of large mullioned windows in the late-medieval manner belies the defensive pretensions of the castle. With wildfowl, waterplants, landscaped parkland and a neatly tended golf course gracing its surrounds, Leeds remains a captivating rather than a grimly imposing castle.

7.15 URQUHART CASTLE *Highland* ▶

The military advantages of this rocky knoll which swells from the shores of Loch Ness have been appreciated since prehistoric times. Not only is it guarded on three sides by the loch and on the other by slopes, but it also dominates the invasion routeways leading outwards from the Western Highlands. An Iron Age promontory fort exploited the site, although its defenceworks are scarcely visible. In the early Middle Ages, one of the most isolated motte and bailey castles which featured a double bailey enclosure was built here but the remains of the stone castle date from the fourteenth, fifteenth and sixteenth centuries.

In the rough and tumble of clan warfare, Urquhart Castle, a royal outpost in the fifteenth century, changed hands many times. Throughout the medieval period the royal grip on the Highland territories was, at best, precarious. The Scottish kings sought to establish a feudal relationship between the Crown and the clan chieftains who exercised *de facto* power in the inaccessible mountains and glens. One of the strategies employed involved the granting of royal charters which confirmed the chiefs both as clan leaders and as vassals of the Crown. Two of these 'sheepskin grants' were given to Ian Moydertach in 1531 and

1534, confirming him as chief of the Clanranald. The title and the castle were inherited by the illegitimate Ian on the death of his father, Alastair – who had himself been installed in the chieftainship after the clansmen had murdered his tyrannical uncle, Dugal. Dugal's son, Ranald, enjoyed the patronage of the powerful Lovat, chief of Clan Fraser, who installed him as an unpopular chieftain, but in 1544, Moydertach, with the support of two other great clan leaders, Cameron of Lochiel and Macdonald of Keppoch, captured Urquhart Castle and Lovat, Ranald and three hundred Fraser clansmen were slain in an ambush by Moydertach and his followers. A virtual Highland civil war followed. Moydertach was outlawed, but later pardoned and reinstated as chief.

In the course of the Jacobite rising of 1689–90, the clan army, which had its victory at Killiecrankie soured by the death of the leader, Viscount Dundee, was penned in the Highlands following the battle of Dunkeld and finally routed by the cavalry of William of Orange on the Haughs of Cromdale. Shortly afterwards, Castle Urquhart was reduced to a romantic ruin by English troops. Gaunt but picturesque it overlooks the black waters of the loch as a prominent symbol and popular sighting-point in monster romance.

Camber Castle and its close relatives like those at Deal, Walmer and St Mawes represent the final stage in medieval castle evolution. It was built in the reign of Henry VIII and by this time the Wars of the Roses had hacked out the heart of the warlike aristocracy, the Tudor monarchs had tightened their grip on the reins of power and the nobility had abandoned the concept of the private fortress in favour of the cosier vision of the country mansion. Almost all the military architecture of the Tudor period was related to the problem of national defence and most of the new fortresses were built on, or close to, the coast.

Though internally strong and secure, the Tudor realm faced threats of foreign invasion. A major invasion scare in 1538–40 prompted Henry to establish a chain of coastal forts which ran from Deal and Walmer in Kent to Pendennis and St Mawes in Cornwall, studding the southern invasion coast with up-to-date strongholds. All tended to be squat and concentric and designed to employ the much-improved artillery pieces: culverins, minions and sakers in a variety of sizes and bores. In the case of some of the forts such as St Mawes, clover leaf plans were adopted but Camber, which was built in 1539 and slighted in 1642, has a more detailed plan. It is strictly functional, providing accommodation for the garrison but none of the frills and luxurious domestic arrangements of many earlier royal and private medieval castles. The emphasis was upon building a formidable artillery platform and hence the adoption of the circular bastions or 'lunettes' which face not only the sea approaches but also guard against shore-based assaults by landed invasion forces.

Originally close to the sea, the growth of shingle banks has stranded the castle over a mile inland and it lies in a bleak and lonely setting beside the Romney Marshes. The photograph shows the gradual colonisation of the shingle beds by plants.

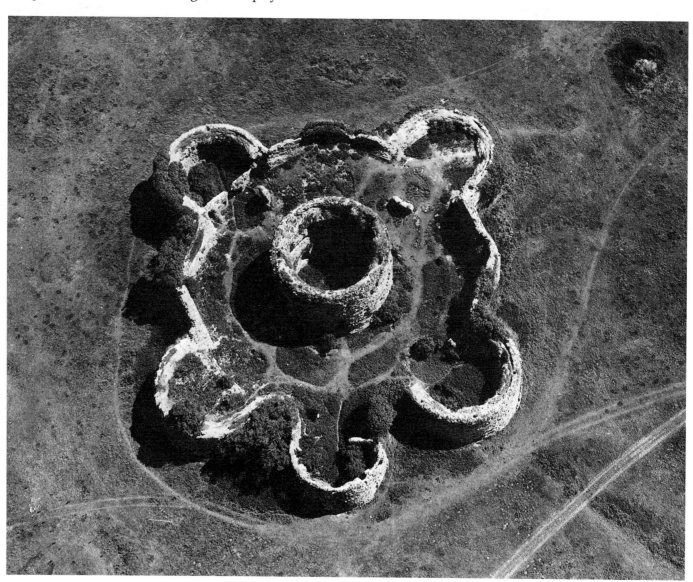

7.17 THE QUEEN'S SCONCE *near Newark-on-Trent, Nottinghamshire*

The central feature of the photograph resembling a great, stranded starfish is sure to perplex most readers. Civil War fortresses are probably the least well-known of our military monuments; several can be found in the vicinity of Newark and the Queen's Sconce is the best preserved.

The Civil War of the seventeenth century erupted too swiftly for new stone castles to be prepared and, in any event, the use of gunpowder and efficient cannon had rendered even the strongest of the medieval fortresses obsolescent. Even so, a number were garrisoned and besieged and even some Iron Age hillforts became the scenes of skirmishes. The Civil War spawned new forms of defence-works which were speedily built, devoid of masonry, but often quite formidable.

The Queen's Sconce is typical, consisting of a rectangular enclosure with its corners guarded by massive arrowhead-shaped earthen bastions and the fortress is surrounded by a moat. Cannon will have been hauled into position and mounted on the bastions, while musketeers patrolled the walkways. Seen from the ground, earthwork castles such as this lack the exciting presence of their medieval, stone-built predecessors but they were well-adapted to the age of artillery and muskets. They are among the few creations of a time of destruction.

8.A *Gregynog Hall, Powys, has the unusual combination of a symmetrical façade and the traditional decorative timber-framing of the west*

8. THE GREAT HOUSES

In this chapter are presented a number of great houses, some celebrated and much-visited and others that are little known. The aristocratic residences are mainly considered at the expense of the homes of common folk because, unless the latter exist as faint relics which are invisible from the ground, as at many deserted village sites, the air photograph is seldom the most effective medium for portraying the smaller houses especially in a rural setting. On the other hand, when urban dwellings are grouped in terraced ranks, middle-class suburban estates or tower blocks, they produce fascinating and informative patterns as pictured in the next chapter on towns.

Where the great houses are concerned, it is an almost infallible rule that a house which seems to be attractively designed, architecturally stylish and harmoniously sited when seen from the ground, will appear equally or more appealing when viewed from above. This phenomenon is not easily explained when we consider that the houses were never intended to be seen from the airman's perspective. The only explanation which can be offered is that the houses were first conceived and sketched as plans rather than as elevations.

As a means of demonstrating the layout of a great house, the air photograph has distinct advantages over the typical ground-level photograph. In the case of the latter, one can normally only see a front, back or side elevation and the plan of the body of the house which lies behind the façade is invisible. Taken from the air, however, the oblique photograph allows one not only to admire the elevations, but also to appreciate the plan. Thus, in the case of late medieval houses for example, one can see over the moat and gate house to the ranges of servants' accommodation and family rooms which flank the courtyard and the great hall, kitchen and solar range which completes the hollow square of buildings. The air photograph is also particularly valuable as a means of demonstrating the layout of a garden and the ways in which the designers have sought to harmonise the juxtaposition between house and gardens. The photographs show a number of gardens that are in the precise and intricate geometrical styles of the sixteenth and seventeenth centuries. Although most of the examples are reconstructions rather than survivals or restorations, the effects are quite stunning and it is plain that although such gardens were never intended to be seen from the air, the formal bedding, hedging and planting arrangements are most effectively stated when viewed from above.

Great houses rather than smaller manor houses were born when changes in the scale and methods of warfare and the emergence of a strong and forceful Tudor dynasty had effectively passed sentence on the aristocratic private fortress. The autonomy which thick walls, moats and towers had offered was no longer obtainable or tolerable in the kingdom of Henry VII and Henry VIII. So, instead of building fortresses, the aristocrats began to discover the comforts of the life which could be enjoyed in the mansion rather than in the cramped and chilly confines of the castle. However, since the great house was a newly fashionable concept, there were few prototypes or blueprints to tell the aspiring owner quite how an aristocratic mansion should appear.

8.B *Ickworth Hall in Suffolk was begun in 1792 by the 4th Earl of Bristol, an unpleasant eccentric who had a great passion for building rotundas. Although the Earl had inherited a considerable fortune, the lavish hall at Ickworth consumed much of his and his successors' wealth*

For several decades, the great house builders clung to the defensive trappings of moats, gatehouses and towers because these were the traditional symbols of high social status. Only gradually was it accepted that size, opulence and a fashionable façade could make the same statement in ways which were as effective but less restrictive upon the planning of the house. The focus of medieval manor and castle life had been the great hall where social activities, administration and day-to-day living all converged. Changes in standards of living and the patterns of domestic life produced demands for greater numbers of more specialised rooms and state and family suites. The medieval concept of the great hall however was even more deeply ingrained than that of defence and the gradual devaluation of the hall from being the key component of a house to a dining or reception chamber which was embraced by suites of specialised rooms and then to a mere entrance vestibule constitutes one of the most important chapters in the history of the British house.

The literature concerning the great houses of Britain is vast, but it is quite strikingly dominated by the Fine Art perspective which tends to regard the house as an example or agglomeration of good, bad or indifferent architecture. Much less has been written about the great house in its primary role as a domestic and social focus. When the house is studied as a home rather than as an architectural exhibit, the development of its layout becomes much clearer and we can see how the changing patterns and norms of domestic life underlay changes in house design. The photographs cover a broad spectrum of buildings of different ages, but the selection is deliberately biased in favour of the period from the mid-fifteenth to the early seventeenth century because this formative timespan covers the transition from the rambling moated medieval house to the more opulent and carefully planned symmetrical houses of the Jacobean aristocracy.

8.c *Built in the course of the seventeenth and eighteenth centuries and surrounded by a park landscaped by Humphry Repton, Woburn Abbey stands on the site of a monastery which was bequeathed to the 1st Earl of Bedford by Henry VIII in 1547*

8.1 OXBOROUGH HALL *Norfolk* and HELMINGHAM HALL *Suffolk*

In the light of changing military and economic circumstances, the austerely fortified strongholds gradually yielded to the great mansion and stately home. These two late fifteenth-century East Anglian halls eloquently reveal a stage in the transition. Both combine the visual trappings of the aristocratic fortress, but neither would be expected to repel a serious attack.

Of the two examples, Oxborough Hall is the most complete, although a fourth range which faced the turreted gatehouse across the courtyard was demolished in 1778. A licence to crenellate, or build a fortified dwelling, was granted to Edward Bedingfield in 1482 – such licences were a handy source of royal income during the medieval period. The design of a square mansion with four ranges enclosing a courtyard and sited within a moat was characteristic of its period, and the massive gatehouse with its paired polygonal turrets is the best survivor of its type.

The mansion was extensively restored in 1835, when the large south-eastern tower at its lower corner on the photograph was added, along with the four towers which 'guard' the kitchen garden – the products of Early Victorian whimsy.

The original design for Helmingham Hall is quite similar, although here the remodelling process has gone further. The Tudor gateway (top of courtyard) is original, but the gabled range (bottom left corner) and the cast iron bridge to its left are by John Nash, while the upper two-thirds of the range on the right-hand side were remodelled by Salvin in 1841, when the remainder of the range, lying nearest to the camera, was added. As at Oxborough, attractive formal gardens are seen across the moat.

Although moated in the manner of many earlier medieval castles and manors and furnished with imposing gatehouses, aristocratic dwellings such as these, with their relatively thin walls (the later examples in the newly fashionable brick) and their large, glazed windows, could not have withstood an artillery bombardment. Before too long even these vestigial defensive features were to lose currency as status symbols, being abandoned in favour of Classically-inspired designs though revived in different forms in the nineteenth century when neo-Gothic architecture became popular.

8.2 COMPTON WYNYATES *Warwickshire*

As well as being a singularly attractive great house and almost perfectly preserved, Compton Wynyates, which lies about eight miles west of Banbury, is also one of the most important landmarks in the development of the aristocratic home in England. The house was built in the 1480s and enlarged in the 1520s. It was therefore an essentially medieval building but it also embodied innovations and was symbolic of the currents of change at the closing decades of the Middle Ages. In its traditional aspects, Compton Wynyates embodied many features of older and less grandiose manor houses and of Oxford and Cambridge colleges. The great hall was a dominating feature, the house was moated and rooms were arranged in blocks around a courtyard, with one room opening into another, as the circulation corridors and symmetrical arrangements which became prominent features of later great houses had not yet been developed.

In other respects, however, Compton Wynyates signified changing patterns of both building and society. Significantly, brick was the chosen building material even though stone was used in the quoins and window details. Until this time, little use had been made of brick, a rare but prestigious material but, in the two centuries which followed, brick displaced timber-framing as a medium for the greater houses and competed with stone even in areas where good quality building stones were available. Bricklaying skills were developed swiftly in late Tudor and Elizabethan times, as the decorative and twisting chimneys of Compton Wynyates proclaim. A virtual forest of these new status symbols crown the house and evidence the new standards of warmth and comfort which aristocrats were able to enjoy as the concept of individually heated rooms supplanted the previously accepted norm of the smoky open hall with its massive fireplace and the older notion of the open central hearth and smoke hole.

Despite the refinements, the layout was an old one. The great hall lies across the courtyard from the showy entrance porch and was built in the traditional manner, with a kitchen at one end and a parlour or solar at the other.

The house also symbolises changes in the political climate. It was constructed during the peace which followed the carnage of the Wars of the Roses. Although it was moated, this trapping of defence aped the status rather than the impregnability of the moated castle, and the house was quite a radical development in that it was expressly built for comfort rather than security, as the chimneys and broad, mullioned windows show. Much later, the moat

was obliged to serve as an actual defencework and in 1644 the house withstood a siege by the Parliamentarian forces for two days. A required condition of the reoccupation of the house by the Compton family was the infilling of the moat.

To the right of the house and finely portrayed in our photograph is a renowned display of topiary, punctuating and framing gardens laid-out in the style that was favoured around 1600. Like so many great houses, Compton Wynyates was created at the cost of a nearby village, emparked and wasted by Sir William Compton.

8.3 KIRBY HALL *Northamptonshire* ▲

Kirby Hall, north of Corby, was built in the early 1570s as a home for Sir Humphrey Stafford. Although it is a post-medieval building and epitomises the splendours of Elizabethan aristocratic life, it also embodies a number of distinctly traditional features. There is still the medieval theme of the great courtyard which is flanked by ranges of lodgings for guests, retainers and serving folk, while the main range of the original building (the lower of the left-to-right running ranges in the photograph) had a distinctly medieval plan. It consisted of a great hall which had a kitchen complex of rooms at one end and a solar

or parlour and bedrooms at the other.

The plan of Kirby Hall also reflects changes which were current at the end of the sixteenth century, when the role of the hall as a splendid focal social, dining and living room was declining and extra rooms designed for particular uses were required. Sir Christopher Hatton, the second owner of Kirby Hall, responded to the changing fashions in aristocratic domestic life by adding a new range of rooms to the solar end of the hall, which formed the stem of the new 'T'-shaped plan. Most of the rooms in this range were for private family use.

In the course of the nineteenth century, the upkeep of the hall was neglected and parts of the courtyard ranges exist only as unroofed shells, although noted rose gardens are maintained in the formal beds to the left of the house. In the closing years of its occupation, the hall was largely derelict and its Hatton range served as a farmhouse. It then came into state ownership and an exploration of the site revealed the outlines of seventeenth-century gardens, a part of which have been restored. Dating from 1680, these gardens are the most authentic relic that we have of garden design in this period, even though the surviving gardens represent only one-third of the original set. A venerable garden feature in the form of a prospect mound can be seen in the lower left corner of the photograph, partly overhung by trees.

8.4 CRATHES CASTLE *Grampian*

The construction of Crathes Castle occupied almost all of the second half of the sixteenth century, a period when English aristocrats were abandoning the concept of the armoured castle and constructing great country houses. The Scottish lords had neither the enormous wealth which was necessary for building mansions on the English scale nor the security from feuding neighbours which strong central government allowed. In consequence, the smaller fortified home had a much longer lifespan in Scotland. Most of the lesser baronial castles adopted the tower-house model and consisted of or included a thick-walled tower some three or more stories in height which was usually furnished with projecting corner turrets to provide flanking fire along the walls. Crathes Castle with its strong tower and turret clusters and later undefended additions was one of the larger tower-houses.

The wing in the Queen Anne style lying to the right of the tower was burned down but reconstructed since this photograph was taken in 1951.

The gardens, which seem rather incongruous in their association with the ruggedly purposeful castle are a celebrated attraction and they date from the early eighteenth century and reflect the growing gentility of life in the larger tower-houses and private castles. The graceful lime avenues and dense and perfectly manicured yew hedges were planted in 1702, dividing the gardens into a series of distinctive units. Despite the rigours of the northern climate, this is one of the most notable collections of plants in Britain and a fine exposition of the gardening tastes of the early eighteenth century.

8.5 WROXTON ABBEY *Oxfordshire*

Many of the great houses of the sixteenth and seventeenth centuries were built on or about the sites of abbeys which had perished as a result of the Dissolution, and the abbey grounds provided choice building sites since they were unencumbered by peasant villages and agriculture. Wroxton Abbey incorporates the remains of a thirteenth-century Augustinian priory.

A comparison of the photograph of this splendid stone-built Jacobean country house with those of Compton Wynyates (pl. 8.2) and Kirby Hall (pl. 8.3) reveals the considerable changes in thinking which had been brought to bear on the design and layout of the aristocratic home during the years preceding the building of Wroxton Abbey in 1618. England had received the ideas and fashions which flowed from the continental Renaissance and these influences were reflected in the fashionable quest for symmetry. This quest had already influenced the appearance

of essentially traditional houses like Kirby Hall, but at Wroxton we see it being earnestly pursued. The house has the form of a main range with greater and lesser cross wings, and the roofline of spiky Gothic gables has a traditional flavour. However, the imposing entrance is centrally placed and the arrangement of the gabled cross wings and vast mullioned windows conform to the symmetrical ideal.

Classical influences were to be current for the two following centuries, in the course of which house layouts evolved and the pursuit of Classical perfection produced many houses which found their inspiration in the buildings of Ancient Greece and Rome. Critics may find them monotonous or incongruous features of the British countryside, whereas Wroxton Abbey succeeded in marrying the fashion for symmetry with a distinctly English and almost traditional appearance.

8.6 KNOLE *Kent*

Knole near Sevenoaks is one of the largest private houses in Britain. At the start of the seventeenth century around 120 servants and retainers were employed here, equal to the population of a quite substantial village of the period. It is a very interesting as well as a very large house, for it was constructed in the closing stages of the medieval period, and expanded and embellished in order to meet the changing demands of aristocratic social and domestic life. Thus the rough and ready if flamboyant standards of medieval hospitality and family life were replaced by post-medieval requirements for opulence, refined accommodation and purpose-built social areas, all housed within an architecturally balanced and imposing house which could support the swarms of specialised servants which high society life expected.

Although the strong Tudor monarchs imposed a stability on England which provided a climate in which the great house could appear, flourish and supplant the castle, personal security was far from being assured in the fifteenth and sixteenth centuries. The uncertainties of the age were experienced at Knole where, in 1456, Archbishop of Canterbury Thomas Bourchier purchased a typically haphazard complex of medieval buildings from the aristocrat William Fiennes. The Archbishop launched the first age of magnificence at Knole, building a palatial retreat used by himself and his successors in office. In a sense, the works were too magnificent, for Knole was coveted by Henry VIII and unwillingly surrendered to the King by Archbishop Cranmer in 1538. Henry invested a small fortune in improvements but appears to have only visited the house once. His daughter, Elizabeth I, granted it to the Earl of Leicester but, following tenancy disputes, it was returned to the crown and granted to the Lord Treasurer, Thomas Sackville, although a sitting tenant had still to be dislodged. In 1603, the year of Elizabeth's death, the Earl finally won control of Knole and a new phase of building was launched. Though now a National Trust property, Knole thereafter remained the Sackville family's home.

The great hall to the rear of the inner courtyard dates from the time of Bourchier's building works and reflects the continuing prominence of the hall as a dominating living, social, dining and administrative focus which was an indispensable part of any great house. Later aristocratic generations expected much more, including suites of private apartments, provided at ground floor level at Knole, state rooms, which here were installed at first floor level and reached by a trend-setting majestic staircase, long galleries in which guests could circulate and converse while admiring the opulent wall hangings, and of course ranks of apartments for servants, which were set around courtyards. After 1603, Thomas Sackville gutted and remodelled the interior of Knole to provide these facilities, built others and embellished the façade, introducing fashionable symmetry and the stylish pageant of Dutch gables.

8.7 WINDSOR CASTLE AND GREAT PARK *Berkshire*

Windsor is arguably the most fascinating and visually impressive of the British royal residences. The association with royalty is a very long one and many monarchs have contributed to the expansion of this remarkable castle, chapel, residential and park complex. The original defences were created by William the Conqueror in the form of a formidable motte and two baileys. At first, they were protected by palisades of timber. These were superseded by the turreted curtain-wall bailey defences and a circular stone shell keep crowning the motte during the twelfth and thirteenth centuries. Although imposing, the Plantagenet round tower was 33 ft lower than the one which is shown in our picture. It was raised in the 1820s to a total height of 230 ft and is said to be the tallest British castle. The addition and raising of other towers and walls took place in the course of the reigns of the nineteenth-

century monarchs.

St George's Chapel – the Chapel of the Dean and Canons of Windsor and of the Order of the Garter, in full – was begun by Edward IV in 1475 on a site within the bailey defences as a chapel for members of the illustrious Order of the Garter. It is a lavish exercise in later medieval ecclesiastical architecture and incorporates a number of royal tombs including those of the chapel's founder, two twentieth-century monarchs and those of Henry VIII and Jane Seymour.

Taken from opposing directions, the photographs show the stunning complex of royal buildings in relation to the attendant town of Windsor, the River Thames and the vast landscaped expanse of Windsor Great Park with its great and lesser avenues, recreational courts and courses, trees and gardens.

*Windsor is arguably the most fascinating and visually impressive of the
British royal residences*

In 1704, John Churchill, Duke of Marlborough, master-minded the defeat of the French armies of Louis XIV at Blenheim on the Danube. In a splendid token of the nation's gratitude, Queen Anne placed the funds to build a palace at the victor's disposal. The great house which resulted was perhaps a royal and national monument rather than a home, putting as it did most of the residences of the monarchy into the second division of magnificence.

John Vanbrugh was a slightly surprising choice of archi-tect, trained as a soldier, experienced in espionage work and best-known as an author of comedies. Nonetheless, the Duke was impressed by the model of the residence of Castle Howard which Vanbrugh had built for the Earl of Carlisle. This was an age when the professional architect was just beginning to emerge and assume the roles which had previously been performed by the master craftsmen of the building trade. Vanbrugh employed another archi-tect, Nicholas Hawksmoor, as his assistant.

In 1705, work began upon what Vanbrugh intended as a monument of '. . . Beauty, Magnificence and Duration': the reader may form his or her own conclusions upon the success of the ambition from the photograph. The overall design displays contemporary Baroque influences, though the weighty rectangular tower-like components hark back romantically to the medieval castle.

The story of the building of Blenheim Palace did not run smoothly; in 1710, Sarah, the strong-willed Duchess of Marlborough, squabbled with the Queen while, upon Anne's death and a change in government, the funds and patronage dried up. In 1712, with the building incomplete and £45,000 owing, the mason sued the Duke, though in 1716 work was resumed at the latter's expense. The Duch-ess for her part disagreed with Vanbrugh, who resigned, and when, in 1725, he attempted to see the finished work for the first time, he was refused entry to the park. Anec-dotes concerning the Duchess and her doings abound. One which is not strictly relevant here, nevertheless appeals because of a certain topicality: it was said by her detractors that she attempted to bribe the Duke of Wales, Frederick, with the sum of £100,000 to marry her granddaughter; marriage did not materialise, but the granddaughter's name was Lady Diana Spencer.

The photograph opposite is unrivalled in its portrayal of the Palace grounds. The original design, in a formal style, was by Vanbrugh and Henry Wise. In the decade following 1764, 'Capability' Brown was employed to remodel the park completely. The grounds were replanted and the lake standing just beyond the Palace was formed by damming a stream. According to this scheme, the lawns swept right up to the walls of the Palace and the close jux-taposition of the formal Palace architecture and the sweep-ing lawns, lake and treescape may have jarred the refined taste of a later age. In 1908–30, Duchêne was employed in the construction of the formal gardens which provide a bridge which helps to reconcile the two contrasting com-ponents. The formal garden to the east (right) of the Palace has a central fountain as its focus, and attempts have been made to reconstruct Sarah's original flower garden. The water terrace gardens to the left, linked by a wall with cascades, appeared in Vanbrugh's plans but were not built until 1925.

Privacy is provided by the thick stockade of woodland which rings the park, and only the airman can view simul-taneously the contrived vista of eighteenth-century land-scaping and the rolling, hedgerow-patterned agricultural landscape of Oxfordshire beyond.

Blenheim photographed from the formal gardens

8.9 MADRESFIELD COURT *Hereford & Worcester*

In several of the preceding entries, it has been seen how the post-medieval enthusiasm for balance, harmony and symmetry helped to transform the basis of new house design, while several venerable houses were remodelled or provided with symmetrical façades according to the dictates of the new fashion. However, in the early years of the nineteenth century, symmetry became distinctly unfashionable and romanticism, in partnership with a sustained vogue for things medieval, fuelled an enthusiasm for Neo-Gothik designs. Symmetry was 'out' and 'Elizabethan' chimneys, spired turrets, spiky Tudor gables and mullioned windows were 'in'. Although it is easy to deride the naive romanticism of much Victorian building, there is no doubt that the pre-Reformation buildings of Britain provided the architects with a delightful repertoire of features and motifs. The better essays in Neo-Gothik architecture always seem to sit comfortably in the English countryside, where the more rigorous exercises on Classical architectural principles seldom seem at ease.

Madresfield Court is largely a Victorian building although it does incorporate some elements of a much older moated house. Professor Pevsner believes that fifteenth-century walling can be detected in the masonry of the moat and possibly in the structures of the minstrel gallery in the great hall. The oldest of the surviving buildings mainly belong, however, to the Elizabethan age when, perhaps between 1546 and 1593, a house was built upon the moated site for the Lygon family. Elements of this brick mansion survive in the gatehouse complex, lower left, with its distinctive stepped gables. Most of the remainder was designed by P. C. Hardwick, begun in 1863 and completed around 1885, although other work was added until the outbreak of the 1914–18 war. 'Elizabethan' chimneys, Dutch gables and less convincingly traditional features met in the Victorian additions, but the results could hardly be described as discordant. Overlooking the undisciplined jumble of buildings is the spired bell turret of 1875.

Although the Victorians generally rejected symmetry in their buildings, particularly the more whimsical ones, they were usually keen to recreate the geometrical formality of sixteenth- and seventeenth-century garden design and the photograph records the immaculate hedging and planting arrangements which accompany the house.

Part of the house seen from the planned garden which dates from the Victorian era but was based on earlier designs

9.A *Trim in Co Meath, with its beautiful churches and medieval castle ruins*

9. TOWNS: OVERVIEWS AND INSIGHTS

Towns are the individualists of the landscape. Each one has its own particular personality and history and, as a result, it is much more difficult to generalise about towns than about, say, fields, roads or even villages. Because the towns of Britain are so diverse and because we want to include the greatest possible number of examples, we have broken from the single entry format in this chapter and grouped examples together under broad headings. No rigid attempt at classification is intended and, in each case, the individuality of the particular town shines through.

Air photography is seen at its most effective in the portrayal of towns. The literal 'man in the street' finds it almost impossible to form an impression of the structure and layout of the town. Metaphorically, he is unable to see the wood for the trees since, from the pavement, the view is limited by the nearest house and shop façades. The key to urban history is usually contained in the street plan and in the relics of abandoned arteries. Even from a vantage point like a church tower or a block of flats, the more distant streets are hidden in the canyons of buildings and the pattern of roads will not be apparent. However, from heights of a thousand or several thousand feet, the town plan begins to emerge in a map-like form and the story of its development can then be explored.

To say that towns vary greatly in size is to state the obvious, but the size of a town affects its portrayal in aerial photography. In the cases of the larger towns, even high-level vertical photographs will not include the full extent of the urban sprawl and, problems of haze apart, by the time that an aeroplane has gained sufficient altitude to capture the whole of a moderately large town like Leicester, Nottingham or Norwich within the camera frame, the fascinating and informative details will virtually have receded from view. However, towns invariably tend to grow outwards from their historic cores, and lower-level photographs of this core will be far more revealing than portraits of sprawling, anonymous acreages of modern suburbs.

In the cases of the smaller towns, all or most of the built-up area can often be incorporated in a low-level oblique photograph. This is apparent in the case of the charming Irish town of Trim in Co Meath, with its beautiful churches and medieval castle ruins. Such photographs often reveal not only the layout but also the history of the town and demonstrate the reasons behind the urban plan.

The picture of Warkworth in Northumberland is a good example. It can be seen how the medieval castle dominates the neck of a meander in the River Coquet, creating a settlement site which is guarded on three sides by water. A planned medieval layout can also be recognised, with the main street of the town running down towards the river crossing from the castle gate, with a broadened branch just below the church that served as a market-place. On closer inspection, other less obvious features emerge – the back lane, for example, which runs parallel and to the right of the main street, and shows that originally the burgage plots were relatively short, terminating at this lane, but then were extended across the lane towards the riverside. Of course, there are always important

9.B *Warkworth in Northumberland lies in a meander of the River Coquet*

9.C *Milngavie, north of Glasgow, looking towards the valley of Strathblane*

details which photographs cannot tell us and which must be sought in the archives. In this case, they include the facts that the church and lands here were presented to Lindisfarne Abbey by the Northumbrian king in 737 and that the medieval town was extended across the river in the form of a segregated new town for mariners and fishermen, as Professor Beresford has described.

Air photographs are also particularly effective through their ability to show settlements in their geographical context or setting. The point is picturesquely made in the case of Milngavie, a northern satellite of Glasgow; the photograph is looking over the town, north-westwards towards the valley of Strathblane, with the knobbly spur of the Campsie Fells to the right and the sterner mountains around Loch Lomond looming faintly through the haze. No less picturesque or informative is the photograph of the Lakeland medieval market town, former mining centre and modern tourist resort of Keswick. The picture leaves one in no doubt of Keswick's suitability for its present role; the town lies just to the left of the centre of the photograph, nestling on a lowland site on the shores of Derwentwater and hemmed around by spectacular mountain scenery.

However, while bearing in mind the ways in which physical features like rivers, hills, bridging and fording points or valley access routes may influence the foundation and development of a town, it is worth remarking that geography does not make a town, and each one is the product of human decisions. Often the decisions can be quirky, subjective or embodying the accidents of history, but there is many a thriving town in Britain which stands on an indifferent site, in a mediocre location, yet was kicked into life by a man of vision or drive and has flourished ever since.

9.D *Keswick in Cumbria nestles on the shores of Derwentwater and is surrounded by stunning scenery*

197

9.1 URBAN ANCESTORS AND FLEDGLINGS

The first thoroughly urban settlements in Britain were Roman creations although, by the time of the Roman Conquest, indigenous developments had carried Britain well along the road towards a town-based civilisation. It is probable that much remains to be discovered about the emergence of proto-towns and one would not be too surprised if large, semi-urban, riverside trading settlements dating to the Bronze Age should be discovered in the course of future British excavations. The substantial and sometimes carefully planned hillfort hut settlements of the Iron Age represent the earliest stride in the direction of urbanism so far discovered in Britain, while in the decades preceding the first Roman landings, a number of extensive tribal capitals were established on lowland sites. Generally shielded by outworks of ramparts, these *oppida* included mints, workshops, royal residences and agglomerations of huts and were involved in administrative, economic and political functions. Even so, they would appear quite untown-like to our eyes, though the Roman towns which succeeded them would impress a modern visitor with their civic provisions and carefully considered layouts.

Of the various *oppida* which have so far been discovered, the Catuvellaunian tribal capital of Camulodunum near Colchester is the most thoroughly known, but even here there is much that remains mysterious. The extensive defended settlement seems to have included two main centres: a royal farm with an adjacent religious sanctuary surrounded by a large rural estate, and the area known

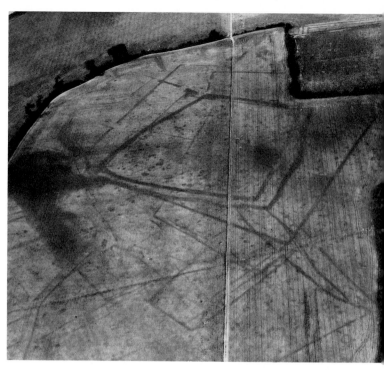

as Sheepen, a trading port and manufacturing centre beside the River Colne which had a mint and pottery, metal and salt-making industries. In due course, the Romans established a *colonia*, a settlement for retired legionaries, on a site next to Sheepen previously occupied by the barracks

A

B

198

of one of their legions. Although this settlement was razed in the Boudicca uprising of AD 60 it was rebuilt to become the direct ancestor of modern Colchester.

The photograph (9.1A) of crop marks at Cheshunt Field, about two miles south-west of Colchester, reveals the outlines of the more rural part of Camulodunum, in which one can recognise ditched enclosures, lanes or droveways, the dark speckles which represent grain storage pits and occasional hut circles. Were we able to reconstruct the sprawling tribal capital from these remains, we would see a settlement which was several evolutionary stages removed from the orderly sophistication of a Roman provincial centre.

The photographs (9.1B–C) of Calleva Atrebatum, Roman Silchester in Hampshire, which succeeded a native capital of the Atrebates tribe on the same site reveals a completely different townscape. In a pioneering excavation of 1890–1909, the Society of Antiquaries laid bare the plan of Silchester and the site remains, arguably, our best-known Roman town. It was surrounded by primary and secondary outer earthworks, and within these by a later earthwork defence, subsequently reinforced by a flint wall, which defined an irregularly roughly 7-sided plan. Gateways in the wall admitted roads from the north, south, east and west, while within its assymetrical confines, a gridwork of streets divided the town into a number of rectangular *insulae* or development plots of various sizes. The photograph shows a section of Silchester, covering roughly one-fifth of the area of the town, from the central forum, clearly shown within its apparently over-large *insula* in

the upper right of the picture, to a stretch of the wall in the north-west, whose bank is covered with a line of trees. The geometrical street pattern is particularly well portrayed by pale lines in the crops, as are the outlines of most of the dwellings, many of them sophisticated, multi-roomed houses of stone. Beneath these vivid traces of the Roman town, a dark band can be followed, running vertically up the photograph near the left-hand side and this marks the line of the broad defensive ditch of the pre-Roman tribal capital.

The second photograph (9.1C) shows a section of the town running from the forum at the right to the south wall of the town at the left. The forum served as an administrative centre and market place and, in this case, a neatly symmetrical plan was adopted, with the basilica running along the western or upper side of the forum while both the forum and the basilica were enhanced by impressive external porticos. A second important civic building, the *mansio*, a sort of hotel, can be recognised near the centre of the left-hand margin. A street can be seen running to the entrance on the right-hand side and we can recognise the suites of rooms surrounding the inner courtyard. Just below, but less easily detected, is an outer courtyard and in its lower left corner there was an imposing bath house.

The double circle between the forum and the mansio is a large temple, more Celtic than Roman in its architectural form.

The photographs show that the buildings of Silchester were not tightly packed as in many Mediterranean cities, but stood in spacious grounds which covered the greater

C

199

parts of most *insulae*. In contrast to Camulodunum, Roman Silchester was a planned, imposing and indeed elegant town. Unlike many other Roman settlements, the site has not been masked or obliterated by later building developments. However, while once serving as home to the Roman and romanised native élites, Calleva Atrebatum now has a less distinguished population, for the small black rectangles which punctuate sections of the photographs are pig shelters.

Like those of other periods, the Roman towns were varied; some had originally been built to house military garrisons, others were deliberately developed as commercial and administrative foci. Some of the centres were created to house retired soldiers, while others still were linked to the development of particular industries. Then there were also the commercial villages or *vici*, of which much remains to be learned. Kenchester (9.1D), a small but walled town in the upper valley of the Wye in Herefordshire, belongs to the top flight of *vici*, for its walls embraced a twenty-two-acre site and it contained several quite grandiose dwellings with porticoed façades, one with a bath suite, as well as more prosaic dwellings. Even so, Kenchester has a distinctly rustic or 'small town' character and the imposing public buildings and gridwork of streets and *insulae* found at the more prestigious settlements are lacking.

The origins and functions of Kenchester are not clear. The town may have begun in the second century and have developed to become a self-governing administrative

E

centre, probably out-living the Roman period but declining in the course of the Dark Ages. As with many other Roman settlements, the townlet initially had earthwork defences which were subsequently enhanced by a stone wall, and then a wide ditch and external towers were added. The photograph shows how Kenchester's kite-shaped wall plan has been respected by the later country roads and hedges. The main street, which ran along the long axis of the kite to gateways opening to the east and west is clearly recognisable, along with the short internal access lanes and the ground-plans of some of the grander houses.

Defensive towns and monastic settlements developed in England in the later stages of the Saxon period, but they may not represent the only steps on a return to urban life in the centuries following the Roman collapse. There are suggestions that defended capitals, perhaps even towns, developed in the northern tribal kingdoms. Dunadd, near Oban, has been suggested as a capital of the Scots; Dundurn in Strath Earn and Burghead (pl. 9.6D) may have been Pictish foci, while Alt Clut or Castle Rock at Dumbarton (9.1E) has long been regarded as a capital of the Britons.

Bede suggested Alt Clut as a political capital that was long established when he mentioned the place in AD 731

and the site is thought to have been destroyed by Dublin Vikings in AD 871. However, as the photograph (9.1E) shows, Castle Rock in the mouth of Dumbarton harbour could hardly have accommodated even the meanest city, while a recent exploration of a number of presumed Dark Age capitals by the archaeologist Leslie Alcock produced no spectacular evidence of lost cities. The lack of obvious archaeological remains may partly reflect the fact that the natural defensive attractions of the presumed early capital sites resulted in the older remains being destroyed in the course of later castle-building operations. At Alt Clut, Alcock dated the earliest outworks discovered to around 1300, while the supposed Dark Age citadel proved to be of the mid-seventeenth century! However, Bede was an unusually reliable chronicler and Alt Clut probably was a Dark Age capital of the Britons; not a bustling metropolis or even a Camelot-like citadel but rather, as Alcock suggests, a place which a ruler would periodically visit on circuit along with his retinue and in which he might install a small garrison. To support this diminished but plausible role for Alt Clut, Alcock discovered the remains of a stone and timber look-out platform and the pommel of a Viking sword, probable relics of the raid of AD 871, but of other more grandiose defenceworks no trace was found.

9.2 FOUR MEDIEVAL TOWNS
Chipping Campden, Lavenham, Hedon and Glastonbury

Contrary to popular belief, medieval towns did not develop from villages following natural process of growth. Each town had its own reason for being and, more often than not, the town owed its status to human actions rather than natural geographical advantages. While there were some towns like London which were so well endowed by geography that growth was almost inevitable, there were many more whose sites and locations were quite mediocre. Scores of medieval towns owed their existence to a founding father and to accidents of history: a noble might have been enticed by the prospects of market revenues to create a new town on his estate; a bishop or abbot might have chosen to expand and elevate the ecclesiastical developments at an ancient and esteemed religious site, or a protected trading settlement might have formed part of a castle-building enterprise at a place really chosen for its contemporary strategic significance.

The completeness of the demise of towns in the centuries following the collapse of Roman power in Britain is still

a controversial question. Some Roman towns became utterly dead; some were apparently deserted although their sites were reoccupied at late dates in the Saxon period; some appear to have become the non-urban foci of Saxon administrations; some shrank into simple agricultural villages and largely disappeared under farmland, while a few may have endured as towns, but on a much reduced scale. An early stage in the revival of town life was marked by the establishment of Saxon *burhs* like Wallingford (pl. 9.5A) in the late ninth and tenth centuries and although the *burhs* may have been conceived as defensive strongpoints in the Wessex-based resistance against Danish invasion, several swiftly developed a commercial life.

The quickening of economic activities, the growth of the church and the expansion of administrative activities stimulated the growth of towns in the later stages of the Saxon kingdom and all these processes were accelerated after the Norman Conquest. A large proportion of British market towns can trace their histories back to an early medieval trading charter granted to the lord of the nearby manor and although borough status was always jealously cherished, such towns generally remained compact, closely linked to the surrounding countryside and scarcely more extensive than a large modern village.

Chipping Campden in Gloucestershire (9.2A) is a fairly typical example. Its existence as a borough can be traced back to a grant to the lord of the local manor in 1173 and the town developed a role as a trading centre for Cotswolds wool merchants. A century after attaining borough status, the town housed around a hundred households and had less than ten shops. Although a new charter of incorporation boosted Chipping Campden's trading activities and a market hall and other public works were provided at the start of the seventeenth century, the character of the medieval town has been well preserved. The medieval market place is represented by a broadening in the main street, now occupied by an island containing private and municipal buildings and a car park.

The burgesses of medieval Chipping Campden occupied dwellings which were set out on either side of the main street and provided with elongated plots or tofts which ran at right angles from the street to the two back lanes which defined the urban area. The outlines of the medieval tofts are plainly apparent in the photograph, even though later development has resulted in a considerable amount of in-filling in the areas behind the main street. Clearly, property boundaries which were defined at a relatively early stage in the Middle Ages still continue to affect the pattern of town growth.

The form and layout of Chipping Campden is typical of many of the smaller medieval trading towns, and although a purely peasant community occupied an outlier

B

of the town, the burgesses owned field land as well as their tofts and the town will have retained a strong rural flavour. The layouts and activities which developed in the larger medieval towns were rather different and recent work shows that, in East Anglia at least, dwellings were often set end-on to the main streets, with the more prestigious dwellings set back in side streets and courtyards rather than fronting on a High Street.

At Lavenham in Suffolk (9.2B), the fossilisation of the medieval townscape is even more complete owing to the demise of the town's textile industry and the failure of other industries to fill the vacuum and spawn new growth. While the majority of medieval towns owed their prosperity, such as it was, to market trading and acted primarily as service centres for the surrounding countryside, Lavenham was essentially an industrial town. Its not inconsiderable wealth is expressed in the sumptuous Perpendicular church, and both church and town owed much to the success and patronage of the Spring family, the leading dynasty amongst the clothiers of Lavenham. The distance from the church to the furthest extremity of the town is scarcely 500 yds and so the whole of the town plan is encapsulated in the photograph. The church and the hall to its left are slightly detached from the economic core of the town which they overlook. Hall Road, to the left, and Church Street, to the right, converge at the apex of a shield-shaped street plan. The market place is visible as a small open triangle of ground about midway between the church and the upper left corner of the photograph. Immediately to its right is the famous guildhall, built in 1529 by the Guild of Corpus Christi which regulated wages, standards and prices in the local cloth-making industry at a time when the industrial fortunes of Lavenham were beginning to dip following a century of prosperity and prominence in the leading English industry of the medieval period.

I have said that most medieval towns were deliberate creations rather than the results of natural or 'organic' growth. Many of the towns were also set out according to deliberate, pre-conceived plans and the geometrical outlines of a medieval street pattern can be recognised in the cores of many British towns. Medieval town planning is particularly well-displayed in the case of Hedon in Humberside (9.2c) where, rather than out-growing its medieval confines, the town has contracted and the planned outlines are displayed in field patterns rather than in street alignments. The town was planted in the late twelfth century as a trading port covering a part of the lands belonging to the older village of Preston which is visible at the top of the photograph. The stream which runs from left to right just below the town was canalised and three channels were cut to give ships access to the heart of Hedon. However, the town's prosperity as an inland trading port of the Humber estuary was short-lived; after less than a century of prime activity, competition from Kingston-upon-Hull and the subsequently inundated Humber port of Ravenserod began a decline which continued throughout the Middle Ages.

Hedon was set out within a square-shaped site which is still visible in the photograph, along with its swiftly gained eastern extension to the right. The square was sub-

C

204

divided into a number of rectangular blocks or *insulae* whose outlines were defined by the main streets, while the *insulae* in turn were divided into plots for the immigrant burgesses; the open area immediately to the left of the church tower was the site of the medieval market. In the course of its decline, Hedon contracted towards its church and market core, and ridge and furrow ploughland covered some of the former townscape; older ridge and furrow patterns are visible in the medieval lands of Preston above Hedon.

It would be difficult to exaggerate the importance of the church in almost every aspect of medieval life, and in the course of the medieval period, great churchmen were as active as lay nobles and entrepreneurs in the establishment, re-modelling and envigoration of towns. In some cases, as at Lichfield, a great ecclesiastical foundation provided the initial magnet for urban growth. But it is also possible that, through the creation of adjacent markets, Saxon monastic communities were, as Michael Aston and James Bond have suggested in *The Landscape of Towns*, 'the instigators of a profitable fashion which was to be copied extensively after the Norman Conquest by ecclesiastics and laymen at many places up and down the country'. Reliable documentary information for the Saxon period is much harder to come by than information for the centuries which followed. Despite the extravagant claims of 'lunatic fringe archaeology', which has Glastonbury in Somerset as a major cult focus, there can be no substance in the legend that Joseph of Arimathea buried the Holy Grail at Glastonbury. However, a monastery seems to have been established at Glastonbury at some stage following the Saxon conversion, and excavation has revealed a bank which could have been built by an early monastic community and which is evidently older than overlying glass-working debris dating from the ninth century.

The town plan of Glastonbury (9.2D) contains hints that the Saxon monks may have established a market just outside their abbey in the subsequently built-up area at the foot of the High Street, at the lower left-hand corner of the photograph. To the right of the High Street are the ruins of the magnificent medieval Abbey buildings which embodied much of the wealth generated by Glastonbury's lucrative role as a destination for pilgrimage; pilgrims' hostels developed along the street, while the majestic church

D

of St John interrupts the outlines of medieval tofts which can still be recognised to the left of the High Street.

The topic of the medieval town is a fascinating one and one which will contain many surprises for those who believed that towns simply grew from villages which were favoured by geographical advantages. Readers who would like to explore the story in more detail can do no better than to refer to *Medieval England, An Aerial Survey* by Professors M. W. Beresford and J. K. S. St Joseph.

A

Of the towns which appeared in the medieval period, a sizable proportion owed their existence to the establishment of a nearby castle. In some cases, royal or baronial castles were built to protect or to intimidate existing urban communities, as at London or York. But many other towns were included as appurtenances to a castle-building project or developed, usually as planned creations, when the lord of the neighbouring castle gained a coveted market charter. As a result, such towns often owed their locations and situations to the accidents of history or their proximity to strategic positions or defensible terrain rather than to any particular local economic geographical advantages. The expansion of English influence into the Celtic lands by Norman kings, warlords and their descendants resulted in the creation of castle-guarded towns which were intrusive and peopled by alien traders, craftsmen and artisans.

The history of Cockermouth (9.3A) in the northern Lake District was quite typical. About 1134, a Norman castle was established on a superbly defensible natural knoll which jutted into the sharply-angled junction between the River Derwent and its tributary, the Cocker, and was thus protected on two of its three sides by rivers. The former Roman fort of Derventio, about a mile away on the opposite side of the Derwent, provided a convenient quarry for building materials. In this case, the castle preceded the town, but in 1221 a market charter was obtained and urban development followed. The market was established on low ground near the upper right corner of the photograph, between the castle and the church, but efforts were made to protect the trading privileges of the more venerable borough of Egremont and so, while Cockermouth had a lawful Monday market, the right to hold a fair was not won until 1638.

The photograph shows how the castle was tailored to the form of the knoll which was enhanced by earthworks, with the Derwent on its left flank and the Cocker on its right. Most of the castle remains now standing date from the thirteenth and fourteenth centuries and one can see how the defended area was divided by buildings into two wards, with a gatehouse to the left and a tower to the right protecting the upper landward approaches, while later, post-medieval buildings were built against the inner face of the wall.

At Bolsover in Derbyshire (9.3B) the pattern was quite similar, if a little more complicated. In late Saxon times, the area was part of a valuable estate but there were probably no fortifications. In the years immediately following the Norman Conquest, when William sought to consolidate his grip on the North, a number of Derbyshire lordships were granted to William Peverell and a pallisaded earthwork castle was built in the wooded area on the left of the photograph. It had a 'B'-shaped form, with inner and outer baileys, although subsequent building operations have largely obliterated its shape.

The building of the castle was soon followed by the plantation of a planned town, which was probably engaged in trading for many years before obtaining an official market charter in 1225. The planned town was set out according to a rectangular grid and aligned on streets leading south-westwards from the bailey gates, diagonally upwards towards the top-left corner of the photograph. A measure of commercial success in the medieval period resulted in the expansion of the town into lands beyond the left-hand margin of the photograph which were taken from surrounding open fields. Modern development has brought the town back towards the castle and in the upper right quadrant of the photograph are some superb specimens of the English 'semi'. Although just a few feet wide, the gaps between the units assert the status and independence of the home-owner, the house façades are derived, however distantly, from the English Gothic, while the ribbons of back garden remind one of the tofts of medieval house and village plots.

The castle in the foreground bears little resemblance to the stone defences which enhanced the castle earthworks after about 1100, and while it seems to ape the form of a Norman keep or a later medieval tower-house, it was begun by Sir Charles Cavendish around 1615, embodying romance, nostalgia and a fine crop of battlements, pinnacles and corner turrets. His son, the 1st Duke of Newcastle, added the symmetrical terrace ranges in 1660, sixteen

years after the palatial mock castle had been stormed and battered by Parliamentary troops.

The castle-building operations enacted at Caernarfon in Gwynned (9.3c) between 1283 and 1322 represented a completely different order of military and strategic thinking. The Edwardian castle took over the site of an older Norman fort which had guarded the Menai Straits and it was one of a number of massive citadels through which the plans of Edward I to consolidate and perpetuate his conquest of North Wales were effected. Today, the castle is a major tourist attraction, but here our attention is focussed on the accompanying town.

The construction of a plantation town was an important element in Edward's plan for Caernarfon and work upon the formidable town wall and ditch was completed before the construction of the castle itself began, with these initial defences also serving as outer fortifications of the citadel. The town wall is still a prominent feature of the Caernarfon townscape although, as the photograph shows, its fronting ditch has been infilled to carry a road. From the air, one can also recognise the original division of the defended town into a gridwork of streets and blocks by a main street, which runs from the east gate in the centre of the wall to the waterside west gate, and three other streets which intersect it at right angles. The *insulae* defined by the streets were partitioned into plots let to burgesses from England – merchants, shopkeepers, artisans and craftsmen – at rents of a shilling a year. As the turmoils of the Middle Ages receded and the need for defence was less strongly felt, the town spilled out beyond its corset of walls and a market-place was established in the open area just below the castle.

c

D

At Denbigh in Clwyd (9.3D) the story of the town's development had some similarities, but there were also important differences. The Edwardian town was preceded by a small Welsh hill-top settlement, the centre of a barony ruled by Dafydd ap Gruffyd. In 1282, the armies of Edward I captured Denbigh following Dafydd's revolt and the surrounding territory was granted to the Earl of Lincoln, who was instructed to fortify the Denbigh site. As at Caernarfon, a town wall was built to defend both a plantation town and the new castle which crowned the hill and a charter of 1290 embodied the division of the defended area into forty-seven burgages, whose holders were each obliged to provide an armed man for the defence of the town. Although the developing castle town was captured by the Welsh in 1294, the plans were brought to fruition following its recapture and the defences were strengthened. However, Denbigh was attacked and burned in the course of the Wars of the Roses and, either as a consequence of the burning or in response to conditions of life on a steeply sloping site which was deprived of good water supplies, the old town site was abandoned and a new town established on a more level site at the foot of the hill. The photograph shows the relative emptiness of the area within the town walls, while the destruction vented upon the castle dates from a Civil War bombardment, the Royalist garrison surrendering in 1646.

The new hill-foot town gained a market-place around 1570 and its tapering triangular outlines are represented on the photograph by the broadening in the modern street just above the road junction, lower right of centre. Standing just within the old town walls are the arcaded ruins of a new church built in the late sixteenth century by the Earl of Leicester, who took advantage of a vacant site in the abandoned settlement, though the project was never brought to fruition.

9.4 THREE LOST TOWNS *Clonmacnois, Dunwich and Torskey*

While thousands of villages disappeared in the course of the Middle Ages, towns had much better prospects of survival. Sometimes the decline of a vital industry would stem the opportunity for future growth and the town would be fossilised as a dwarf amongst the urban giants of the industrial age; Thaxted in Essex and Lavenham (pl. 9.2B) are examples. A handful of towns did perish utterly; Clonmines in Co Wexford, Kincardine near Stonehaven in the north of Scotland and Caus in Shropshire are cases in point, while the three examples included here which, though not entirely without life, are nevertheless dead as towns.

Clonmacnois in Co Offaly (9.4A) is arguably the most important religious focus in Ireland even though the once remarkably resilient urban component has long since surrendered to fate. The monastic tradition was born in Ireland at a time when England was a European backwater divided between a small host of pagan kingdoms. Clonmacnois was founded by St Cíarán, an ecclesiastical classmate of St Columba and pupil of St Finnian in 545 and in the ninth century, when England was beset by Danish wars, Clonmacnois was a major focus of European Christian civilisation. A substantial town developed around the monastic core and, in one form or another, it endured for about a thousand years. When Clonmacnois was terminally reduced by the English garrison of Athlone in 1552, the town and monastery had survived literally dozens of assaults and raids by native Irish chieftains and rivals, Viking plunderers and English forces. The aerial photograph cannot reveal the beauties of the carved early Christian stone crosses (*below*) and tombstones, although the twelfth-century round towers and medieval church buildings are clearly portrayed while the faint outlines of the accompanying settlement can be traced in the pasture. The ruins of a motte and bailey castle can be seen above and to the left of the monastic complex, overlooking the broad channel of the Shannon.

One of the beautifully carved early Christian stone crosses at Clonmacnois

Whereas Clonmacnois fell victim to human intolerance, Dunwich in Suffolk (9.4B) is one of Nature's casualties. Although Dunwich is probably the most widely-known lost settlement in Britain, its site is one of the least revealing – for the simple reason that the greater part of it is now eroded by the sea and the village which perpetuates the town's name is less than a fag end of what was once a leading east coast port. Dunwich was an important Saxon town and much of its importance was retained in the medieval period. However, in the course of the Middle Ages five churches were lost in the relentless retreat of the Suffolk coastline. Two more churches followed in the later sixteenth and early seventeenth centuries; in 1677 the market place was lost and with little of Dunwich remaining, another church has joined the rubble on the beach. This

photograph was taken in 1951 and the cliff-line is seen to be corrugated and scalloped by small landslips. Today, the cliff is much closer to the old holloway which runs diagonally upwards from the village road junction and before too long, this road to nowhere will also have been lost.

The causes of Dunwich's fate are quite clear-cut, but less is known about the demise of Torksey in Lincolnshire (9.4C) and, as the photograph shows, ploughing has so obliterated the evidence that the site is scarcely more revealing than that of Dunwich. Like Wallingford (pl. 9.5A), Torksey was a Saxon *burh* and its subsequent prosperity owed much to its position beside the Foss Dyke, a Roman canal which joins the Trent at the foot of the photograph. The town ran from the canal to the modern shrunken vil-

B

c

lage of Torksey, just left of centre, a distance of almost half a mile. The decay of Torksey seems to have been quite advanced by the thirteenth century and by the fifteenth, Torksey was little more than a largish village. The fortunes of Torksey seem to have been bound to those of Lincoln, which it served as a river outport. The medieval silting of the Foss Dyke was probably a symptom of Torksey's decline rather than its cause, for had there been the trade to justify it, the canal would have been scoured. Professor Beresford has suggested in *Medieval England: An Aerial Survey* that the post-Conquest growth of the port of Boston led to a reorientation of trade, while in the late thirteenth century Boston also captured Lincoln's wool trading functions. Standing in the river meadows between Torksey village and the Trent are the ruins of Torksey 'castle'. This is not a relic of the town, for Torksey was already reduced to a village when this mansion was built from stone pillaged from the old priory in the Elizabethan period.

From the ruins of Torksey 'castle' one looks across the Trent to a modern power station

213

A

9.5 THREE DEFENDED TOWNS *Wallingford, Berwick-upon-Tweed and Londonderry*

Many of our old or middle-aged towns were embraced by a corset of walls or ramparts, but the true functions of these defenceworks are not always as obvious as they might seem. Walls could and did serve as protective screens against foreign or native invaders, but in the medieval period and probably in the Roman period too, walls also proclaimed the urban status and prestige of the defended settlement – in the same way that the castle moat was an important aristocratic status symbol in the Middle Ages. Walls could also play a useful role in towns where trading was a vital function and market tolls an important source of revenue, because the provision of a limited number of gates helped to control the comings and goings of traders. In many cases, the town walls seem to have been primarily status symbols and, just as the castle and the moat passed into redundancy in the closing years of the Middle Ages, so town walls tended to be neglected and became lawful or illegal quarries for building stone although, in the meantime, the restrictions on urban growth which the ring or rings of walls had created become indelibly stamped in the layout of streets.

The following examples of urban defences of different ages responded to sterner military challenges. Wallingford in Oxfordshire (9.5A), the first example, is by far the oldest and it still preserves the outlines of a Saxon fortified town or *burh*. There is still much to learn about the Saxon *burhs*; some always seem to have had important economic as well as military functions, some were sited on earlier Saxon or Roman administrative foci and a few seem to have predated the Danish threat. Most, however, were created after 865, when a total Danish conquest of England had become a distinct possibility, and were established by King Alfred and his successor to defend Wessex and its approaches. After the Danish threat had receded, some of the *burhs* withered but others developed economic functions and survived. Wallingford seems to have been one of a number of *burhs* which was established on a previously empty site. Whether it was conceived as a trading centre as well as a fortress from the outset, we cannot be sure, but the Saxon planned layout of a grid of streets surrounded by a rectangular earthen rampart – rather Roman-like in concept – is still plainly evident. The main axis of the town now runs across the photograph opposite from left to right towards the bridge across the Thames (below).

The main axis of Wallingford runs across the bridge over the Thames and into the town

The walls of Berwick upon Tweed in Northumberland (9.5B) represent a very different chapter in the development of town defences, one which is much more evident on the continent than in Britain. In the course of the post-medieval centuries, religious, dynastic and imperial struggles spawned patterns of massive and intricate urban defences in the north-west of continental Europe. But, shielded by the great moat of the English Channel, the English concentrated on studding their coastline with anti-invasion works while the towns of the soft interior lay undefended inside the hard shell of coastal defences. Berwick was rather unusual, being exposed principally to landward invasion from Scotland, and the resultant defences endow the town with a rather continental aura. In the frantic traumas of the Civil War and in the course of the hostilities many English towns found themselves unprepared against assault and were hastily fortified in a superficially similar style, but these defences took the form of earthworks rather than the formidable girdle of masonry which is such a striking feature of Berwick.

The original town wall was built in the reign of Edward I; Henry VIII strengthened the castle defences and furnished the wall with a gun tower, while a 'modern' star-shaped fortress was planned in the reign of Edward VI.

B

216

c

In 1558, however, a completely new defensive system was introduced in the face of a major Scottish invasion scare. Although the work was never entirely completed, a large area of the north of the town and a smaller section in the south were abandoned in order to create a more compact defensive perimeter, and the remainder of the town was ringed by a curtain wall which was itself shielded by flanking fire from great projecting arrow-shaped bastions. In the 1640s and early '50s additional defenceworks included earthwork parapets which can be seen rising above the bastions. The old medieval wall still provided riverside defences, while running to the right of the lower right bastion is a stretch of the Edwardian wall formerly guarding the northern section of the town, abandoned at the close of the Middle Ages and then completely dwarfed by the massive wall and bastion of 1558–9.

At Londonderry (9.5c) the town walls constitute probably the most important physical symbol in the iconogra-

phy of a nation which suffers from an excess of history. The town arose as a creation of the Protestant plantation of Ulster and was the last great fortified 'bastide' town to be built in Europe. It was built on the banks of the River Foyle as an urban focus for estates owned by London companies and a planned grid-iron pattern of streets was constructed within the encircling walls. In 1688 the townspeople were prepared to admit a Royalist and Catholic garrison when thirteen Presbyterian apprentices slammed the town gates. From April to July of 1689 the town lay under siege until it was relieved by a Williamite fleet. Thenceforth, the apprentice boys' slogan of 'No Surrender' has been a watchword of the Ulster loyalists in a land where the currents of history are reversed. Although later industrial expansion has carried the town far beyond the confines of its seventeenth-century defences, the roughly oblong walled core with its internal gridwork of streets is still plainly apparent in the town plan.

9.6 THE MODERNISM OF TIMES PAST *Bath, Edinburgh and Burghead*

It has been seen that the concept of the planned town is not a modern phenomenon, and while the Roman achievements in creating ordered urban landscapes are well known, pre-conceived layouts governed the forms of some Saxon *burhs* and were the norm in the new town foundations of the Middle Ages. While haphazard 'organic' growth was also a feature of urban development in all parts of Britain and at all periods in history, planning was seldom less, and often more, important. With the passing of the Middle Ages and a weakening of the orthodoxy imposed by the Roman church, interest in the pagan Classical civilisations, particularly those of Greece and Rome, grew enormously.

Classical influences affected many aspects of art and life. At the level of the house, they were reflected in the fashion for symmetrical elevations or even Palladian façades, while in the landscape there was a quest for orderly arrangements, expressed in scenic tastes or the layout of gardens, parks and villages. In urban developments, too, the desire for order and symmetry was apparent and expressed in straight and stately avenues, stylish terrace developments in which the house façades were identical or the flourishes of a loftier central block were exactly balanced by symmetrical flanking rows or in harmonious compositions of avenues, squares and crescents.

The aspirations of eighteenth-century civilisation are perfectly expressed in the Royal Crescent and Queen Square district of Bath (9.6A–B). The town had been famed for its mineral springs since at least Roman times, but a fashionable revival began in 1702 when Queen Anne arrived to sample the medicinal waters. Following the royal patronage and under the influential promotion of Beau Nash, Bath developed as an elegant and fashionable spa whose presumed medicinal attributes provided the pretext for high living in every conceivable form. In order to accommodate its new aristocratic clientele, Bath developed an appropriately stately and refined complex of residences.

A

B

John Wood the Elder, a local architect, began the building of Queen Square in 1729, serving both as architect and as speculator when the Corporation of Bath shied away from the ambitious undertaking. Influenced by the design of London's Cavendish Square, Wood aligned the residences behind a single pedimented Classical façade. He laid out the street pattern of Bath's fashionable core and, following his death in 1754, the work was brought to fruition by his son, with the Circus being started in 1754 and the Royal Crescent in 1767. By 1775, the district had assumed the appearance shown in the photograph (9.6A), with elegant buildings in the creamy-white local limestone arranged in rows and curves behind palatial façades in a manner which blended the Classical and Picturesque architectural movements.

Royal Crescent, which set the trend for prestigious housing developments in several other British towns, appears on the left of the photograph. It is linked by Brock Street to the Circus and just above the Circus are the Assembly Rooms, while Gay Street runs off to the right to define the upper margin of Queen Square.

When the low-level oblique photograph (9.6A) is compared to the much broader vista shown on the high-altitude vertical photograph, it is seen that the fashionable eighteenth-century core forms a relatively small component of Bath, although the Crescent and Circus are clearly recognisable in the upper left quadrant. Scarcely less obvious are the distinctive working class terraces, inter-war suburban semis and select post-war estate developments, all contributing to the tangle that made the city of Bath a motorist's nightmare in the days preceding the motorway.

The photograph of Edinburgh (9.6c) shows a remarkable juxtaposition of older and newer urban development. Although only the central fraction of the modern city is shown, the whole of medieval Edinburgh was incorporated in the area above the castle (lower right-hand corner) and to the right of the railway. When John Rocque mapped the city in the middle of the eighteenth century, its size had scarcely changed and Edinburgh was aligned upon the medieval axis of the Land Market and Canongate roads, clearly visible, running upwards from the castle.

In 1755, Edinburgh housed around 31,000 people and was hemmed in by the waters and bogs of the Nor Loch, which lay just to the left of the castle and over the railway. Between 1770 and 1800, a New Town was laid out across the Loch and its spacious, geometrically planned streets and elegant housing provided a striking contrast to the Old Town with its cramped dwellings and the undisciplined alleys with names like Grassmarket and Cowgate advertising their medieval age and functions. The Nor Loch was drained and a bridge provided across its valley to link the two towns. By 1800, the city had a population of 162,000 and continued to grow rapidly. However, the New Town as planned by James Craig was a coherent entity and not readily amenable to expansion, and although Edinburgh developed outwards in several direc-

tions, the pressure of population in the Old Town resulted in the division and subdivision of old properties to create increasingly cramped and squalid apartments. Meanwhile, imperfections in the drainage of the Nor Loch had left the ground too damp for building purposes, allowing the railway developments of the mid-nineteenth century to reach right into the heart of the city. The railway marks the alignment of the old Nor Loch, whose former shores are carpeted by elegantly landscaped gardens.

The photograph shows a number of landmarks that will be familiar to tourists and Festival visitors. The castle, which perches upon a plug of volcanic rock, needs no introduction, while the medieval alignment above follows a tail of glacial debris eastwards or upwards, along Canongate towards the Palace of Holyroodhouse, which is just below the upper margin of the photograph. Running parallel and to the left of the railway is Princes Street, defining the southern margin of the New Town while the National Monument and Nelson's Monument stand on Carlton Hill at the head of the street. St Giles Cathedral can be seen about midway between Waverley Station and the right-hand margin of the photograph.

The orderly planning which was a hallmark of the Age of Reason was not confined to sections of leading or fashionable cities, but was also a feature of new village and

c

D

small town development – particularly in the north-east of Scotland, where estate owners often competely reorganised the pre-Culloden landscapes of tenant farming hamlets. Grid-iron layouts were popular, not only because they mirrored the general fashion for geometrical order, but also because, if successful, the new town or village could easily be enlarged by extending the grid plan of streets. However, the latter argument could not be advanced in the case of Burghead on the shores of the Moray Firth (9.6D), since the townlet is confined by the peninsula on which it stands. Close inspection of the photograph shows that the dwellings portrayed are not fully-fledged terraces, but adjoining small stone cottages.

In this case, the historical significance of the site extends far beyond the days of the planned settlement. Largely destroyed in the course of the construction works of 1808 were the remains of a massive Pictish promontory fort, dated AD 400–800. Fortunately, the ruins were surveyed before the building of the town and port of Burghead when in the 1740s the Duke of Cumberland requested General Roy to plan the monuments. The survey shows that the neck of the peninsula was spanned by three sets of ramparts, each about half a mile in length. Thus Burghead is unique amongst the repetitive, perhaps monotonous, late eighteenth- and early-nineteenth-century planned villages and townlets of north-east Scotland in standing on the site of a major Pictish regional capital which some regard as an indigenous proto-town. Developed by joint proprietors in the early years of the nineteenth century, Burghead obliterated not only the Pictish defences but also the unplanned fishing village from which it inherited its site.

9.7 THREE MODERN TOWNSCAPES *Newcastle upon Tyne, Cumbernauld and Glasgow*

The effects of the Industrial Revolution of the eighteenth and nineteenth centuries upon the townscapes of Britain were profound. In all the larger British towns, the pre-industrial cores form relatively small islands surrounded by oceans of post-industrial development, while in many cases, twentieth-century suburban sprawl dwarfs the earlier urban expanse. In the post-war period, urban planning policies became increasingly influential in the years before 1980, with attempts to check suburban sprawl by the creation of Green Belts, the establishment of satellite New Towns to relieve the pressures for growth on the larger metropolises, attempts to zone and segregate residential and industrial areas and efforts to modernise and rehabilitate congested or decrepit inner city areas.

Each phase of the nineteenth- and twentieth-century urban explosion has been marked by the adoption of different answers to the problem of mass housing. In the early and middle phases of the Industrial Revolution, the terraced row was universally popular. The earlier generation of terraces were spontaneous answers to the problems of providing cheap, high-density housing in constricted industrial areas and the dwellings tended to be standard cottages which happened to be joined together and which often constituted considerable improvements on other contemporary forms of working-class housing. Although the image of the terrace has been blackened by the tendency to associate it with the gruesome and unhygienic back-to-backs of Victorian industrialisation, which were developed to maximise the density of dwellings while ruthlessly minimising their cost, the terrace was in fact a very versatile form of housing. It could be elaborated and embellished to provide upper-middle-class suburban accommodation while subtle but vital variations in size, room arrangements and decoration distinguished the different grades of middle- and working-class terraced housing.

While terraces continued to be built on a massive scale in the earlier part of the twentieth century, the suburban middle-class semi became the archetypal dwelling of the democratic society. Though seldom held in much esteem by the arbiters of architectural taste, the semi tempted the aspiring middle-class owner with the illusion of privacy and independence and it was built according to designs which satisfied both the desires for conformity and individualism, with tiny variations in elevation and decoration meeting the latter demand.

If the semi represented a victory for the wishes of the home-buyer over the preconceptions of the architect, the tower block represented quite the reverse. It seemed to offer the solution to post-war political demands for a massive housing programme at a minimal cost, appealed to developers by economising on the need for costly building land and reflected the contemporary fancies of architectural fad merchants. Most parties now agree that in general the tower-block concept was a horrifying mistake. Low-level forms of high-density housing have proved to be as economical of land, while the terrible social consequences of life in the worst of the tower-block estates are now familiar to all and the coalitions of political, developmental and architectural interests are now exploring different and more diversified forms of mass housing.

In the photograph of a segment of Newcastle upon Tyne (9.7A), we see an intricate patchwork of largely pre-war housing, mainly established before stricter town planning policies created a more rigid ordering of our urban landscapes. The photograph is looking along the A69 which roughly follows the course of Hadrian's Wall, towards the heart of the city. The city centre lies near the upper left margin of the picture and is linked via the various Tyne bridges to Gateshead, where nineteenth-century industrialisation spawned some of the most deprived terraced slums. Scarcely visible amongst the jumble of development in the angle between the A69 and the river is the famous Scotswood Road, bound for Blaydon which lies across the river a little beyond the right-hand margin.

The Roman fort of Condercum lay in the very bottom left corner of the photograph, but the picture is dominated by the patterns of nineteenth- and early twentieth-century inner suburban development. The interlocking patterns of terraces, semis, civic buildings like the large hospital complex at the centre of the left-hand margin and occasional rows of prestigious detached villas reflect the characteristically piecemeal nature of development. The theme of disorganised growth is apparent in the upper section of the photograph, where the nineteenth-century landscape of factories, workshops and terraces is gradually surrendering to the residential and commercial tower blocks of modern city centre redevelopment.

A

B

The integrated and disciplined landscape of Cumbernauld in Strathclyde (9.7B) presents a complete contrast, for this is a scene which was born in the minds of planners and architects rather than developing from the rough and tumble of 'organic' urban and industrial growth. The first crop of fourteen New Towns created under the New Towns Act of 1946 were joined by later additions in the 50s and 60s. Glasgow overspill was diverted to East Kilbride, Glenrothes and the newer developments of Cumbernauld, begun in 1955 and Livingston, begun in 1962.

Cumbernauld is 12 miles from Glasgow and the photograph shows the imaginative, integrated development which was possible on this open site. Efforts were made to create a varied townscape, and though the by now traditional tower blocks are not absent, the photograph clearly shows the attempt to create high-density low-rise housing. In the foreground are futuristic developments of the old terrace concept and, just above, geometrical patterns of three-storey terraces which embrace courtyards and seem to derive some of their inspiration from the traditional Scottish tenements. Wholesale planning and integration allowed an efficient provision of main and access roads and the zoning of residential and industrial areas. From the air, we see a designer's eye view of the New Town, much as it will have appeared upon the drawing-board and the modernistic geometry is certainly impressive – although it is worth remarking that the residents of Cumbernauld will never see their home from this vantage point and the most impressive effects are not apparent to the man or woman on the street.

A less progressive modern townscape is shown in the photograph of the Springburn suburb of Glasgow (9.7c). In the foreground are tenements and tenement-inspired blocks of housing but the picture is dominated by the two clusters of four tower blocks and the remarkable curtain wall of seven-storey blocks which follows the road like a concrete python and houses more people than Lavenham (pl. 9.2B). At the upper extremity of the curtain wall is an older Glaswegian cameo of tenements and allotments, a deprived environment but one which may have been more conducive to the development of strong community relationships. In the upper right section of the photograph, the large building is – conveniently, the cynic may say – a mental hospital.

c

10.A *The Roman road of King Street ran along the edge of the Lincolnshire fen from Durobrivae near Peterborough to Bourne. As is so often the case, its outline is still traced in part by existing country roads. In the foreground, we see a typical situation with the surfaced road suddenly abandoning the old Roman routeway which then degenerates into an overgrown trackway. The essential straightness of the Roman route remains impressive*

10. INDUSTRY AND TRANSPORT

Ever since the products of the Neolithic stone axe factories were first dispersed across Britain by long-distance trackways (and probably by sea-routes, too), there has been a tight bond between industry and transport. The two activities are closely linked, for a developing industry will demand efficient communications for the assembly of its raw materials and the export of its products, while the establishment of a transport artery will stimulate the emergence of new manufacturing activities at key points along its route. Both industry and transport reflect the political and social conditions of their times. So, for example, the political fragmentation and instability of the Iron Age and the Dark Ages were reflected respectively in the lack of and the neglect of efficient long-distance routeways. Similarly, the invigoration of commerce during the Roman overlordship and the vitalisation of manufacturing during the early years of the Industrial Revolution helped to stimulate and sustain vital improvements to the transport system.

From the air as from the ground, routeways can be notoriously difficult to date: a skim of tarmac can endow a country track of an Iron Age vintage with a misleadingly modern appearance, while the abandonment of a section of eighteenth-century turnpike can result in an overgrown holloway which might seem medieval or prehistoric.

The prehistoric landscape of Britain developed a variety of different types of routeway, so that by the Iron Age there were the already ancient Stone Age routeways, younger trading routes, local trackways radiating from defensive and political centres, country lanes and field access tracks, river ferries and coastal and continental shipping routes. Indeed, it is quite probable that the framework of our rural road network was achieved before the close of the prehistoric period. Even so, the legacy of communications which the Romans inherited was an unplanned tangle of trackways set out by peoples who had no political vision of a united British realm and little or no enthusiasm for the engineering and maintenance of sophisticated transport arteries. The Romans had both the vision and the technology necessary, and they provided a coherent 'national' system of integrated long-distance and intra-regional roads which served both the military and commercial needs of the day.

The same roads were obliged to serve the same needs in many later days too, when the political and administrative talents for transport planning on the grand scale had been lost. For well over a millennium after the Roman withdrawal, many of the Roman alignments provided the main highways of the realm and new road-building undertakings tended to be of a localised, piecemeal and pragmatic nature. Some new or revitalised routeways developed in relation to commercial activities such as salt-trading and cattle-droving, but most improvements had to wait until the turnpike era, mainly of the eighteenth and early nineteenth centuries. Even then, the improving Trusts operated at local or regional levels and so though the roads that they built or revitalised were far superior to their muddy, rutted predecessors, they hardly amounted to an integrated national network. It took a century and some twenty separate Acts for the turnpiking of the whole London to Carlisle road to be accomplished.

10.B *This landscape is the product of post-medieval Fenland colonisation and nineteenth-century railway development. The disciplined labyrinth of tracks constitutes the marshalling yards at the small Cambridgeshire town of March, at once both an East Anglian hub and an outpost of the rail transport industry whose past and future hang upon the nail of rail policy*

The scale of medieval river traffic was quite considerable, but this transport system was of course constrained by the natural endowment of navigable streams. The first stirrings of the Industrial Revolution highlighted the need for purpose-built waterways designed to link the emerging manufacturing centres to their raw materials and market areas. The first genuinely impressive canal was constructed by employees of the Duke of Bridgewater to link the products of his Worsley coalfield to the industrial and domestic markets of Manchester. The canal system developed as the lifelines of young industry, but in due course the canal network was eclipsed by that of the railways. Although the canals like railways could move along tunnels and bridges (or aqueducts), they were more susceptible to the problems of gravity and where the terrain was steep or lofty, expensive flights of canal locks, high level reservoirs and pumping systems were required. By the middle of the nineteenth century, the general outlines of the British railway network had been established. Even so, despite its apparent modernity, the system was less planned and integrated than the Roman road network. Rival companies duplicated alignments, speculation and optimism often exceeded the real economic potential of many tracks and the system was divided between a jumble of competing interests.

It can be argued that twentieth-century governments have been too ready to dismiss the canal system as outmoded, too reluctant to rationalise, reorganise and invest in the

10.c *Tilbury Docks, photographed in 1973 in the early days of the container revolution. Here we see a bustling junction between land and water transport with warehouses, heavy lorries, seagoing freighters, their attendant tugs and shoals of river barges converged at this important transhipment centre*

railway system, whilst responding too readily to the demands of the road transport lobbies. In the three fields of land, sea and air transport, the container revolution has made vital contributions to efficiency, but even the phenomenon of containerisation has been overshadowed by the post-war motorway revolution. The motorways are not really an indigenous development, being foreshadowed by the *autobahns* of pre-war Germany and the futuristic national, state and urban routeways of the USA.

Until well into the 1950s, the British road transport system was based upon piecemeal improvements to a haphazard tangle of inadequate routeways which was composed of fragments of road inherited from every preceding road or track-making era. While the priorities and policies of modern transport thinking can be questioned, the motorways are a principal component of what is arguably the first coherent transport and industrial development policy to be operated in Britain since Roman times. Modern improvements in power transmission, the reduction in the demands for bulky raw materials and the progress in miniaturisation and technological innovation have all tended to highlight the importance of industrial access to markets. No modern industrialist would consider establishing a new factory at any distance from a motorway without an unusual and compelling reason, and so the next chapters in the industrialisation of Britain will be closely guided by the motorway pattern which is now approaching completion.

10.1 GRIME'S GRAVES *Norfolk*

Although the topography in the air photograph may confuse the layman, this bit of countryside near Brandon has often been hailed as Britain's first factory. What we see are the overgrown relics of an efficient flint-mining industry which dates back to the later stages of the Neolithic period. Although the miners – like most of their medieval counterparts – were probably part-time workers, there was nothing haphazard or 'primitive' about the Stone Age activities at Grime's Graves. Flint occurs here in a number of roughly horizontal seams and the miners dug through the inferior 'topstone' and 'wallstone' layers to reach a band known as the 'floorstone', which contained the top-quality industrial flints.

The floorstone was found at depths of down to forty feet and it was quarried by sinking broad shafts vertically until the desired level was reached and then a series of radiating galleries were tunnelled into the horizontal floor-stone beds. Eventually the mining activities extended over an area of almost a hundred acres and the pocked and hummocky landscape which we see today consists of mounds of flint flakes interspersed with the depressions which result from the subsidence and compaction of the shaft back-fill. The masses of worked flint debris show that axeheads were prepared on site for export, probably as rough-outs which could be finished and polished elsewhere. From Grime's Graves, the axes were traded widely across England and even beyond, along important routeways such as the Icknield Way and Ridgeway (see pl. 10.2).

The buildings that are visible in the photograph relate to the modern existence of Grime's Graves as a popular historic monument: this is an exceptional site to visit with one of the excavated shafts normally open to the public.

The entrance to one of the galleries cut by Neolithic flint miners at Grime's Graves

A

Roads and trackways are amongst the oldest features of the man-made landscape. We know very little about the communication networks of the Old or Middle Stone Ages, when hunters may have followed the migration trails used by their prey. Certain ancient trackways such as the Ridgeway of Wessex and the southern Midlands and the East Anglian Icknield Way are known to have been used during the New Stone Age when communities were much less parochial and more the masters of their environment than the traditional views of prehistory allowed. The peasants of this period will have forged comprehensive networks of field-access tracks and local routeways but there were also the long-distance trade routes which seem particularly to have been associated with the distribution of the products of the leading stone axe factories.

The Ridgeway is probably the best known of these ancient highways; scores of stone axes have been found close to its line and it runs near to the Avebury complex of Stone Age monuments and beside the great long barrow and chambered tomb of Wayland's Smithy (which lies only a quarter of a mile from the lower margin of plate 10.2A).

Here can be seen one of the most dramatic sections of the Ridgeway, which ascends the chalk downs beside the well-preserved Iron Age hillfort of Uffington Castle in the lower part of the photograph and continues to follow the crest of the downland scarp eastwards for many miles. To the left of the hillfort is the familiar outline of the Uffington White Horse, one of two British hill figures of a probably Iron Age or Roman date and which may be a tribal totem engraved in the scarp face to symbolise territorial control.

Today the Ridgeway exists as a single trackway used by ramblers, farm vehicles and, sadly, by trail riders on motorcycles. In its Neolithic heyday, it probably appeared very differently, although it is unlikely to have existed as a forest trail for woodland clearance by the early farmers will have produced a downland landscape which was probably as thinly wooded as that which we see today. However, rather than existing as a single trackway, like other ancient routeways, the Ridgeway will have consisted of a 'zone of movement' containing many branching, sub-parallel tracks, worn and slightly hollowed by the passage of feet and hooves. It will have been unsurfaced, although we know that Neolithic communities were capable of engineering artificial timber causeways across areas of marshy terrain such as the Somerset Levels.

In plate 10.2B, which shows a section of Postern Hill just to the south-east of Marlborough, we see the evidence of a zone of movement as previously described. The Ridgeway runs in a north-south direction about four miles to the west of this site and no specific date is available for this complex of old hollowed tracks which ascend the hill flanks. Even so, the branching, fanning and joining form of these holloways suggest the original form and appearance of the major prehistoric routeways.

B

We tend to regard Roman roads as being the most ancient elements in our networks of communications. Even so, they may be relatively youthful in comparison with the majority of our winding, undated and for most purposes undatable country lanes and trackways, which probably have Iron Age or older origins. Although the British province of the Roman Empire will have been traversed by a close pattern of tracks and routeways, the Romans were the first rulers to form a comprehensive vision and plan of the territory. The integrated system of roads which they created was arguably their greatest and most enduring development. The Roman network provided the basis not only of the Dark Age communication system, but also that of the medieval period and such achievements in planning and road engineering were not again approached until the turnpike era of the eighteenth and early nineteenth centuries. Arguably, they were not equalled until the post-war motorway age.

Most if not all of the Roman roads were constructed by the military. The first generation of Roman roads were inspired by the problems of conquest and political power transmission. Although the later roads in the northern and western uplands were heavily influenced by the needs to patrol and pacify the more remote and unruly territories, the roads of the lowland zone became important commercial arteries and urban links whilst retaining their military value.

The older lanes and trackways remained in use during the occupation and the Roman roads themselves came in many forms. The more important routeways ran on raised, ditch-flanked banks or aggers, were surfaced with sand, gravel or cobbles and stood upon rubble foundations to assist drainage. They were straight, but not uncompromisingly so, and where natural hill or river features demanded diversions, the sweeping curves that resulted often consisted of a number of short, straight sections. Perhaps the most impressive feature of the major Roman arteries concerns the sureness with which they are sighted on the distant target town or camp and much is still to be learned about Roman long-distance survey techniques.

While the Roman roads varied in their size, importance and constructional details they are even more varied as features of the modern landscape. Some still carry long-distance highways, some are ploughed out and others emerge as holloways or overgrown aggers under pasture. Many carry surfaced country lanes for short distances before degenerating into footpaths or field tracks and then re-emerging into the pattern of modern roads. The photographs reveal two formerly important Roman roads in different stages of use.

Dere Street, pl. 10.3A, ran from the Yorkshire Ouse to the Forth and was the eastern partner in a pair of major Roman routeways into Scotland. It provided a northern continuation of Ermine Street from York through the town and military base at Corbridge near Hadrian's Wall. The road survived into the medieval period and is known by a Saxon name which probably means 'beast' or 'deer'. The section in the photograph endures as a grassy, tree-flanked avenue and lies near to Ancrum in the former county of Roxburghshire.

The second photograph, pl. 10.3B, reveals a section of the Fosse Way surviving as a country road near Moreton Morrell in Warwickshire. The Fosse Way was an important highway running from Exeter to Lincoln. It originated as a lateral line of communication during an early phase of the Roman conquest of our island, when the frontier zone corresponded roughly to the Trent and Severn valleys, but it continued in use after the frontier had been pushed north as a vital long-distance routeway.

A

10.4 RELICS OF THE PEASANT MINER *Garrow Downs, Cornwall*

Many forms of industrial activity were practised in the medieval period but the scale and productivity of manufacturing were at relatively low levels. The industrial workers were often part-timers and this was particularly true of those who were active in the extractive industries such as coal, lead and tin mining. Often the mining took place on commons where the mineral rights were generally owned by and leased from the lords of the relevant manors. In Cornwall, the extraction of tin has been important since the Bronze Age and beside the stream in the lower part of the photograph, evidence can be seen of pre-industrial tin working. Particularly well-represented are the relics of the farmstead and land-holding of a medieval tin miner.

We know little about the families of peasant-miners who lived and laboured in this barren setting on Bodmin Moor, but we can be sure that they were all as tough as old boots. The thin acid soils of these granite slopes will have offered damp peat, masses of rocks and boulders and little encouragement to the part-time farmers, yet we can see how stones were gathered to provide the farmstead and field

walls in the farmed area in the lower left quadrant. We can also see how narrow plough ridges were built up and the kinks and wiggles in the ridges where the plough was deflected by intransigent rocky outcrops.

Tin working and farming must have provided a bare subsistence here until some unknown date when the family fortunes finally decayed. Other banks or lynchets just above right of centre offer hints that Bronze Age peasants, perhaps wedded to similar lifestyles, may once have been settled here.

10.5 COAL MINES ▶
Catherton Common, Shropshire

On Catherton Common near Hopton Wafers, the relics of medieval coal mining are quite spectacular when seen from the air. In most respects, the mining technology which was available to the medieval coal workers was far closer to that which was employed by the Stone Age flint quarriers of Grime's Graves than to the shaft mining capabilities

which developed in the course of the Industrial Revolution.

Coal was a significant fuel and raw material during the medieval period but its potential was held in check by the inability to employ it effectively as a smelting fuel in the iron industry. As a domestic fuel, the importance of coal was constrained by the general medieval inability to plan or maintain an efficient road transport network and by practical difficulties in mining techniques. Some coal was obtained by open cast and adit mining methods, but on Catherton Common we see the effects of bell-pit mining which was commonly practised in the period before the development of pumping systems to permit deeper shaft mining.

Rather in the manner of the Grime's Graves miners, the coal workers would dig a vertical pit and then exploit the seams around its base. The undercutting of the base of the pit produced a bell-shaped excavation and when the pit was abandoned, the collapse of the narrower bell top produces ring-doughnut-like features such as these in the photograph. When seen *en masse* in areas where successive pits have been dug close together, the aerial view of the relict workings reminds me of frogspawn.

Irregular as well as planned enclosures have colonised some of the extensive former workings, but the most severely pitted areas with their unstable and dross-strewn lands and steeply rolling contorsions remain unenclosed.

This section of the Severn Gorge has a better claim than any other place to the title of 'the cradle of world industry'. A local industrial tradition, based on readily available resources of coal and iron as well as the water transport provided by the Severn, was deeply rooted, but the small scale of the operations and the primitive technology employed was not such as to launch an Industrial Revolution.

The greatest single achievement which set the wheels of industry in motion was Abraham Darby's successful application of coal as a fuel in iron smelting. Darby leased a small charcoal blast furnace at Coalbrookdale in 1708. Perhaps influenced by experiments carried out by Dud Dudley, Darby realised that coal might be employed in smelting if it were first converted into coke, a purer form of carbon and free from unwanted gases and contaminants. By good fortune or design, he was able to exploit the local coals which had low sulphur contents. Darby died in 1717 and a decade passed before his son was old enough to continue the expansion of the Coalbrookdale Company; by 1798, three generations of the family had created Britain's largest iron-making business, then valued at £95,424.

The extensive Darby operations were surrounded by other activities including lead smelting and cottage pottery industries and, in the closing decades of the eighteenth century, porcelain, bitumen, brick and chain-making industries developed. Although the Severn was a vital artery for the shipment of raw materials and manufactures, it was also a hazardous barrier to meet across its valley. The challenge was met by Abraham Darby III who produced castings for a revolutionary iron bridge which was completed in 1781. By this time, according to most modern opinions, the Industrial Revolution was entering its third decade.

The aerial photograph shows a view up the Severn Gorge. The Iron Bridge spans the river in the middle distance and above and beyond lie the Darby works at Coalbrookdale. In the foreground are the still-intact bottle kilns of the Coalport porcelain works while the coal and ironstone mines, brick and tile works and potteries of Calcutts, Jackfield and Broseley punctuate the scene.

This is a vintage and valuable air photograph, taken in 1948 when several of the small and venerable works portrayed were still going concerns, although by-passed by modern patterns of industrial development. Thus the picture precedes both the closure and partial destruction of the sites and the magnificent conservation and display achievements enacted at so many of the works in recent years. It also provides a vivid record of a fossilised and typical early industrial landscape, for while the initial development of the Gorge produced scenes that seemed outlandish and even Satanic to contemporary folk, we can see that the scenery preserved much of its rural character. Although this area was a leading British seedbed of industry at the turn of the eighteenth century, the works were small by modern standards and quite loosely distributed in a countryside of small industrial villages like Jackfield, Broseley, Benthall, Madeley and Iron Bridge. Each phase in the industrialisation of Britain created its own characteristic scenery, as a comparison of this picture with those of Hanley (pl. 10.7A) and Milton Keynes (pl. 10.9) will plainly show.

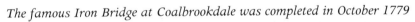

The famous Iron Bridge at Coalbrookdale was completed in October 1779

A

10.7 THE POTTERIES *Hanley, Staffordshire*

Taken in 1949, this is a vintage air photograph and it serves to demonstrate that air photographs are valuable not only as specialist research aids revealing unsuspected archaeological features as crop, soil or shadow marks, but also as historic documents in their own right. The plumes of smoke rising from some of the chimneys and bottle kilns show that in 1949 this venerable industrial landscape was still a going concern. I visited this area in 1964 as a geography student and our research project involved a survey of industrial dereliction. In 1971, I returned as an Open University summer school tutor and by this time gas-firing had been adopted in the surviving pottery workshops and the bottle kiln had become a curio in a landscape experiencing both industrial decline and imaginative environmental rehabilitation. Meanwhile, Hanley was re-emerging as a shopping and commercial centre for the Potteries towns.

The photograph shows an area close to the joining of the Grand Junction (or Trent and Mersey) and Caldon canals and the A50 runs across the former canal from centre left to lower right.

This is an area closely associated with the greatest pioneer of the British pottery industry, Josiah Wedgwood. In 1760, at the very dawn of the Industrial Revolution, the local pottery industry employed about 7000 workers. Nine years later, Wedgwood opened his famous Etruria works on a site which is about a mile beyond the left-hand margin of the photograph. The Grand Junction Canal was completed in 1777 providing economical water transport for the china clay which was imported from Cornwall to combine with the local coal and flints from eastern counties in the pottery processes, while also facilitating the export of the delicate wares. When John Wesley described the area a few years later, he told of people flowing in from every side and the springing up of houses, villages and towns: 'Hence the wilderness is literally become a fruitful field.' By 1785, Wedgwood estimated that the local pottery industry employed 15,000 people.

The landscape displayed in the photograph is redolent of the earlier phases of industrialisation in Britain: an ugly but gutsy hotch-potch of small workshops, belching furnaces, blackened terraces of workers' dwellings all bound together by polluted waterways. The growth of the industry in this corner of Hanley outstripped any feeble efforts to plan the development, resulting in a typically congested and chaotic scene which was once brimful of activity, craftsmanship and character.

The second photograph, pl. 10.7B, shows a scene which is characteristic of the areas where the china clay for the Staffordshire potteries was quarried. The snow-white kaolin is a natural by-product of the decomposition of granite. These workings lie around St Stephen in Cornwall; a quarry is seen as a broad white gash just below the centre of the photograph and glaring mounds of kaolin and waste superimpose an outlandish lunar character on the mellow Cornish countryside. The great bleached cones of quarrying debris provide insalubrious environments for most plants and the pioneering colonists establish themselves but slowly. As a result, the level of plant establishment is a good guide to the age of the workings and in the lower left part of the photograph can be seen a close juxtaposition of new and old waste mounds.

B

241

10.8 BUILDWAS POWER STATION *Shropshire*

This photograph was taken in 1970, shortly after the opening of the vast new electric power station at Buildwas beside the Severn. It provides us with a particularly fine opportunity to compare the contrasting landscapes of modern and early industrialisation for the area of eighteenth- and nineteenth-century development around Coalbrookdale and the Severn Gorge lies a little more than a mile downstream to the south-east.

Dominating the setting are the four great cooling towers whose construction was denounced by many conservationists in the area and which are visible in the semi-rural landscape for miles around. On closer inspection of the photograph, one can recognise the feeder railway track, coal trucks, conveyors and, radiating outwards, the power transmission lines which also produce a serious disfiguration of the countryside. A few miles from the power station and just beyond the upper left margin of our photograph, the new town of Telford, named after the great early nineteenth-century road-builder and civil engineer Thomas Telford, is extending over the Shropshire coalfield as an overspill centre for the industrial Midlands.

The photograph also serves reminders that each new development in Britain is superimposed upon many layers of previous human history and endeavour. Buildwas is a

significant historical site, the setting of a Domesday village and manor which appear to have been absorbed after the establishment of the Cistercian Buildwas Abbey in 1135. During the medieval period, the Abbey experienced Welsh raids, the abbot being kidnapped in 1350 and the estates wasted in 1406. In 1535 the Abbey was dissolved and the glimmerings of industrialisation could be recognised in the decades which followed when the monastic iron forge was taken over by private entrepreneurs and, in due course, by pioneers of the Industrial Revolution including the Darbys who developed Coalbrookdale.

10.9 MODERN DEVELOPMENT ▶ *Milton Keynes, Buckinghamshire*

In 1801, the population of Great Britain was less than 11 million and the majority of people lived in rural settings. As the Industrial Revolution continued to gather momentum during the nineteenth century, so population and urbanisation grew. The census of 1861 showed a population of 23 million and by this time town-dwellers had be-

gun to outnumber country folk. In the 1950s, population topped the 50 million mark but the increase had been concentrated in urban areas and townsfolk now made up more than three-quarters of the nation. Although population in general has tended to stabilise in recent years, detailed figures have revealed areas of industrial decline and others with high rates of growth. The expansion of the favoured centres has resulted in urban growth across thousands of previously rural acres while the post-war motorway revolution has made its own massive advances across the countryside.

During the post-war period, the uneven nature of British development gave rise to fears that the dynamic south-east and London in particular were acting as a whirlpool, sucking more and more development into the area of massive economic advantage and this trend foreshadowed many problems of hyperconcentration. In the late 1940s, a number of New Town satellites were designated to receive London overspill but continuing high levels of growth in and around London suggested the need for a broader strategy. The South-East Study of 1964 advocated the establishment of major new cities at Bletchley, Newbury and Southampton to redistribute population growth and economic development; the Strategy for the South-East of 1967 envisaged Bletchley—Milton Keynes as one of a number of counter-magnets to the pull of London, while the Milton

Keynes—Northampton—Wellingborough zone was highlighted as a major growth zone in the Strategic Plan for the South-East in 1970. The 1971 census revealed a population of 46,500 already established in Milton Keynes.

The photograph, which was taken two years later, reveals a part of the landscape of new town creation at Milton Keynes. The pattern of modern urban and industrial growth contrasts enormously with the unplanned nineteenth-century urban chaos displayed in the photograph of Hanley (pl. 10.7A).

The photograph is looking northwards along the construction works of the A4146 and the junction with the emerging A421 is at the foot of the picture. The colossal developments are superimposed upon fields which still display the traces of medieval ridge and furrow, while the old village of Woughton on the Green near the top of the photograph is about to be lassoed by development. Since this photograph was taken, urban development has spread across most of the fields in the left and centre of the picture. The old Grand Union canal runs diagonally across the upper right corner of the photograph, a relic of a different industrial era. Beyond it is the River Ouzel, while many resourceful and hard-working readers will be interested to note that the buildings which are just visible in the upper right corner are those of The Open University, Walton Hall.

10.10 THE AGE OF THE MOTORWAY

We are familiar with the designation of different periods of the past as the 'Bronze Age', the 'Railway Age' and so on and it is interesting to speculate on how our descendants will label the times in which we live. Unless we are careful, this might be the Nuclear Age, but optimism suggests that the historians may refer to our period as the Motorway Age. Like the Roman roads and the railways of previous eras, the motorways have transformed our industrial activities, our lifestyles and large stretches of our landscape. For better or for worse they have captured a large share of the transport trade from the railways and profoundly expanded the opportunities for high speed travel.

Unlike most other landscape features, the nature and development of motorways require no explanation here but the aerial pageant of landscape history would be incomplete if motorways were omitted. As many travellers will know, motorways can be both tedious and frightening, but from the air the ribbons of road metal, the spiralling access and departure lanes and the tanglesome interchanges produce strange, almost unearthly patterns.

The first photograph, pl. 10.10A, portrays one of the most dramatic sections of motorway where the M6 north-western routeway sweeps south through the steep confines of the Lune valley between Lancaster and Penrith. The dual carriageways, which have been obliged to separate by the steep terrain, converge in the lower part of the photograph before passing through the swirl of access and departure lanes at the junction with the A685 by the village of Tebay. The massive scale of the motorway helps to distort our senses of perception, for the road bridge beyond the roundabout which carries the A685 across the M6 en route for Kendal is more than a mile from the interchange.

The second photograph, pl. 10.10B reveals the almost Gordian knot of routeways at the junction between two motorways, the M23 and M25 near Caterham in Surrey. Motorway design seeks to maintain a rapid and uninterrupted flow of traffic by ensuring that all vehicles enter or leave the routeway via slip roads to the left and, bearing in mind that traffic in Britain drives on the left, one can pick a way through this photograph and see how traffic arriving from any one direction can leave this interchange in any of the other three.

A

B

10.11 HEATHROW AIRPORT

For millions of the British and their visitors, this is almost the first and last view of the United Kingdom. The photograph, which is unusual in this collection in being a high level vertical view, reveals the striking geometry of the airport buildings, runways and taxiways. The tiny barbed darts which are airliners can be seen, neatly marshalled at the different terminals; one is near the centre of the upper runway and another can be glimpsed close to the left-hand margin of the photograph, about to enter the lower runway and commence its take-off run.

11.A *The monastic ruins of Bardney Abbey in Lincolnshire are virtually levelled*

11. CHRISTIANITY IN BRITAIN: A DIFFERENT PERSPECTIVE

Christian monuments of different sizes and ages provide some of our most attractive essays in architectural development. Usually they also have interesting histories, whether concerning the missionary activities of the conversion period, the majestic building operations of the High Middle Ages, the accumulation of vast monastic empires or the destruction of centuries-old communities during the Dissolution. The pages which follow provide an unusual perspective upon the church in Britain.

Each viewing point has its advantages and disadvantages. In the course of a conventional church visit, one has an opportunity to admire the medieval mastery of carpentry or stone-carving as displayed in roofing timbers, pews, screens, gargoyles, capitals or façades. When viewing churches from above, the interior details remain mysterious and we are poorly placed to appraise the quality of the decoration. Instead, one is rewarded with a view of the totality of the external architectural achievement and the churches are seen in a way which was denied even to the master masons and sponsors who designed them.

One is also in a better position to appreciate their plan and layout. This is particularly valuable in the case of the larger, ruinous monastic houses. Many visitors to these monuments have great difficulty in understanding how the different and apparently amorphous collections of tumbled walls and foundation relics fitted together to produce a complex of monastic buildings. These layouts seem much more comprehensible when they are viewed from above and so the onlooker is an important step closer to an understanding of the buildings before their destruction.

This point is particularly well made by the photograph of Bardney Abbey in Lincolnshire, where the monastic ruins are virtually levelled. It had an unusual origin which it shared with early foundations at Whitby, Ely and four other houses, some endowed by Saxon queens or princesses, as a double monastery of men and women under the rule of an abbess. Although the monastic relics are scarcely perceptible from the ground, from the air the snow-dusted landscape reveals the outlines of buildings, cloisters and fishponds, while the cruciform outline of the abbey church is particularly well-displayed, with a double row of 'studs' marking the positions of the piers which flanked the aisle.

The country surrounding Castle Acre Priory in Norfolk has also received a light dusting of snow, highlighting the earthworks which lie beyond the immediate confines of the abbey. They represent a variety of structures and, to select a rather prosaic example, the channel which runs diagonally from the upper right corner of the abbey buildings to the upper right corner of the photograph reveals a former artificial stream course. It was constructed to run through the monastic kitchen (which appears as the detached rectangular building to the right of the bottom-right corner of the abbey complex), before flowing onwards to flush the 'reredorter' or monastic lavatory which is built over the stream. The 'dorter' or dormitory adjoins the reredorter at a right angle and is linked to the great abbey church, which runs along the left-hand side of the complex, by the

11.B *The light fall of snow has highlighted the earthworks of Castle Acre Priory in Norfolk*

chapter house. The cloister occupies the rectangular space between the church and dorter while the Prior's lodgings stand at the lower left of the abbey buildings.

As well as providing more comprehensible perspectives on the layouts of the greater churches and religious houses, air photographs also help us to see the buildings in terms of their setting. From the ground, the visitor will often find that the surroundings of these ecclesiastical *tours de force* are dominated and obscured by the massive, towering religious buildings. The effect of a soaring tower or finely-detailed façade may be diminished when it is seen from above, but from the air the buildings are seen in their environmental context.

This statement is underlined by the fine photograph of Wells cathedral (pl. 11.5), which portrays the domestic ecclesiastical buildings that are the neighbours of the great cathedral, and the point is equally apparent in the following photograph of Canterbury cathedral. Not only does it provide a comprehensive view of this magnificent accumulation of medieval building which dates from the Norman rebuilding of an older church destroyed by fire in 1174 to the completion of the magnificent central Bell Harry tower in the late fifteenth century, but it plainly reveals the outlines of the great cathedral close. At some cathedrals, the buildings of the surrounding town were allowed to huddle and straggle close to the walls of the church, but others which were associated with monastic orders required a certain aloofness and separation from the lay dwellings. Writing of Canterbury cathedral close, Batsford and Fry remarked that it was '. . . one of the most fascinating architectural mazes in England, and it is a morning's task to explore with a plan its several green courts and walled alleys, its ruined arcades and pleasant Georgian canons' houses.' They were writing in 1934, when few air photographs were available and there is no doubt that our photograph would have given them better service than their plan!

The selection of photographs which follows is heavily biased in favour of the larger churches and religious houses at the expense of the humbler parish churches. The logic behind the choice is simple and centres on the 'horses for courses' maxim: most parish churches have simple plans based upon the tower, nave and chancel components. Their homelier charms are best enjoyed from the ground and, in portraying the larger and more complicated foundations, we are playing to the strengths of the air photographic medium.

11.C *A comprehensive view of Canterbury Cathedral, including the great cathedral close*

11.D *Surrounding streets press close to the walls of York Minster*

A

11.1 KNOWLTON *Dorset*

Long after the beliefs of the Neolithic religion had been forgotten, its temples and monuments continued to be revered by other pagan cults. During the conversion of the English kingdoms to Christianity, a number of pagan temples, shrines and holy wells were adopted by the missionaries and the Christianisation of places which had been hallowed in pagan worship was indeed official policy of the Roman church. This was expressed in a letter sent by Pope Gregory to Abbot Mellitus in 601, in which the Abbot was instructed that the old temples '. . . must be purified from the worship of demons and dedicated to the service of the true God'.

The surviving church at Knowlton does not date from the age of conversion, the body of the building being Norman and the tower dating from the fifteenth century. It does stand, however, within a massive Neolithic henge

monument, the central and best preserved member of a group of three, which has a diameter of about 320 ft. To its upper left in pl. 11.1A can be seen the faint outlines of a much larger henge which is cut by the B3078 Cranborne—Wimborne road, but the third henge in the group is scarcely visible. There is also a large round barrow masked by a circular clump of trees to the left of the central henge.

The village which Knowlton church served is now deserted. It lay some distance away on the flanks of a valley, so the decision to build its church in a remote location demonstrates the magnetism of the ancient pagan earthworks.

On pl. 11.1B, the outlines of the old churchyard can be seen on the flat ground inside the henge ditch.

B

The first monastery on Holy Island was a very early foundation dating from 634 when King Oswald of Northumbria established a community of Celtic monks from Iona on the island. Their mission was the conversion of the northern part of the kingdom to Christianity. The first bishop and abbot was St Aidan and later in the seventh century St Cuthbert led the community. During this early period of greatness, the glorious Lindisfarne Gospels were produced. Troubled times were to follow, and in 793 the monastery experienced the first Danish raid on English territory. In 875, following a succession of barbarian raids, the monks abandoned their island and the relics of St Cuthbert were lodged in the relative security of Durham.

In 1083, following the Norman Conquest and with the Viking threat virtually extinguished, William of St Calais, Bishop of Durham, decided to re-establish a community on the island as a dependent priory of Durham cathedral. In the fourteenth century, Holy Island became a strategic base used in the distribution of supplies for English armies engaged in Scottish and border campaigns. As a result, fortifications against Scottish attack were installed. A ridge of basalt which runs across the upper right corner of the photograph carries a small medieval fort. Near the upper central portion of the monastic ruins, the massive chimney of the warming house is a prominent landmark and just above it are the thick walls of a defensive suite of chambers which carried a tower in their uppermost angle.

Some Norman masonry survives but most of the buildings displayed are of the thirteenth and fourteenth centuries. Running along the left side of the ruins is the early twelfth-century church which was extended later in the century by the lengthening of the chancel which forms its upper left portion. The cloister lay to its right and was flanked by cellars and the pantry (below) and the chapter house (above). To the right of the cloister was the frater or refrectory and beyond the frater, the large rectangular enclosure of the outer court. Immediately below the monastic buildings is the island's impressive thirteenth-century parish church.

11.3 RECULVER *Kent*

There are several associations between early Christian churches and Roman shore-forts. Around 630, the Irish missionary St Fursey founded a monastery inside the walls of Burgh Castle in Suffolk and about 654, St Cedd established the still surviving chapel of St Peter-on-the-Walls astride one wall of the fort of Othona, near Bradwell-on-Sea in Essex and the ruined fortifications provided a quarry for building materials. At Reculver, half of the eight-acre Saxon Shore fort of Regulbium has been eroded by the sea, but the portion containing the church survives. A section of the defensive Roman wall can be seen directly below the church.

The church was built around 669 when Egbert, the Ken-

tish King, donated the site to a priest called Bassa. Whatever other attractions the ruined fort may have had, its walls yielded copious supplies of tile-like bricks and other building materials. The most prominent remains comprise the twin Norman towers which are still important navigational aids to coastal shipping. Excavation has revealed the outlines of the original Saxon church and the photograph shows the bright outlines of the nave, the rounded apsidal chapel and flanking porticus which lie inside the tumbled masonry of the larger medieval church. Human figures, most of them staring up at the Cambridge University aeroplane provide an impression of the scale of the remains.

One of the most interesting but less well-known aspects of Christianity in the British landscape concerns the ways in which the rules and history of different monastic orders found expression in the architecture and layout of the houses which they founded. The Carthusian House of the Assumption of the Most Blessed Virgin and St Nicholas of Mount Grace in Ingelby – to give this Charterhouse its full title – was built near Northallerton by one of the less prominent orders. The Carthusians originated from a community of hermits founded by St Bruno in 1084. Their first Charterhouse was established on a bleak, mountainous site in the diocese of Grenoble; other hermit communities were spawned in Italy, and the first house of the order in England was created in 1178, as part of the penance of Henry II for his part in the murder of Thomas à Becket.

The Carthusians followed a rugged and ascetic lifestyle and deliberately avoided the expansion of their houses into vast and richly-endowed establishments. Mount Grace was a late arrival on the monastic stage, being founded in 1398 and then precipitated into an endowment dispute when the founder, Thomas Holland, suffered execution and forfeiture by the new king, Henry VI, in 1400. The monastic buildings were unostentatious, in accordance with the principles of their order; for most of the community's existence there was a prior, sixteen monks, three novices and six lay-brothers. Unlike most other orders, the Carthusians rejected communal dormitories and, perpetuating the hermit tradition, each monk had a private cell to which a patch of land was attached. The lozenge-shaped enclosure near the centre of the photograph opposite was the great cloister and the cells and their adjoining gardens were set around the sides of the cloister. One of the cells has been reconstructed and one can see the doorways to a number of others and just discern a few of the adjacent food hatches, through which the monks were given food. Just below and slightly to the right of the main cloister was a lesser cloister surrounded by six cells, but only its outlines are visible. Below the great and lesser cloisters was the outer court and between it and the cloisters can be seen the ruins of the priory church, a simple building only 88 ft in length. Below and to the left of the church can be seen a well-preserved range of buildings representing one of the two original guest houses which has been preserved as a result of its conversion into a private dwelling in the mid-seventeenth century by Sir Thomas Lascelles.

The Carthusians were often criticised by members of other monastic orders for their introspection, the apparent dullness of their contemplative life and lack of missionary zeal. Although they avoided the accumulation of wealth and assets or the corruption which afflicted some of the more powerful orders, they did not escape the Dissolution. In 1534, four monks from Mount Grace were imprisoned for refusing the Oath of Supremacy, although the Archbishop of York managed to persuade the Prior to take the Oath. In 1539, the Prior surrendered his foundation to the king.

Mount Grace is the best-preserved Charterhouse in the country

11.5 WELLS CATHEDRAL *Somerset*

Many connoisseurs of church building regard Wells as the loveliest of the British medieval cathedrals. From the air, we are in a poor position to appraise the splendour of the ornate carving which graces the West Front, but are well-placed to appreciate the lovely and historically fascinating cathedral setting.

A church has stood here since the start of the eighth century, while a recent excavation has produced hints that a Roman settlement may have occupied the same site. Wells became a diocesan centre in 909; the Saxon church was replaced by a Norman cathedral in the reign of Stephen and the building was consecrated in 1148. The cathedral that we see today results from the remodelling of the Norman building during the episcopate of Reginald de Bohun (1174–91), and further building in the thirteenth and early fourteenth centuries. The central tower was completed in 1322, by which time the exterior of the cathedral had developed most of the form that we see today.

The original foundation seems to have been closely linked to the Holy Well of St Andrew, which lies in the bushes just to the right of the cathedral. The recent excavations helped to resolve the puzzle presented by the lack of alignment between the cathedral and the planned market place of Wells (which in our photograph runs diagonally towards the gatehouse below the cathedral cloister and has a central parking reservation). It was demonstrated that the Saxon cathedral was aligned between the Holy Well and market place, but when the buildings were redesigned during Bishop Reginald's construction of the new church in the Early English manner, the old alignment was abandoned for a more orthodox east-west orientation.

The medieval cathedral close survives virtually intact and is surrounded by the dwellings of church dignitaries. Running diagonally upwards from the central tower to the upper left corner of the photograph is Vicars' Close. In the twelfth and thirteenth centuries, the vicars, who were the appointed deputies of the fifty canons and who were required to be in quire for the daily masses, had scattered lodgings in the town. Convenient accommodation in the form of Vicars' Close was planned in 1348, but owing to the arrival of the Black Death in this year, the work was not completed until 1360 and was an early exercise in terraced building. The tall but standardised chimneys were added a century later, following new domestic fashions.

Below the cathedral and to its right is the medieval moat inside which is the Bishop's palace. The moat and the formidable wall with corner and gatehouse turrets which follows its inner bank were built in 1340. Many cathedrals preserve their medieval masonry but have become encircled by nondescript post-medieval buildings. At Wells, most of the medieval setting has survived and so one can appreciate the close and the domestic accommodation for greater and lesser churchmen who composed the numerous community which was attendant to each great cathedral.

11.6 SWEETHEART ABBEY *Dumfries & Galloway*

Built of mellow red sandstone according to the architectural principles of the Early English style then current, Sweetheart Abbey was founded in 1273. Its pretty name in fact derives from a rather gruesome relic, for the foundress of the abbey was Lady Devorguilla, wife of John Balliol, the father of the Scottish puppet king of the same name. On John's death, she carried his embalmed heart in an ivory and silver casket. Sweetheart was one of three religious houses which Devorguilla founded, two were occupied by friars, while Sweetheart was a Cistercian foundation colonised from Dundrennan twenty miles to the south-west which dated from 1142 and which was itself a daughter house of Rievaulx Abbey.

The Catholic mass was officially abolished in Scotland in 1560 but, in 1565, Gilbert Brown of Carsluith became the abbot of Sweetheart and displayed a determined and courageous adherence to the old faith. Three times he was arrested and exiled to France for his defence and celebration of the Catholic rites before his death in France in 1612.

Better preserved than most such ruins, the abbey church displays a simple cruciform plan and, though roofless, most of the walls stand to their original heights. The remaining monastic buildings are very poorly preserved, but to the right of the south (right-hand) transept, the chambers outlined by masonry were, from left to right, the sacristy and library; the chapter house; the narrow treasury; the parlour, and the warming house. The other buildings have almost completely vanished through the ravages of stone-robbers and the survival of the abbey church results from its voluntary protection and conservation by the local community in the years before 1928 when the responsibilities were assumed by the government.

Though roofless, most of the walls of Sweetheart Abbey stand to their original heights

11.7 LIVERPOOL ANGLICAN CATHEDRAL *Mersey*

There is a line in a popular Merseyside song that relates 'If you want a cathedral, we've got one to spare.' It is not so tactless as to specify which cathedral is on offer, for Liverpool is unusual in having two cathedrals, one Anglican, the other Roman Catholic – and both are twentieth-century creations. The Anglican cathedral is shown in our photographs and although its recent completion attracted far less national publicity than the rebuilding of the bomb-damaged cathedral at Coventry, it became the second largest cathedral in the world, surpassed only by St Peter's in Rome. Unlike the modernistic designs employed at Liverpool's Catholic cathedral and at Coventry, the Anglican building is more conservative and has a superficially medieval appearance. Both cathedrals became widely discussed when they were seen on television at the time of Pope John Paul II's visit in 1982.

It also bears some comparison with medieval cathedrals in terms of the time taken to complete the colossal structure. Sir Giles Gilbert Scott, a grandson of the great Victorian architect Sir George Gilbert Scott, won the competition for the cathedral design in 1901, at the age of twenty-one. Construction work began in 1904 but was delayed by shortages of funds, design changes and the disruption caused by two World Wars. Work in the 1970s centred on the completion of the nave interior.

Although the layout of the cathedral has some resemblances to that of St Paul's, it is primarily an unusual twentieth-century application of Gothic principles being less ornately fussy than much of nineteenth-century Gothic architecture. Despite the relative lack of media publicity, the design, in its final version, has been widely praised. The cathedral is undoubtedly the last of the line of stone-build cathedrals in Britain and the pinkish local sandstone is crowned by a green roof of copper. Unusually, the cathedral has a roughly north-south orientation rather than the conventional east-west alignment. This is determined by the form of the natural ridge which bears the great building. An abandoned graveyard lies in a deep, wooded former quarry and the tree-grown ridge provides an attractive frontage to the cathedral when it is approached from the left, or west. To the east lies the Merseyside dockland and

The second largest cathedral in the world, the Anglican Cathedral of Liverpool is built on a natural ridge

an elongated block of riverside warehouses can be seen in the upper right corner of the photograph. Rising above the jumble of nineteenth- and twentieth-century residential and industrial property and patches of slum clearance, the gigantic cathedral is a most imposing landmark. Although the impact of the terrain and of the 331-ft tower are diminished when viewed from the air, we are in a better position to appreciate the industrial setting and the unusual plan, with its emphasis on symmetry which is so unusual in a Gothic-based building, the paired transepts which flank the entrance porches and the small octagonal chapter house (upper left).

APPENDIX

AND ACKNOWLEDGEMENTS

The following list gives the dates on which the photographs were taken. All photographs marked with an * are the copyright of the University of Cambridge; the remaining photographs in these columns are Crown Copyright and are reproduced with the kind permission of the Controller of Her Majesty's Stationery Office.

Introduction

A	11. 7.55
B	5. 7.49
C	10. 7.49
D	20. 6.49

Chapter 1

A	18. 7.72*
B	27. 7.47*
C	22. 6.77*
1A	5. 7.49
B	3.10.73*
2A	4. 6.70*
B	26.11.73*
3	14. 6.73*
4	24.11.72*
5	25. 7.79*
6	24. 4.75*
7A	20. 3.55
B	13. 6.67*
8	14. 4.57
9	19. 7.49
10	24. 6.49
11A	3. 4.69*
B	17. 4.69*
C	26. 5.78*

Chapter 2

A	14. 7.51
B	14. 7.51
1A	24. 7.81*
B	22. 6.76*
2A	10. 7.58*
B	23. 1.76*
3	19. 7.51

4	1. 8.57
5	19. 5.71*
6	8.12.75*
7	10. 7.49
8	11. 7.49
9	31. 5.66*
10	9. 4.49
11	8. 4.56
12	20. 6.48*
13	27. 4.54

Chapter 3

A	24.11.72*
B	20. 4.71*
C	4. 7.53
1	4. 8.74*
2	30. 4.66*
3	29. 4.66*
4	4. 2.71*
5	24. 5.60*
6	21.11.75*
7	10. 3.54
8A	3. 4.63
B	23. 5.62*
9	25. 6.55
10	13.11.69*
11	28. 6.76*
12	25. 6.63*
13	2. 5.53
14	13. 7.57*
15	18. 6.51
16	29. 4.66*
17A	21. 6.77*
B	11. 7.51
18A	22. 6.77*

18B	3. 8.65*
19	25. 7.64*
20A	3. 7.75*
B	6.10.67*

Chapter 4

A	14. 7.51
B	2. 7.57*
C	6. 6.62
1	21. 6.66*
2	9. 7.62
3	24. 6.52
4	2. 1.67*
5	8. 6.62
6	3. 7.69*
7	26. 3.56
8A	16. 6.51
B	16. 6.51
9	3. 6.65*
10	28. 4.76*
11	11. 8.53
12	17. 6.51
13	15. 7.52
14	18.10.67*
15	6. 7.52
16	21. 7.55
17A	15. 7.59*
B	14. 7.51
18	21. 7.74*
19	7. 7.72*

Chapter 5

A	12. 4.63
B	4. 8.65*
C	13. 1.79*

1A 20. 1.78*
B 27. 1.69*
C 28.11.72*
D 27. 1.69*
E 27. 1.69*
F 20. 4.53
G 3. 1.66*
H 12. 3.66*
I 11. 6.50
J 27. 4.54
K 18.10.79*
2 25. 6.49
3 14. 6.62
4 3. 5.71*
5 29. 3.65*
6 21.12.68*
7 5.11.69*
8 1. 6.62*
9 13.11.69*
10 15. 7.52
11A 17. 6.51
B 5. 7.52
12 20.11.69*
13 11. 1.67*

Chapter 6
A 13. 5.68*
1A 16. 1.73*
B 17. 5.80*
2 28. 7.76*
3 16. 6.57*
4 1.10.73*

Chapter 7
A 14. 4.57
B 21.11.75*
16. 2.70*
1A 22. 7.49
B 4. 8.75*
2A 11. 6.50
B 18. 6.52
3 25. 5.62*
4 20. 7.48*
5 17. 5.70*
6 19. 6.48*
7 24. 6.54

8 25. 6.63*
9 14. 7.51
10 30. 7.68*
11 30. 6.49
12 26. 6.48*
13 24. 6.59*
14 23. 5.69*
15 15. 7.58
16 24. 7.48*
17 2. 5.67*

Chapter 8
A 1. 9.76*
B 30.11.70*
C 16. 6.48*
1A 20. 6.51
B 24. 6.49
2 4. 6.50
3 10. 6.50
4 14. 7.51
5 4. 6.50
6 29. 6.53
7A 25. 6.55
B 18. 6.48*
8 16. 6.48*
9 4. 6.50

Chapter 9
A 8. 7.64*
B 17. 7.61*
C 11. 7.51
D 21. 6.77*
1A 27. 6.60*
B 23. 6.70*
C 23. 6.70*
D 7. 7.75*
E 11. 7.51
2A 13. 4.53
B 2. 8.51
C 28. 3.55
D 22. 7.56
3A 11. 7.49
B 11. 7.74*
C 20. 7.48*
D 14. 6.56
4A 16. 7.68*

4B 2. 8.51
C 21. 4.53
5A 19. 6.51
B 13. 7.47*
C 12. 7.55
6A 22. 7.56
B 16. 4.74*
C 28. 7.68*
D 25. 7.64*
7A 21. 6.77*
B 9. 7.71*
C 8. 8.77*

Chapter 10
A 23. 7.58*
B 13.11.70*
C 25. 4.73*
1 15. 1.75*
2A 1.10.73*
B 22. 4.53
3A 26. 7.53
B 3. 6.53
4 7. 6.62
5 2. 2.79*
6 27. 6.48*
7A 23. 7.49
B 28. 4.66*
8 18. 5.70*
9 14. 2.73*
10A 21. 6.77*
B 18. 6.76*
11 30.10.81*

Chapter 11
A 10. 2.78*
B 10. 2.69*
C 29. 6.73*
D 30. 5.74*
1A 1.12.65*
B 19.10.72*
2 10. 7.48*
3 19. 7.49
4 24. 7.60*
5 9. 6.69*
6 11. 7.49
7 10. 7.81*

The ground level photographs which appear also are reproduced with kind permission of: Richard Muir: 35, 46, 52, 130, 146, 154, 168, 171, 211, 213, 215, 239. Royal Commission on Historical Monuments (England): 63, 193. British Tourist Authority: 167, 189, 230, 261, 263. Walter Scott (Bradford) Ltd: 257.

INDEX

DATE DUE